COMING OF AGE

Andy Murray was born on 15 May 1987 in Dunblane, Scotland. In September 2004 he won the boys' singles title at the US Open in New York, and that December he was crowned BBC Young Sports Personality of the Year. The following year he became the youngest-ever player to represent Britain in the Davis Cup, reached the third round in his debut at Wimbledon, and broke into the Top 100 at the Thailand Open. In 2006 he won his first ATP title at San José, and ended 2007 ranked number 11 in the world, having won the St Petersburg Open. 2009 saw Andy off to a career-best 45-7 start, capturing four ATP World Tour titles, including becoming the first British player since Bunny Austin in 1938 to earn the title at Queen's Club.

Sue Mott is a freelance sports writer. She was the *Sunday Times* tennis correspondent before going on to become an award-winning feature writer, columnist and interviewer for the *Daily Telegraph*. She has written books, co-presented a BBC TV sports investigation programme and regularly contributes to television and radio. She is an Arsenal supporter but has a very poor backhand.

ANDY MURRAY

COMING OF AGE

The Autobiography

arrow books

Published in the United Kingdom by Arrow Books in 2009

1 3 5 7 9 10 8 6 4 2

First published in the United Kingdom in 2008 by Century

Arrow Books
The Random House Group Limited
20 Vauxhall Bridge Road, London, SW1V 2SA

Addresses for companies within The Random House Group Limited can be
found at: www.randomhouse.co.uk/offices.htm

The Random House Group Limited Reg. No. 954009

www.rbooks.co.uk

A CIP catalogue record for this book
is available from the British Library

ISBN 9780099505655

The Random House Group Limited supports The Forest Stewardship
Council (FSC), the leading international forest certification organisation.
All our titles that are printed on Greenpeace approved FSC certified paper
carry the FSC logo. Our paper procurement policy can be found at:
www.rbooks.co.uk/environment

Typeset by SX Composing DTP, Rayleigh, Essex
Printed and bound in the United Kingdom by
CPI Bookmarque, Croydon, CR0 4TD

Cover photography by Carlos Serrao.
Inset photography by Getty, Corbis, PA Photos; Wimbledon 2009 by Rob
Stewart and Malaria No More photo by Simon Mooney.

To all my fans – for all the support you have given me
through the good times and the tough times.

Acknowledgements

Thanks to – my family for keeping me grounded.

To my mum and dad for always encouraging me to pursue my tennis career.

To all my coaches for helping me to get to the level I'm at – Leon Smith, Pato Alvarez, Mark Petchey, Brad Gilbert – and to everyone who is with me now – Miles Maclagan, Matt Little, Jez Green, Andy Ireland and Alex Corretja.

To Tennis Scotland, Sportscotland, Scottish Institute of Sport, the LTA, RBS, Robinsons and Edmund Cohen for providing the funding and support I needed to train in Spain.

To all my sponsors for their continued support – RBS, Fred Perry, Head, and Highland Spring and my former agent Patricio Apey and Ace Group

To everyone who gets involved with www.andymurray.com

To my former physio Jean-Pierre Bruyere for taking such good care of me and teaching me how to look after my body.

To Stuart Higgins for helping me to understand the media better and Neil Granger for taking care of my money!

To Sue Mott for all her help in the writing of this book.

And thanks to Random House.

To Simon Fuller and the team at 19 for their advice and support.

And to Kim, Carlos, Dani, Rob and Ross for always being there when I need them.

Contents

COMING OF AGE

Chapter One:
The Two Impostors

Kipling's wrong, by the way. You can't treat them exactly the same, Triumph and Disaster. I don't. Triumph is clearly better. I have never liked losing. When I was a little boy I'd overturn the Monopoly board in a rage if I was losing – so my gran tells me anyway – but you could say I have matured with age. I understand I'm not going to win every tennis match I play. I come off the court and I'm disappointed, but I don't beat myself up over it. I'm competitive, I want to win, but I'm not an idiot.

I wanted to win that day I stood under the Rudyard Kipling quote at the entrance to the Centre Court at Wimbledon for the very first time in my life. There's hardly a more famous spot in the whole tennis world. You don't even have to look up to know that it's there . . .

> If you can meet with Triumph and Disaster
> And treat those two impostors just the same.

It was my first Centre Court match, at my first Wimbledon, in my first grand slam against a man who had played in a

Wimbledon final. Oh, and ten million people were watching on television and I had this massive bag of drinks over my shoulder that was way too heavy to carry.

I had been sitting in the champions' locker room when they came to get me for the match. It wasn't a mistake. I was allowed to be in there because I'd been part of the Davis Cup squad for Britain, but it was seriously weird being there, with attendants offering you towels and John McEnroe doing stretching exercises on the floor. The walk from the locker room to the court just made things even more unbelievable.

The corridor was lined with framed photographs of all the former champions. Some I would play against one day – and one day surprisingly soon – like Roger Federer and Lleyton Hewitt. One I had already played against, no less a hero than John McEnroe who had deliberately ignored me the first time we met. Some had been runners up, like my childhood hero Andre Agassi – I used to own a pair of pink Lycra and denim shorts thanks to him, which may not be something to boast about. Some I had loved watching on TV like Björn Borg and Jimmy Connors. Others I only knew about from the history books, like Fred Perry, who as everyone knows – because we are always being reminded – was the last British man to win Wimbledon in 1936. That's a very long time ago. Now I was walking down the corridor, listening to 'Let's Get It Started' by Black Eyed Peas on my iPod, reckoning it was probably too soon for me to change all that.

I was eighteen years old – just – and this was about to become the most amazing time of my life. We walked past the back entrance to the royal box. Sir Sean Connery was in there, but I didn't know it at the time. We were led down a set of stairs beside the trophy cabinet, through the main hallway and then, just to maximise the intimidation, they made me stand underneath that famous Kipling sign carved over the doorway.

All the names of all the Wimbledon champions were lettered in gold on the wall next to me. A television camera was pointing at my face and my opponent was standing there with me, obviously much more relaxed than I was, having played on the tour for eight years, an established Top 10 guy. As competitors go, David Nalbandian was a heavyweight. No one said anything. It took an effort to believe this was actually happening.

I love boxing and sometimes tennis is pretty similar. No one gets punched in the face, but waiting to go on court was like waiting to walk into the ring. The two of us would go out together, but only one of us would survive.

This was my first Wimbledon – my first Wimbledon as a senior professional. I'd played the junior tournament three times before and lost twice in the first round. It wasn't exactly my most successful stomping ground; I'd never played well there. I'd never really played well on grass before. It was only my third senior tournament and here I was, about to play on some of the most famous courts in the world, amongst all the best players, with 14,000 people watching and a huge television audience at home. Two months before that I was playing – and losing – in front of four or five people at a Challenger event in Germany.

That's why that Wimbledon experience was so special in 2005. It was *so* new. I was a schoolboy's age, ranked 317th in the world, I had no experience playing at that level, so going into the tournament my expectations were pretty low. Why wouldn't they be? I'd never done anything at Wimbledon before. This could so easily have been one of Kipling's Disasters.

And yet, by the end of the tournament I'd become a friend of Sir Sean Connery, was being stalked by television crews, had received proposals of marriage and had had my first taste of 'Murray-mania'. It was surreal.

I'd only started practising on the Friday before Wimbledon because I'd twisted my ankle at Queen's. That had caused quite a stir. Because I cramped up two points from winning my third-round match against Thomas Johansson, the Swede who won the Australian Open in 2002, people were saying I was unfit. It had been a good match in many ways for me, but going wide for a ball at 30–15 5–4 in the deciding set (my coaches will tell you I usually remember every single point I play) I had turned my ankle badly. I seemed to be on the ground for about ten minutes before they decided to do something about it. The trainer taped up the injury, but when I went back out to play I couldn't because the ankle was shot and my legs started cramping badly. I couldn't finish the match and didn't step on any court for another week. I didn't know if I was going to be able to play Wimbledon at all.

When I walked into Wimbledon for my first match there as a professional, I already knew that I was playing first match on Court Two, known as 'the Graveyard of the Champions'. That was all right. I wasn't a champion. I had won precisely two matches in my life on the ATP tour.

It was weird. Many things would be weird this week. First of all I had to get used to being in that main locker room with the stars who had no clue who I was. Normally someone with my ranking, the second lowest in the entire draw, would be in the upstairs locker room with the lower-ranked players – and Andy Roddick, because he refused to go in the main one until he won Wimbledon. I think that's OK for him, if that's how he feels, but being downstairs was a perk I was prepared to take.

It was still very strange. Roger Federer was in there. All the top players were in there – plus John McEnroe, Pat Cash and all the commentators who were going to be playing in the Over-35s tournament in the second week. I felt out of place because no one knew who I was, and I felt them staring at me and thinking: 'What are you doing in here?' Maybe they thought I was a stray ball boy.

These guys were all much older and more famous than I was. I felt awkward. Obviously I knew nothing compared with them. The only thing I could do was keep my head down and not speak unless spoken to. Some people might find that hard to believe when they see me on court, but it's true. I didn't think it was right to go up to these guys and start acting like we were friends. I was sure they wouldn't like it.

McEnroe, of course, is an icon and everybody loves him at Wimbledon. I wouldn't have said a word to him if we hadn't met before but I knew him – or sort of knew him – because we'd met a few months earlier at an exhibition tournament at the Wembley Arena. It is not a memory I treasure. In fact, it was pretty embarrassing, but at least it broke the ice – almost – with one of the greatest players of all time.

It was a $250,000, eight-player, one-set, straight knock-out, winner-takes-all event at the back end of 2004 and I had no business being there at all. At the time I was just a 17-year-old junior, but Tim Henman had pulled out with an injury and I had just won the US Open Juniors, so I had had a surprise call asking if I would be able to go down and play.

That was another one of those surreal experiences. I was invited to the press conference the day before play started and found myself sitting between Boris Becker, Goran Ivanisevic and John McEnroe, three legends of the game. I was stuck right in the middle, feeling so nervous and so intimidated I could hardly speak.

I was such a nobody, even more than I would be at Wimbledon. It didn't help that I was due to play McEnroe in the opening round and he was taking the match very seriously. I worked this out after the press conference when the photographers asked the two of us to square up and stare into one another's eyes. It was just desperately embarrassing and a little scary.

McEnroe wasn't speaking to me. He wasn't putting me at my ease – which was fine. I didn't mind – but I couldn't believe they were making me do this: a 17-year-old kid doing a boxing stare-out with someone like John McEnroe. He was loving it. You could tell he was enjoying it and I was just hating it.

Result: he won 6–1. It was the first time I'd played in front of a decent-size crowd and I was so nervous I couldn't play at all well. I hadn't been practising, I'd been taking a break after the US Open and I hadn't even turned professional yet. It was a last-minute call-up and I was playing horribly. It was awful. Being on court with McEnroe was awesome, but feeling so inadequate was just terrible. At the end of it I said: 'Mr McEnroe. It has been an honour to play against you.' Seeing him again six months later at Wimbledon, I didn't know whether to be horrified or pleased.

I'd come straight from junior tournaments and low-grade senior events when no one cared whether you won or lost, except your mother, and the entire audience was one man and his dog. I'd stayed in rubbish hotels, family digs, boarding school dormitories and sometimes you ran out of money for food. Now suddenly I was part of the biggest tournament in the world, staying in the basement flat of a house in Wimbledon village with my mum and my brother and being offered a courtesy car just to drive down the hill to the courts. It was hard to believe. Some days I just walked. It didn't matter. Despite my brief showing at Queen's, nobody recognised me. No one took any notice of me. But after my second match, it changed. That was when it all went a little bit mad.

First, however, I had to survive that opening match, my debut as a senior professional at Wimbledon. I was a bit nervous when I woke up after a decent sleep but I was also really, really focused. My opponent was George Bastl of Switzerland, a good player ranked higher than me – but then everyone was ranked higher than me. The bad news was that he had beaten Pete Sampras, one of the greatest grass-court players of all time, at Wimbledon three years before. The good news was that I still thought I had a chance of winning.

As I said, we were on Court Two – the scene of his famous triumph against Sampras, who had won Wimbledon seven times – but that didn't worry me. I walked out there with 'Let's Get It Started' on my iPod and it turned out to be quite a theme tune for the week that would change my life.

There weren't many people watching as we started, but the crowd grew as the match went on. I played really well and my serve didn't get broken the entire match. I won 6–4 6–2 6–2 and then I delayed Venus Williams coming on court for the second match because I was trying to sign so many autographs.

That wasn't just me being naïve. It was a promise I had made to myself years before on my first ever trip to Wimbledon as a kid with friends on a minibus from Dunblane Sports Club. I was seven years old and my hero at the time was Andre Agassi. I really wanted his autograph but I couldn't get near him. I had to come away without it and was really disappointed. I promised myself there and then that if I was ever a famous player I wouldn't ignore the kids who wanted my autograph. I'd sign as many as I could. Sorry Venus, I just didn't realise how long it would take.

It was ages before I got back to the locker room. I was still a little amazed to be in there. It was old-fashioned but unbelievably clean. Next to every sink was deodorant and shaving foam – not that I used it. Two locker-room attendants were available to get you towels. There was drinking water, Coke and Sprite. They'd got everything in there. I'd never experienced anything like it in my life.

It wasn't long ago that I'd been in some horrible places in junior tournaments round the world, where the kids don't care where they pee and everything stinks. You'd see insects like large black beetles scurrying about and some of the showers were just pipes sticking out of a wall, pouring dirty, bad-smelling water. There are no towels and usually no loo roll. You just take one from your hotel. You get used to it. It's fine. But, for this and many other reasons, Wimbledon was a massive culture shock.

That night, after my first win, we went out for a Pizza Express takeaway. We've always joked that my mum's cooking is not the best. Actually it's not a joke. So most nights we ate out or ordered in. I didn't celebrate though. I was obviously really happy that I'd won, but the tournament was so important to me, I just wanted to make sure I was ready for my next match. This one would be a really tough test, against a player with a bit of a reputation for gamesmanship, Radek Stepanek from the Czech Republic. However, there was more to it than that.

Stepanek's coach at the time was Tony Pickard, the former British Davis Cup captain who had famously coached the Swede Stefan Edberg when he won Wimbledon in 1988 and 1990.

Some time before Wimbledon he'd met my mum at a tournament and decided to have a conversation with her about what I was doing at the Sanchez-Casal Academy in Barcelona and why I was playing Futures events in Spain.

'What's Andy doing playing in Spain and not in British Futures events?' he asked her. 'He should be back here, competing at home. It shows fear that he's leaving his country. He will lose locker-room respect if he goes on avoiding British players.'

My mum told him that she just wanted me to be happy and that I was doing very well in Spain. It didn't seem as though he was very impressed.

'I do know the men's tour,' he said, implying that she didn't. 'I used to coach Stefan Edberg.' Then he walked off.

I don't know what he thought when his player and I were drawn against each other in the second round at Wimbledon but word reached us that people in Stepanek's camp were saying things like: 'This kid's got nothing to beat us with. He can't hurt us.' I didn't need the incentive to win at Wimbledon. I'm competitive about absolutely everything. I really wanted to win this next match.

Meanwhile, things were getting seriously weird. People came to watch my practice sessions, which I had never experienced before. I was signing autographs and when I walked into the press conference room for the first time after the Bastl match there were more people in there than had ever stood round the court to watch my matches.

Press conferences aren't easy. I was quite shy when I was younger and all of a sudden I was being asked to be quite open with strangers who were firing questions at me – and not just about tennis either.

I was asked about my girlfriend. I didn't even have a girlfriend any more. I'd gone out with a German girl in Spain but that was all over now. Yet – this is how crazy it was – two journalists and a photographer flew over to Barcelona and offered her money to do an interview and take pictures. (She took the money but she didn't say anything bad.) I couldn't believe it. This whole Wimbledon thing was amazing. I'd never experienced anything like it and I never expected anything like it. How could I? I'm ranked 300 in the world and there are photographers following me around. It wasn't right.

So with all that going on, I had to try and concentrate for the Stepanek match that I really, really wanted to win. It was the one I was most nervous for. When I woke up that morning I couldn't believe it. I had a raging temperature, and was sweating buckets. My mum called Jean-Pierre Bruyere, my physio, and asked what she should do. He suggested a cool bath at some awful temperature so she rushed out to buy a thermometer. I took the bath and sat around with some cold towels on my forehead, drinking lots of water. I managed to practise for a bit with Mark Petchey, the former British player who was helping me on a part-time basis, and by the time my match was called, I was feeling OK. The next day some of the papers blamed it on a dodgy curry, a pretty wild guess of theirs because I hadn't even had a curry.

The match was taking place on Court One, the court shaped like a bullring that you reach by walking along this underground tunnel that seems to go on for miles. It was quiet and intimidating down there. All you've got for company are two security guards and your opponent. When that opponent is someone like Stepanek, seeded 14th, with loads of experience and coached by the coach of a Wimbledon champion, it was enough to make anyone nervous. I'd never been on Court One in my life, not even to practise, and now I was, officially, the lowest-ranked player left in the tournament.

We walked and walked. It felt like for ever. The butterflies were going and when we finally arrived in the open, I looked around me and the court felt huge. Then the crowd saw me and gave me such a big cheer that the butterflies began to subside and it settled me down a little bit. I looked up at the players' box to see my mum, my brother and Petch, and that settled me down even more. I don't find the support of a crowd intimidating. I like it. It was nice to know they were on my side. They obviously wanted me to win but didn't really expect me to.

The match started and my nerves seemed to melt away. I was ahead all the time. I broke his serve early in every set and he broke me once during the whole match. It really couldn't have gone any more smoothly. I returned well and countered everything he tried. He probably didn't expect me to play as well as I did and at 6–4 6–4 5–3 I had two match points.

The first one he saved with an unbelievably hard diving volley which I hit long because I wasn't expecting it. He saved the next one with a really good pick-up which hit the net and just dropped over on to my side. He walked up and kissed the net and then walked back to the baseline, pointing to his head like I was choking or getting nervous or something.

I didn't know what to do. I had no experience of tennis at that level and wasn't sure whether players were supposed to behave like that, but in the next game at 30–all I hit a forehand that just touched the top of the net and dropped over. I ran up to kiss the net. Doing the same thing back to him was my way of letting him know that I may be younger but I wouldn't be intimidated.

Winning that match was pretty special. He was the highest-ranked player I'd ever beaten by a pretty long way and when I walked into the press interview room later it was absolutely packed. I was asked about the gamesmanship. I said he was trying to put me off, but in the end he was the one looking silly because he'd lost to an 18-year-old ranked 317 in the world. That got a bit of a laugh.

Later, Petch told me that he shook hands with Tony Pickard in the players' box at the end of the match and said: 'Tough luck.' Pickard just said: 'That was a terrible match. Both of them played badly. It was embarrassing. I can't believe that was on Court One.'

Mark just said: 'I suppose Andy did what he had to do to win,' and left it at that. I didn't get upset; I found it quite funny. This kind of backbiting was typical of British tennis at the time. I'd grown used to some players and coaches not wanting me to win because I was doing well, this was just an extension of the same thing. I knew what he had said to my mum and I thought it was very rude. It was basically someone who thought he knew better trying to tell Mum what she should be doing. I don't mind people offering advice, but only when you ask for it.

I woke up early the next morning, really excited to see what was being said about me. Obviously being in the papers at that time was pretty cool. I was on the back pages of all of them. However, the thing I found most weird then was the live TV interview, because you couldn't pause to think. There was no room for error. The BBC reporter Gary Richardson was coming round almost every morning to talk to me. We didn't know how to say 'no' in those days. It was irritating the first time it happened because my mum hadn't told me she had agreed I'd do it and I got woken up really early. She'll tell you that I never like getting up in the morning. I'm always at my grumpiest then (although I'm absolutely nothing compared to Jamie). It is not my favourite time of day.

It wasn't all bad. We were staying in the basement of this house in the village and a BBC crew wanted to film me coming upstairs from my flat, and the cameraman taking the shot was walking backwards when he tripped and fell over and smacked his head on the ground. Understandably he then completely snapped at the guy who was supposed to be guiding him. I didn't laugh out loud at the time – I waited ten seconds until I was in the car taking me to the courts. It was awesome. Right up there with one of the funniest things I've seen.

I'd made the third round of Wimbledon. I'd gone from a Court Two nobody to a Court One winner. Next stop the Centre Court against David Nalbandian, a player so famous in Cordoba he had a bus stop and hot-dog stand named after him – but that wasn't his real claim to fame. He was a brutal player, one who could run all day, and a hero in his home country for making the Wimbledon final three years ago against Lleyton Hewitt. He had lost, but he was a huge opponent for me.

I couldn't wait to play him. It was one of the biggest matches of my life and I thought I had a chance.

The morning of the match I was fine. I've always been good at killing time. I just went down to the courts and practised in my 'Ronaldinho' shirt, a souvenir from my time in Barcelona. I could pretend and say it was just like any other practice, but I'd be lying. There were people and cameras everywhere. Tim Henman had been knocked out in the second round to Dmitry Tursunov, 8–6 in the fifth set, and I was the last Brit left in the tournament.

I didn't feel as nervous as for the Stepanek match, but I think, subconsciously, I was. I just didn't want to understand the situation I was in. Maybe I was trying to blank it. I went to the toilet a lot of times before the match and my legs were heavy, all signs of nerves that I was desperate to ignore.

I've talked about boxing. I love the sport and I really do compare tennis with it sometimes. It's about performing well in front of a big crowd with one man out to stop you. You've got two competitors. You have to beat the other one. You have to come up with a game plan. You've got to know his weakness, your weaknesses. Tennis is hard on the mind as well as the legs. You can go from feeling really comfortable and confident to seeing it all slip away. You've got to be mentally strong. When it starts to go wrong, you have to make sure you don't get angry, don't get annoyed. Actually, now I come to think of it, it's fine to get angry and annoyed. Just don't let it affect your game.

I have had my moments of madness on court. I know that everyone's seen me on TV roaring with frustration or getting pumped up. It's just the way I am. I got defaulted once when I was twelve at the Scottish Junior Championships at

Craiglockhart. I was playing one of my brother's best friends and in a moment of frustration I flung my racket towards the chair. It went underneath the fence and just seemed to keep going forever. The assistant referee defaulted me and I had to trudge off the court to pick up my racket. Afterwards I ran off to my mum. I was really upset and wanted her support but she was just annoyed. I thought that was a bit unfair, considering her history. Mum got defaulted when she was a junior and my gran was so disgusted she drove home without her. My mum had to call one of my gran's friends to come and pick her up. So it's definitely there in the family, the fury, but you've got to keep it under control.

Getting ready for the match, I just tried to stay focused. Tactics, stretching, warm-up, I'd done everything I could to prepare. I wanted to walk out on court with no excuses. If I won I won, if I didn't I had done everything I possibly could to win.

The thing I find most amazing about the whole Centre Court experience is not the stadium, not the crowd but the actual court. It's perfect. The grass is so well cut; the lines are so perfectly drawn. After years and years of junior tournaments, and playing on surfaces like car parks, the courts at Wimbledon are incredible.

The only thing about the court that isn't so good – and I'm not joking – is the bottom of the umpire's chair. You might say I'm nit-picking, but the wheels are black and it looks really ugly in comparison to the rest of the court. The chair is green. The grass, obviously, is green. I don't understand the wheels being black when everything else is perfect.

The main difference though between the Centre Court at Wimbledon and the main stadium court anywhere else in the world is the quietness. You hear the ball being hit so clearly. It sounds so clean. At the US Open, people in the crowd are talking, shouting, arguing, eating. At Wimbledon, if someone opened a packet of crisps at the back, you'd hear it all over the court. It's *that* quiet. It's so silent it's almost intimidating, especially when you know they're all watching you.

Tennis is one of probably only two sports – golf is the other one – where the players get pretty wound up over noise. I actually don't mind that much. I think players need to get on with it more. Obviously, I don't like it when you're reaching up for a lob and then you hear the clicks of thirty cameras as you're about to hit your overhead, but I don't mind when the crowd shouts out between points. It adds to the atmosphere.

I don't think quiet was the right word that afternoon when I finally stepped on the Centre Court. I don't know exactly how loud it was because I still had my iPod on, but it was loud enough. Luckily, I didn't have to stop and bow to the royal box because they had stopped all that by then. That's a good thing, because I wouldn't have known what to do. I'd never done it before and I'd never met royalty. Well, I'd met the Duchess of Gloucester once, I think, but I didn't have to bow then either.

I walked to the umpire's chair, put down that ridiculously heavy drinks bag and prepared to play the match. It was great that my dad had come down from Scotland to watch me in person, among all the other people supporting me.

What happened next was nearly unbelievable. The atmosphere was fantastic and I won the really long first set in the tie-break. The second set was the best set of tennis I'd played all year and I found myself leading 7–6 6–1. I had loads of chances in the third set but that was when the momentum started to change a little bit. We were playing points of a really high intensity. I had game points in the first three games but suddenly found myself 0–3 down. That's when I decided to give Nalbandian the set. People might not have realised at the time, but it seemed like a good idea to start fresh in the fourth. The trouble is I'd never played a four-set, let alone five-set, game in my life except in the Davis Cup doubles. In the singles, never.

I took a toilet break. One of the security guards had to keep me company. I'll never forget him because all the time we were walking, he was muttering: 'Come on, Andy. Come on, Andy. You can do it!'

The fourth set was really close. I had chances. He had chances. You'd think I'd be nervous at 4–4 in the fourth, against one of the best players in the world, but actually it was great. I'd never played anywhere near that level of tennis before. Then I had a break point on his serve. He hit a shot on to the baseline. The line judge called it out, but the umpire over-ruled him. I knew it was in – I saw chalk – but it was one of those that you hope the umpire will leave alone. He didn't. I lost the game. I lost the set. It wasn't a mental let-down. It was just inexperience. Nalbandian knew that the most important thing to do was stay solid and make few mistakes. I was more impetuous. I was in too much of a rush to finish off the point.

He broke me early in the fifth set. To be honest, I can't remember much about it any more. I was starting to hurt a lot and I was cold. This was the last match on and it was getting late. Whenever I stood up after the changeovers I was feeling really stiff. My legs were hurting. It was the longest match I'd ever played. My legs and my backside were really sore because of the low bounce of the ball. All that bending. That was when I understood what playing professional tennis at the highest level was all about. I realised that I had the potential to play at that level, but I was still a little kid.

In the locker room afterwards I saw Mark, my coach. We'd hardly worked together for any length of time yet. I didn't really know him that well. Both of us were trying to be brave and hold back the tears. It was really difficult. I apologised to him for losing and he looked quite shocked. He said: 'You've nothing to apologise for. It was a great effort.'

I just sat there for about fifteen minutes by myself, trying to take it all in. Actually, trying to get my legs working again. When I went for my shower I could hardly stand up. My legs buckled. I was absolutely exhausted, but somehow I gathered myself. I went and did my press conference and that was – nearly – the end of my first Wimbledon.

I say 'nearly', because I had to come back on the Monday to play in the mixed doubles with Shahar Peer of Israel. She must have wished I hadn't. I was rubbish. We lost in the first round, but there was a huge crowd round Court Three where we played. They told me later that it was the first time in living memory that an unseeded player losing in the first round of the mixed doubles had been asked to hold a press conference. It was quite a fun conversation. They asked me about all the female attention I was getting. I just said: 'That's the best thing about this. It's great.'

I wasn't being strictly honest. The Nalbandian match hurt for a few days but looking back on it now, it was the match that made me understand what I needed to do to become one of the best players in the world. It was maybe a good thing I didn't win. I played really well all week and just lost to a better player who knew how to pace himself. If I'd won in three or four sets, I might not have realised I needed to be much fitter and much stronger.

There was a pretty funny mixture of responses to what I'd done. Jimmy Connors, Boris Becker, John McEnroe and Martina Navratilova said encouraging things, which was nice, but there were quotes in the papers from some former British Davis Cup captains that were pretty critical.

David Lloyd said: 'For an 18-year-old kid to be getting tired like that on grass is a big worry. Two weeks in a row, at Queen's and Wimbledon, he got tired. The worst thing in tennis is to have a weakness. Everybody else homes in on it pretty quick.'

Tony Pickard said my temper was a problem: 'Obviously, nobody has been able to bounce it out of him. Now it will be a hell of a problem to get rid of it. To be doing that shows that when the going gets tough, somebody can't handle it. He isn't John McEnroe. He used it to break everybody else's concentration. Murray is only breaking his own.'

Lloyd also said that Jimmy Connors had gone over the top about me, 'saying Murray was the greatest thing since sliced bread. He should not have made a comment like that about a kid who didn't try in the fifth set against Nalbandian. You can't say he is going to win a grand slam. But because we're so desperate, he already has a noose around his neck.'

In some ways, they were right. I went away afterwards and tried to grow up fast. I wanted to play at that level. Once you get that sort of buzz from playing the biggest tennis tournament in the world, you want to play that sort of tournament consistently. You don't want to go back and play in Challenger and Futures events, the lower-ranked tournaments, where there's no one watching, no atmosphere and not that much fun.

You don't get Sean Connery phoning you after playing some lowly event in South America. I didn't know he was in the royal box that Saturday, but I saw it in the papers the next day. Then he called me. I might have thought it was a wind-up but my management company at the time had told me he'd asked for my phone number – and anyway, I recognised his voice. It was just like talking to James Bond.

I didn't do much of the talking. I just listened to that voice I knew so well from all the Bond films I used to watch. Every Christmas there was a two-for-one offer and I had built up the entire set. Now, suddenly, after three matches at Wimbledon, I'm having a conversation with 007 himself.

I was getting phone calls from James Bond and being followed by the so-called paparazzi. I had gone from being an absolute nobody to finding myself in the papers every day. However, I didn't confuse myself with a national hero. I just felt as if something had changed. I can tell you the exact moment that that began to sink in. It was when I walked out of our Wimbledon house with friends to have a day's go-karting the day after the Nalbandian match. There was a line of white vans with blacked-out windows outside in the street. As our car pulled out, so did they and they followed us all the way to the track. It was like being in a spy movie.

At the beginning of that year I had been really struggling. I'd lost a lot of matches at senior tournaments. I didn't know if I was going to make it. I didn't know if I was good enough. That Wimbledon was where it all clicked. It was like a light bulb going on. I'd started playing tennis when I was three years old, and I'd made a lot of sacrifices over the years. I'd gone to Spain, left my family, and it had been a long, long road – but now I'd just played five sets in the third round of Wimbledon. I'd lost but it was close. I didn't feel I had made it yet, but that tournament was like a payback to me for all the hard times.

Now I had to start working even harder. I had to start spending more time in the gym, being more professional. I was eighteen and still physically under-developed. I was still growing and hadn't put on much muscle. Basically, I just needed to grow up and after that Wimbledon I did.

Chapter Two:
But I'm Not Sorry

People think that I'm stroppy, that my mum's pushy and that my big brother fancied his mixed doubles partner at Wimbledon 2007. It just goes to show how appearances can be deceptive, although I'm not so sure about Jamie and Jelena Jankovic. But that's his story. My story is that I am not stroppy at all. I can't remember the last time I had an argument with my mum. I genuinely can't remember. I never slammed a door, never shouted 'I hate you.' I never did either of those things to my parents. I think Mum is the one person who gets me. She understands me really well. I can't count the number of times I've been called a bad-tempered brat, but that is not how it felt growing up. I would say it was relaxed, easy-going, full of sport and loads of fun.

Obviously I can't remember the very early years too clearly. I can vaguely recollect playing swingball, but I can't picture a time or place. I have a memory of going to France with Mum and Dad, but nothing specific comes back to me except I can remember a babysitter giving me a little sip of her coffee and I spat it out. I've never touched coffee since.

*

I was born Andrew Barron Murray on the 15th of May, 1987, in Glasgow. Only two weeks before, the family had moved to Dunblane, a little cathedral town not far from Stirling which at the time seemed very relaxed, very friendly and very safe – except at Halloween when Jamie and I and our friends would go out with our pals and throw eggs at people's houses.

I definitely cannot remember a time without Jamie, my elder brother by fifteen and a half months. That's relevant because growing up aged five, six, seven, eight, he was better than me at stuff purely because he was older, stronger and cleverer. It took me until I was ten to beat him at tennis and I've got a funny fingernail to prove it.

We were playing in a national tournament for the Under-10s at Solihull when he was ten, and we both reached the final. I don't remember the match with any clarity, but what I do remember is coming back home with him on the minibus with all the Scottish players – there must have been about fifteen of us – and I was winding him up about beating him. Mum was driving. It was difficult for him to get away from it because I was sitting beside him at the time with my arm lying on the armrest. After about fifteen minutes of this, he'd had enough of my goading. He shouted at me and his fist came down on my hand. I got this huge whack on my finger which went black and blue and I had to go to the doctor's for a tetanus injection the next day. It never did grow back properly. So that was the first time I beat Jamie in competition and that was my return for it.

I was obviously very competitive with him. That was why I started to hate – I still hate – losing so much. My whole tennis career happened purely because, when I was growing up, my big brother was much better than me at most things. He was better in school than me, he was better at tennis than me and even when we pretended to be professional wrestlers, he only ever let me win the Women's belts.

My mum, my first tennis coach, will tell you that when I started playing tennis she thought I was useless. I was only about three or four and she used to spend hours throwing balls for me to hit. She says I kept missing whereas Jamie could do it right away. It wasn't really until I was about seven that I started to become noticeably better. I had bad concentration, bad coordination and a temper. It was not a good combination.

Gran tells me that regardless of whether we were playing Snap, Monopoly or dominoes, I had to win at all costs. If I didn't, I'd storm off in a terrible huff. I don't believe any of this, but pretty much everyone in the family tells me the same thing. They even tell me that Jamie used to let me win things for a quiet life, but I don't believe that either. Maybe it would have been just to shut me up but I don't remember being that bad.

I suppose I was what you might call 'vocal' on the tennis court when I was young. I have heard stories about me playing at a junior tournament in Edinburgh and the father of the guy I was playing was standing right behind the court, applauding my double faults and cheering when I hit the ball out. I was getting angrier and angrier. Mum and Gran had even started to edge away because they could see what was coming and wanted to pretend it was nothing to do with them.

I suddenly snapped, turned round and slammed a ball into the netting where the man was standing. To all intents and purposes, I was smashing the ball straight at him. Of course, I got into trouble. The match was stopped, the referee was called and Gran said she could hear me, even though she was hiding, announce with some defiance: 'Well, I'm sorry, but I'm *not* sorry.'

Gran and Grandpa played a big part in my life for lots of reasons. One was pure geography. We used to live about 200 yards from the Sports Club at Dunblane where the tennis courts were. Gran and Grandpa lived about 200 yards in the opposite direction. They used to pick us up from school, drive us to training, and feed us tea whenever Mum and Dad were out. Mum was usually working as a tennis coach by then and Dad worked for the retail company, R.S. McColl.

I remember being around Gran a lot of the time. She ran a toy and children's clothes shop in Dunblane high street and we would often go there after school, play with the toys we didn't consider embarrassing and see if we could tease some money out of her for sweets. Most memorable were the car journeys we took together. We make jokes about her driving to this day. She used to indicate three miles before she had to turn off and I've never seen her overtake anyone. It always used to take a little bit longer to get anywhere in the car with Gran.

Another reason they play such a significant part in our lives is probably their genes. Grandpa, Roy Erskine, had played for Hibernian Football Club in the 1950s with some of the biggest names in Scottish football at the time: Willie Ormond, Lawrie Reilly, Eddie Turnbull, Gordon Smith, Tommy Younger. Eventually he moved on to Stirling Albion (for £8 a week, and £1 a point), at the same time working as a qualified optician.

There was sporting prowess on Gran's side of the family as well. She had an English father who for some reason was called Jock. Maybe it was because they lived in Berwick-on-Tweed, right on the Scottish border. Jock Edney was a brilliant sportsman. Gran says he was the Victor Ludorum of his school for three years running, which is obviously a good thing, but I've never been too sure what it means. I do know that he represented the county of Northumberland at athletics, cricket and tennis.

Gran's mother was a Scot, an Anderson, and a gym and ballet teacher before her premature death when Gran was only thirteen. A great-uncle once traced the name back as far as he could go and found a connection with some Scandinavian called Anderssen, but I think it might be pushing it to see me descended from the Vikings just because of that.

Gran was sent to boarding school in Scotland, which is how she met Grandpa and the first time she saw him was on a Sunday afternoon covered in mud from a football match. She remembers it clearly being a Sunday because his father was very strict and thoroughly disapproved of him playing football on the Sabbath. He did it anyway. Maybe that's where I get my independent streak from.

Obviously growing up we all supported Hibs. I still do. We used to go and watch games pretty often when we were young. We even joined the Hibs Kids Club. I didn't enjoy it at first. It always seemed to be freezing cold and wet and everyone shouted and swore, but we got more into it over time.

Grandpa is really nice and really funny but when we were younger, Jamie and I didn't always like him that much because he was pretty strict and used to wind us up so badly. He'd say things like: 'Tuck your shirt in' or 'Take your hat off.' No hats were allowed indoors. Once we got a bit older, it started to change and now we have a really good relationship with him, but he used to give us a lot of trouble when we were boys.

He always loved dogs and he used to sit next to his Golden Retriever saying to her things like: 'Pathetic little boy, isn't he,

Nina?' He also used to call me a 'little wart'. When I asked him why, he said, 'You are something I'd like to get rid of but can't.' Obviously, he didn't mean it – or at least I don't think he did. He was just teasing me. He still does it sometimes, but now I have the sense to laugh.

He was really keen on collecting old stamps and envelopes as a hobby. I remember sitting in their living room watching cartoons after school and Grandpa would be in the other room at the huge table, fiddling about with his stamps. He is really into it still and is pretty much an expert in postal history. He didn't manage to get me interested though. Stamp collecting is definitely not my thing. I was more into football stickers and Teenage Mutant Ninja Turtles.

I remember that dining table well for another reason: Gran's Christmas lunch. She's a great cook, although she doesn't ever make enough of it. It was fine when we were 10-year-olds but she's been making the same amount of food through the years and as Jamie and I have grown to 6'3", it seems as if it has got less and less. We've usually finished ours before she has served everyone else's.

I've seen a few pictures of us as children. There is one on my website of Jamie and I wearing little Wimbledon tennis shirts with rackets in hand, but we weren't really playing tennis. In those days when we were really young, Mum would try and hit our legs with a soft ball and Jamie and I would use the rackets to try and stop it. She called it French cricket. We may have been on a tennis court a few times, but we didn't start properly until we were about five or six.

I'm told my first tournament was in Dunblane when I was five and I went down south for the first time to play in an Under-10s event in Wrexham when I was six. My mum thinks it was a significant moment in my life even though it's a complete blank to me now. Apparently, I had lost two one-set matches to much older boys, but was leading 6–2 in the tie-break of my final match when a drop shot I'd played bounced three times on my opponent's side of the net. As I walked up to shake hands, the guy smashed the ball past me and claimed the point. Nobody came to rescue the situation – we were playing without umpires – and I never won another point. I was absolutely distraught afterwards, but Mum reckons it toughened me up. I made sure nobody ever cheated me that badly again.

I have vague memories of playing for the Dunblane Third Team when I was eight and my partner was a 51-year-old architect called John Clark. Gran tells me that after a couple of points, I went up to him and said: 'You're standing a bit close to the net. You should stand back a bit because I want to serve and volley and you'll get lobbed.'

I used to play for the men's team quite often and travel around the Central District playing matches. I enjoyed it because it was more challenging than playing at the club with the other kids there, and I used to love beating the old men. They didn't like it so much though and some of them tried to introduce a rule at the district AGM that no kids under twelve were allowed to play in the men's leagues.

The first tournament I remember winning was the Under-10s at Solihull when I was eight. That was where I would beat Jamie two years later. I always loved going down there. It must have been a nightmare to organise because it was held at seven different venues, with tournaments for the Under-10s to the Under-18s, plus singles and doubles. I know that is where I won my first prize money. £50 cash! I was so excited.

I came straight home and splashed out on computer games.

Everyone used to love it at Solihull. The courts were either side of a car park where it was cool for me and Jamie to hang out with the older boys. I must have liked it because I won there every year from age eight to twelve. I don't remember the score that first time when I was eight, but I know it was three sets and Jamie had a cold. He kept coughing. I accused him of doing it mid-rally to put me off. Somewhere we've got it on video. It is really funny watching yourself that young. I see things that I still do now. The fist-pump when I win points, getting angry when I lose points, the number of times I bounce the ball when I serve.

I used to bleach my hair blond in those days and keep it really short. Sometimes it was spiky. Maybe I looked a bit like Bart Simpson. I used to have a red jumper with a big Bart on the front and there's a picture of me in it at my mum's house with a cheeky grin and teeth missing.

There are pictures of me and Abby too, my secret weapon when I was ten. She was blonde and cute, and whenever I played a tournament I used to cut off a lock of her hair to take with me for good luck. Abby was the Golden Retriever pup that Gran and Grandpa said was my dog, though she always lived at their house. She is still alive and Gran had her portrait painted one Christmas for my flat down in London. Although she is getting on a bit now; her good luck has held pretty true.

At school I never really enjoyed studying. I loved doing sports, but you did so few of them. We only had about two hours a week. In the classroom I found it tough to concentrate when all I was thinking about was playing football or tennis or whatever it was. I always hated getting homework after doing so much work in class. It didn't seem fair.

In the end, I took my exams in Spain not Scotland, when I was playing at the Sanchez-Casal Academy in Barcelona. I don't know what my exact grades were. I wasn't that interested. I did well in Maths and French. How I did well in French, I shall never know. You learn stuff you're never going to use, like what you have in your garden. I remember thinking at the time how ridiculous that was. When are you ever going to ask anyone about that?

I had a lot of friends when I was growing up because I used to play football all the time. Even when I was ten I was trying to balance it with playing tennis. I loved it. I played striker or left midfield and when I was twelve I was actually playing more football than tennis. I spent a while playing for Gairdoch United, but the coach wouldn't put me in the team often because I couldn't make all the training sessions.

They were a feeder team for Rangers and when I was thirteen I was offered a place at their Academy. I remember being told about it when I was eating at McDonald's. I thought, we all thought, that would be great. But then it came to crunch time. I was at tennis practice with my coach Leon Smith at the Stirling University courts and my dad came to pick me up after only forty-five minutes because I had to go to football. I just looked at Dad and said: 'I can't do this. I can't leave now. I want to go back and finish my practice,' and Dad said, 'Fine.' He never tried to stop me. I didn't play football for another seven months after that.

I was a good footballer, but how was I to know whether I was the 1,000th best player in Britain or 10th best? There isn't a ranking system like there is in tennis. I preferred playing football at that age, but I didn't know how good I was. It is a risky business. It can come down to a scout's decision. If the day he comes to watch, you play badly, there might not be another chance. In tennis by that stage I'd won some competitions. I knew I was a good tennis player, one of the best in Europe, and that kind of swung my decision.

I'd also been through a few times when I thought I wanted to stop playing tennis. I'd say to my mum: 'I don't want to play any more' and give up for a couple of weeks, but then I'd think: 'Maybe I do want to play after all.' I never got pushed into playing tennis which was good of my parents because they could see I had talent. Mum and Dad always said to me: 'As long as you're happy, that's the most important thing. As long as you are doing something.' They impressed on me that even if you're earning lots of money, it's no good if you are doing something you hate.

I'm sure that's why I stayed in tennis. Mum was a tennis coach but she was never pushy in any way. You hear so many stories of tennis parents pushing their kids to play every single day, three hours a day, home-schooling their kids, and it's tough. It works sometimes, but they might not necessarily be happy. In an individual sport like tennis you need to enjoy it to continue playing.

Gradually we went to more and more tournaments, and the one that really stands out in my mind is the Orange Bowl I won in Miami when I was eleven. It was recognised as the unofficial World Championships for the Under-12s and it was the first time I'd ever left Europe.

I went over there with Leon, first to prepare at the Harry Hopman School at Saddlebrook. I could hardly believe the place with its massive swimming pool, loads of courts and a golf course designed by Arnold Palmer – not to mention sunshine in December, which would be a pretty rare sight for a Scottish boy like me. It was awesome. I really enjoyed it.

But funnily enough, though, the thing I most remember – maybe typically – is losing a practice match. I was playing a guy called Jose Muguruza. He was two years older than me and I lost a close set. I was really annoyed on the way back to the villa where Leon and I were staying with three other boys.

'What's wrong with you? Why are you so annoyed?' Leon said. 'You don't see Pete Sampras and Andre Agassi getting like that on court, do you?'

'It's because they are where I want to be and I won't be happy until I get there,' I replied.

Maybe that was the fire that took me through the whole tournament. I don't think anybody really expected me to get that far. I know that because I didn't have enough clothes with me. When Mum and Gran came out to Miami to watch, the first thing they had to do was find a laundry somewhere and wash all my things.

The Under-12s event was played in a public park, not glamorous at all, with a small clubhouse alongside and the crowd watching from the roof of the building. I could see Leon at one end of the roof and my mum at the other, because she doesn't like to talk to people when she's watching me. Gran was in the middle, sewing sponsors' labels on new shirts that she and Mum had run out to buy.

When I won the tournament, beating a Czech guy called Tomas Piskacek 6–4 6–1 in the final, it was the day before Christmas Eve. Apparently, I presented the Orange Bowl trophy to my gran and said: 'Here you are, Gran. Take that home and fill it with one of your fresh fruit salads and we can have it with vanilla ice cream for Christmas Day.' She did. She was very reliable like that.

There were only a couple of other junior tournaments that made a real impression. One was Les Petits, an Under-14s in Tarbes, France, a sort of European equivalent of the Orange Bowl. It provided the best competition on the continent, plus my favourite brand of French vanilla yoghurt. No wonder I've always remembered it. Previous winners of the title included Rafa Nadal, Richard Gasquet and Martina Hingis, so it can't be a bad sign of a player's progress. Pretty much anyone who has won there has gone on to become a Top 100 player and I reached the final.

To get there, I'd beaten Novak Djokovic, who was a week younger than me, in the semi-final, and then in the final I faced the Russian Alexander Krasnokutsky and held a match point against him. He was serving – game point for him, match point for me because of the sudden-death deuce rule we were playing. I can still remember the shot that I missed. It was a backhand. I'd hit a drop shot, he came to the net, I went for the backhand but couldn't quite reach. Then I lost the final set 6–3.

I definitely remember crying afterwards. I called my mum and told her I'd lost when I should have won. It made it worse that I'd seen the trophy and the engraved names of all the star players who had won there. Mum said a lot of brilliant players had played in the final and lost, like Mario Ancic, so that made me feel a bit better, but I was still pretty down because I knew how big the tournament was. Everyone was so disappointed for me. I felt it badly. A lot of people had come to watch. The crowd was about two thousand strong. As junior tournaments go, it was second only to the Slams.

Almost every other weekend I was playing somewhere. Most

I can't remember any more. I know I won the warm-up event for Tarbes at Telford because I earned myself a scooter, one of those little metal fold-ups that were popular at the time. My doubles partner Andrew Kennaugh and I promptly set up a racing track round our hotel car park which was a little bit ridiculous but fun at the time. I've still got that scooter in the garage.

It wasn't all about winning, though. At that age, I went through a stage of losing confidence and struggling. I was suddenly losing to Andrew who I usually used to beat easily. Everyone seemed to be getting stronger than me. I was growing in height but I wasn't filling out. I was quite weak. It took me to the middle of my fifteenth year to beat Andrew 6–0 6–1 in an ITF event in Nottingham. By then I'd given up football. I'd decided to devote myself to tennis and that commitment made a big difference.

I loved all sports, I was obsessed with sport, but at some point in life you have to make up your mind to specialise. As I got older I started playing golf and going to loads of boxing, which is now my favourite sport to watch. I went to my first live boxing match in Glasgow to see Audley Harrison top the bill. I'll never forget it. We walked through the door, Jamie and I, and there was a little guy with his gloves and boxing shorts on walking towards us, shouting, swearing and completely gone. His face was battered and bright red. He looked completely beaten up. He walked right past us and out of the door.

When we got to our seats the people sitting next to us said: 'You should have seen what's just happened. The last guy nearly got killed.' It was intense and intimidating and like nothing I'd experienced before. I realised that tennis was a completely different thing altogether. Tennis matches can be tense but these guys are getting lumps hit out of them. I have so much respect for them.

I don't really know why I love boxing so much. It's not bloodlust. I've never been in a fight in my life. I'm not a violent type. It's not my nature off the court. I don't particularly like arguing. I can't think of anything worse, to be honest, than to be in a punch-up with someone. I've been in the ring with Amir Khan, but the only thing I hit with a glove was his punchbag.

But when you're there at ringside, it's so intense, the anticipation is so great, the fighters are so close to one another in the ring, I get really nervous. I've been close enough to get slightly splattered in blood when Scott Harrison fought in Glasgow. Even that didn't put me off. It puts tennis in perspective. I can't believe how tough those guys have to be. It's scary.

I've been a bit of a geek when it comes to boxing ever since. I'm friends with the Scottish super featherweight, Alex Arthur. I think I surprised him when we met by knowing so much about him. It's because, whenever boxing is on TV, whether it's the Portuguese national championships or a heavyweight title fight, I'll watch it. I know the results of almost all the fights for the last three or four years. I am that bad.

I suppose the only sport you could say I didn't enjoy much was rugby. I hardly played it at all, but for some reason I remember going along, aged eight, to mini rugby at Stirling county for the first time. The coach had never seen me before and I had never watched a rugby match, never mind played in one. So when I got the ball and started running in the opposite direction from our try line, everyone was shouting: 'You're going the wrong way! YOU'RE GOING THE WRONG

WAY!' All I was doing was running in a half-moon, round the defence, and going down to score a try.

It's not my kind of sport. It seems to me the same thing is happening all the time. A guy kicks a ball into touch and gets a round of applause. I don't understand that at all.

Golf Jamie and I took up as we got older. We were members at the country club at Gleneagles and that had a short 9-hole course which was perfect for us. Also Gran and Grandpa were members of the Dunblane Golf Club and used to take us out if we pestered them enough. I think they quite liked the fact that they could still beat us. They were pretty sick and tired of losing to us at tennis. They were both self-taught tennis players and had really odd strokes. Gran tells me that I used to get really cross with them when I was little and shout: 'Grandpa, play properly' when he was playing one of his weird-looking forehands. He maintains he invented topspin.

Jamie became really good at golf at one stage, playing off a handicap of three. Maybe he was taking after my Uncle Keith who is a golf pro in America. Gran always says she feels sorry for my other uncle, Niall, because by the time she had ferried Keith to all his golf tournaments and my mum to all her tennis tournaments, there was no time to ferry Niall anywhere. He became an optician.

My dad is a really good golfer too: he still plays off nine. He's also a member of a squash team and he still plays five-a-side football. It was fun for Jamie and me to play any sport with him because he is as competitive as we are.

Obviously, I saw so much of Mum when I was younger because she was my first tennis coach, but there are many things for which I can thank my dad. He was the one who used to discipline me more, and who used to be hard on me about getting into trouble at school or not doing my homework or saying a swear word by mistake. I still don't swear in front of my dad to this day – in front of millions on the television in matches, but never in front of Dad.

However, I do remember him saying once: 'Don't take shit from anyone.' This was brilliant advice for when I was sent to Spain and had to look after myself. When you're that age, kids will tease you and you can get into fights. The stuff Dad had told me and the discipline he gave me when I was younger, really helped once I was out there on my own.

My parents separated when I was about ten. I guess when any couple separates, it is difficult, but we were so young, we didn't really understand. You understand it more as you get older. Obviously it was a bit strange at the time to see Mum and Dad in different houses, but I reckon the experience will help me in later life with certain things. I will always want to try and achieve a steady relationship because it is not the nicest thing when your parents split up. I've had the same girlfriend, Kim, for a long time now and I will try hard to make it work.

But although it was difficult at the time, Jamie and I love Mum and Dad just the same. If you take into account all the things they have done for us both, I am sure they took us into consideration. It certainly was not made as awkward as it could be for us. I've seen what some parents can be like during a divorce, but ours obviously tried to keep any hard feelings away from us. We were lucky, Jamie and I, that as brothers we could do so many things together, but we never talked about the separation much. We speak about things more now than we did when we were younger.

*

Most people don't have a childhood that comes to an abrupt end on a certain date. Things change slowly. In my case, however, everything changed one day in September 2002: country, weather, family, friends, language, food, life. I went from being a boy in Dunblane to a tennis player in Spain. It was scary, but it was awesome too.

Dunblane

On Wednesday the 13th of March, 1996, Thomas Hamilton, 43, walked into Dunblane Primary School with two 9mm Browning pistols and two Smith and Wesson revolvers. He made his way to the gym where he fired multiple shots at point-blank range at a first-year primary class and their teacher, Gwen Mayor. He murdered sixteen children between five and six years old and the teacher before turning one of the guns on himself and committing suicide. It was the deadliest attack on children in the history of the UK.

Jamie and I were at the school that day. Most people know that. I have been asked about it in press conferences a few times and I've always said that, because I was so young, I don't have any real recollection of the day. That is true. I genuinely can't remember much and it's not something I have ever wanted to go back and find out about because it's so uncomfortable.

It doesn't belong in my childhood at all. It seems randomly attached to my history, but in a way that I can't describe. To me, Dunblane was, and still is, one of the safest places in the world. Last Christmas I said to Mum that I could imagine people there not bothering to lock their front doors. That might seem strange when something so terrible happened in the middle of the town while I was there, but that is the way I have always felt. I don't want to dig deeper. I want that sense of comfort to stay the same. I don't think something so crazy and horrific should scar my feelings for my hometown. I think I am lucky I don't remember.

JUDY MURRAY: The boys have always said they were too young to appreciate the enormity of what happened and I'm grateful for that. I have never said much about it except that it was, unquestionably, the worst day of my life. Everybody in the town would say the same thing. We never forget it, but what gives me the most pride and comfort is that Dunblane has not surrendered its spirit. It makes me proud that Andy and Jamie have played a small part in that. When people talk about Dunblane, they don't just think of the shootings, they might also think: 'That's where the Murrays come from.'

We have moved on, but, of course, you never forget. Having spent my childhood here and then come back in my twenties to raise the boys, I still find it really hard to believe something like that happened in what feels like a little village to me. It is such a quiet, lovely place to live.

My mother and I ran a children's toy and clothing shop in the middle of the town. That morning I was working in the shop with another woman who often came in to help. The phone rang and my colleague answered it. It was her daughter ringing to say she'd just heard on the radio that there had been a shooting at Dunblane Primary School and that a man with a gun was in the playground.

'Are you sure?' I said, when she told me. It seemed utterly beyond belief. We were still trying to make sense of it when my mum came flying through the door, shouting: 'Have you heard? Have you heard! There's been a shooting up at the primary school.' I didn't hear any more, I just picked up my car keys and ran out of the door. I don't even remember saying anything to her.

I got in the car and drove off. Of course, lots of other people were driving the same way at the same time. I can just remember slamming on my horn and swearing at the top of my voice while shouting: GET OUT OF THE WAY! GET OUT OF THE WAY! Eventually I had to stop the car and pull over somewhere. You couldn't get near the school for all the police vehicles and other cars that lined the road. I ran towards the school gates. You couldn't get near those either. There were dozens and dozens of other parents there, all barred from entry and desperate to find out what was going on. No one knew. There were rumours, whispers, but no one knew anything for sure.

At last someone came and escorted the parents who had children in the school to a small guest house on the same road. I remember sitting there with a crowd of people and yet no one was saying anything, everyone gripped by the same terrible fear. More people came in, the room was filling up. We talked in whispers. I was sitting opposite a woman who was a head teacher at a primary school in the next town. Her son was one of Jamie's best pals and she said she had heard a rumour that a primary one class was involved, but she didn't know whether or not it was true. It was starting to get pretty crowded and I budged up on my chair to share it with a girl I had been at primary and secondary school with.

Eventually, someone came in and asked all the parents with children in Mrs Mayor's class to please leave with them. There was a part of me in that moment that almost collapsed in relief. But the next second I was feeling so guilty because the woman I'd been sitting with jumped up and cried: 'That's my daughter's class!' I stood up to go with her because she was shaking terribly, but we were told that no one could go except the parents of the children involved. It was horrendous beyond words.

This had all taken hours and hours. The shootings happened at

9.30am and it was now way beyond lunchtime. It was taking ages to organise the evacuation of the children in all the other classes. The authorities needed to make sure they were kept away from the scene of the gym and shielded from all the police cars and ambulances.

I was finally given the boys at 2.30pm. I was trying to stay calm but I probably hugged them harder than they have ever been hugged in their lives. I have to say the school did an unbelievable job because they managed to get Andy and Jamie out to me together, despite them being in different classes, and it was obvious that they had absolutely no idea what had happened. They had simply been told that a man with a gun had been found in the school. The teachers had even managed to feed them lunch in their classrooms.

By that time, we had heard that the murderer was this guy Thomas Hamilton who had run a Boys Club at the primary school and at Dunblane High School for years. We were all aware who he was. Andy and Jamie used to go to his club.

So I stopped the car on the way home and explained to them what had happened. I didn't want them to find out from somebody else. It was my job to tell them as gently and carefully as I could. To this day Jamie never talks about it. He never asks any questions and he never mentioned it again. But Andy said immediately: 'Why would Mr Hamilton do a thing like that? Why wouldn't he just shoot himself?' I have never forgotten him saying that. I said: 'I think he must have just gone mad, Andy. Only a crazy person might do something like that.'

For days after it happened the children were kept off school and the town was eerily quiet. If you went out, even for a newspaper, there were journalists waiting to stop you and ask questions: 'Did you know so-and-so?' So we stayed home, watching everything we could on television and still not being able to believe that it had happened just down the road.

COMING OF AGE

We'd all thought Dunblane was such a safe place. It was. It *is*. Yet somewhere in our past is this terrible tragedy that doesn't fit in. At the time, we just did our best to cope. The school was closed for about a week and when the children finally went back, everything had changed. Suddenly, you had to sign in and there were many changes in terms of security. I can't remember now whether the gym had already been knocked down, but it was eventually turned into a memorial garden.

The extent of the teachers' ordeal soon became clear. Somebody told me that the nursery teachers were asked to go in and identify the bodies of the children who had been shot. Their own teacher had been killed and many of those children didn't have names on their gym kit. The only people who would know them, apart from the parents, were those who had taught them the year before. Can you imagine anything more terrible and more sad than that?

I still couldn't believe how – with all those children in the school and with all that furore and upset going on – the teachers had managed to keep the rest of the children in the classroom fed, watered and completely unaware of the horror so close to them. Those teachers saved the children from a million nightmares. Can you imagine if they had seen something? It could have haunted them for life. It was a heroic job the teachers did that day, and continued to do by getting themselves back to work when it was over.

It went round in our minds for a long time afterwards. There had always been question marks about Hamilton, but for all that he was an oddball, I never, ever thought he was dangerous. It was only later when you read things about his collection of guns, that he lived on his own, ran the Boys Club . . . did you realise the problem was perhaps there all along.

I'd given him a lift from the Boys Club to the train station a few times because he lived in Stirling and he didn't have a car of his own.

I had actually sat beside him and spoken to him. I didn't know him well by any means. He was definitely odd and a loner, but we had no idea that he had the potential to be a murderer.

I think the police had tried to investigate him over the years because people had expressed concerns, but nobody had ever been able to prove anything. I think there was an effort to stop him setting up a boys club somewhere else but he took the case to the local ombudsman and they overturned the ban. There was obviously a major investigation later into the failings of the authorities. One parent, little Sophie North's father, continues to fight an anti-gun campaign. His story is so tragic because he lost his wife to cancer and all he had was his beautiful little 5-year-old daughter. Suddenly he'd lost her too in a way you could never imagine.

You still see the parents of some of the children who were killed – down the street, at the golf club – trying to get on with their lives. A few moved away. Not many. The rest of us can never imagine what it must be like to lose a young child in such a way. It goes unspoken now. I can't remember the last time I heard anyone talking about it locally. That doesn't mean it will ever be forgotten.

ANDY: I have always found it difficult to talk about Dunblane. It is not something I want to look back on or think about in huge detail. Some of my friends' brothers and sisters were killed. I have been asked about it in press conferences from time to time, but it's hard to get the words right. I can't remember much, but I don't want to sound as though I am holding anything back. The trouble is I don't have anything to hold back. I was too young to understand the magnitude of it. But if I said that, people might think I didn't care.

I have only retained patchy impressions of that day, such as being in a classroom singing songs. I don't remember which songs exactly, but I do remember that the school headmaster had told us to go into a classroom – not our usual classroom – because we'd been on our way to the gym. That is a pretty devastating thought.

I know I asked my mum lots of questions about it afterwards. We had eight or nine days off school and I obviously wanted to know why it happened. The weirdest thing was that we knew the guy. He had been in my mum's car. It's obviously weird to think you had a murderer in your car, sitting next to your mum. That is probably another reason why I don't want to look back at it. It is just so uncomfortable to think that it was someone we knew from the Boys Club. We used to go to the club and have fun. Then to find out he's a murderer was something my brain couldn't cope with.

When you're eight years old and you go on an aeroplane, you don't have any nerves or fear. You're not scared of anything. Once you start to get older, you hear about plane crashes, then you experience turbulence and you begin to feel fear because you understand a little more about the way the world works. I never minded flying at all, then after 9/11 I was pretty uncomfortable. It was the same with the shootings. I was completely naïve and the reality just went way over my head.

I understand now that the person who did it must have been mad, but I've never wanted to find out the psychological reasons behind it. Perhaps it's too close for comfort. I could have been one of those children.

In the end, I think I decided it was just this freak thing. I think if I had been fourteen or fifteen, it would have shocked me far more deeply. Mentally, it would have scarred me. But I was so young, it just didn't affect me like that.

When we went back to school, it was very different. We had to use a buzzer to get into the school and key cards to go through doors. I remember listening all the time to a song released to commemorate those who were killed. I think it was 'Knock, Knock,

Knocking on Heaven's Door'. Quite a few kids in my school sang the chorus.* The money from the sale of the song went to a charity to help rebuild the school.

A lot of people say that everything happens for a reason but I can't believe that. I don't know if what happened that day changed the way I thought about religion. I think it's great to believe in stuff. I have no problem with that. But I haven't looked into any particular religion, so I wouldn't know which one to believe in. I've tried to understand space and how the world works, but my head starts hurting after twenty minutes. Quite a few of my friends are religious and that's absolutely fine with me. I just wish people didn't fight.

I don't really think it was a belief that helped Jamie and me come through it all. It was the way family, friends, teachers, everyone pulled together. In some ways, it probably made the town much friendlier and more polite because of the mutual compassion. It seemed to make the place stronger.

Since I left as a pupil, I've never been back to the primary school. But Jamie and I have been in touch with the secondary school. They named the new assembly hall after us. It's great to be remembered like that. I would like to go back one day and see what it's like, maybe visit the memorial garden at the primary school. I'm glad it's still a school and that children still play there. Dunblane is still the quiet, lovely place I remember from when I was a kid. What happened was a terrible, horrible tragedy but I think it's important that one madman didn't destroy the place I'm proud to come from.

*With Bob Dylan's consent, the song was re-recorded with a new verse written by Dunblane musician Ted Christopher. The new version has the brothers and sisters of those killed singing the chorus.

Chapter Three:
El Kid

Murrays don't like leaving home as a rule. My mum had joined the women's pro tour when she left school and only lasted a few months because of homesickness. My brother left home at twelve to go to an LTA training school in Cambridge and spent seven miserable months there. Somehow I broke the mould. By the time I was fifteen, I was desperate to go. I lived in a cold, damp climate with limited facilities and county-standard players to practise with. What I needed was sunshine, hard work, open-air courts and world-class opposition. Maybe going to Barcelona wasn't too hard a choice.

Jamie's stay in Cambridge was a terrible mistake. After what happened to him I would never advise a kid to leave home so young. When he came back seven months later, I practised with him. He looked upset and unhappy, the complete opposite of his old self. He used to enjoy himself on court but all that had changed. I remember Mum walking to the back of the court and muttering: 'I can't believe what they've done to him,' with tears in her eyes. She was so upset.

It wasn't just that Jamie was homesick. It was amazing how quickly he went from being a happy kid to missing his home, missing his parents and not enjoying his tennis. I made head-lines once, during the Aberdeen Cup in 2005, by saying the LTA had 'ruined' Jamie. The press asked me about him and I just said what I believed: 'He was number two junior in the world when he was around age twelve. Then he went down to an LTA academy in Cambridge and they ruined him for a few years. It was their fault.' I have stuck by that opinion ever since. I am not saying the LTA, as a whole, was to blame, but that set-up at Cambridge did not work for him.

So there was no way I wanted to leave home at that age, but once I'd made the decision that tennis was my chosen sport, it all changed. If I wanted to make it, then I had to go away.

Sometimes you need a kick-start. That came when I played in the European Under-16 team championships in Andorra. We lost in the final against Spain and Rafa Nadal was playing. I've known him since we were about thirteen and after the match a few of us were hanging round a racket-ball court, just talking. He started telling me that he practised with people like Carlos Moya, one of the Spaniards on the tour ranked in the World Top 10. He said he'd never beaten him, never even broken his serve, but it was significant that he was playing him at all.

I started thinking. And steaming. I never got the chance to practise with Tim Henman. I didn't even meet him properly until I was sixteen. I went home and said to Mum: 'Rafa Nadal is practising with Moya! And I'm having to practise with a few county-level players, my brother and my mum. Rafa's out in the sun all day – he hardly goes to school and he's playing four and a half hours a day. I'm playing four and a half hours a week. It's not enough!'

That's when it began, my determination to go and live in

another country, possibly Spain. We went over to look at a couple of Academies, one run by the Catalan Tennis Federation and then the Sanchez-Casal Tennis Academy at the Open Sports Club in Barcelona. It even occurred to me to try the Harry Hopman School at Saddlebrook in the USA that I remembered so well from my Orange Bowl win in 1999. I was due to spend a month there in May 2002. However, the night before I was due to leave for Florida, I was playing a game of football for a team called Auchterarder Primrose as a bit of fun and I had just run three-quarters of the length of the pitch when this guy, who was probably a bit fed up with me, stood on my foot just as I was about to cross the ball. That was me done for six weeks. Badly sprained ankle. I couldn't walk or anything and I wasn't much fun because I had to sit around the house doing nothing. I didn't even have an excuse not to do my homework.

The Sanchez-Casal Academy was the one that attracted me most. I went there with Mum to have a look around and played a match against Emilio Sanchez, one of the founders of the Academy and a five-times grand slam doubles champion. I beat him 6–3 6–1. I loved it already. I was playing against a guy who, even though he had retired a few years previously, had been in the World Top 10, and had won a silver medal at the 1988 Olympics. I came off court dripping with sweat. I saw loads of kids, good tennis players, all around me. This was what I wanted.

I told Mum that I'd just beaten Emilio in straight sets and she said: 'Andy, I'm not sure that was such a good idea.' But I wanted to play really well against him to show I was a good player. He didn't ban me; I enrolled at the Academy.

It hadn't been that hard a decision to go abroad. It wasn't

just what happened to Jamie. I didn't want to train at one of the national centres in the UK because of the attitude of the players and some of the coaches. That scene wasn't me. It was the wrong environment. Everything is paid for and they're spoiled and pretty lazy. Not every single player, but most. The majority didn't want to be top tennis players, and it brings everyone else down.

Everyone at Sanchez wanted to be there. They had all *paid* to be there. It cost about £25,000 a year plus competition costs which I had to find from somewhere: sponsorships, the LTA, sportscotland and my parents. I was lucky that during my time there the Royal Bank of Scotland started to sponsor me and have done ever since. It was, and still is, really difficult to convince companies to invest in young players with potential and RBS had never got involved with tennis before. But they took a chance on me and I hope I have repaid their faith.

If I had stayed in Britain I would have been practising with kids my age who didn't have the right attitude and there is a chance I would have been spoiled myself. In Spain I was practising with guys up to thirty years old, some of them already on the Men's Tour, some who had just started, but all of them with highish world rankings and ambition. To me, it was perfect. I was fifteen and the next youngest guy to me in that group was nineteen.

I had to look after myself, be disciplined, hard-working and get used to playing on clay in hot conditions. I learned so much just being away from home. There's so much bitching that goes on in British tennis, between parents and players and everyone. It's ridiculous. I still have friends from that age group, and I remember well what it was like. We laugh about it now, but it wasn't fun to be around at the time. When you went to tournaments, the parents were saying things about you, hoping you would lose because you were one of the best players. There was way, way too much jealousy. In Spain there was no jealousy, just hard work.

That is a huge part of the reason I left home. I remember leaving my house feeling a kind of pang of regret. I don't know what caused it exactly. Whether it was going into the unknown in a foreign culture or worrying that I might be homesick, I don't know, but once I was in Spain, I didn't want to come back.

That does not mean that all went smoothly for me. There were twenty-nine courts at the Academy, clay for the elite, hard for the average players and another type of hard court for the beginners. I remembered my mum telling me to go over to the clay courts, say who I was and start practising. So I walked over and the coach had never heard of me.

'I don't know anything about you,' he said. 'Go and practise on the hard courts.' So, OK, I went over to the hard courts and the first person I found there was a guy called Danny Valverdu from Venezuela and he was quite rude to me. I didn't know anyone. I had lunch on my own, dinner on my own. It was awkward.

Then, at dinner on the second day, Danny said: 'Come and sit over here.' He's one of my best friends now. We played doubles together for a while on the junior circuit and never lost a match. We had to surrender the final of the Canadian Open Juniors because I had to go and play the qualifying event for the US Open, but we have never lost a match together on court.

Very soon Barcelona seemed perfect to me. I lived in the dormitory above the school block and every night we would play football on the artificial pitch, copy each other's homework and have fun on the PlayStation. There were always people around. I liked that. You could be immature and mess around, and not get told off by your parents. I must have got quite a few things out of my system at that age. Lights out was midnight and there was a woman called Arantxa to make sure we all went to bed in time. Of course, we didn't. We'd be making a noise or annoying one another. Then you would hear Arantxa open a door, march down the hall and we would all have to pretend to be asleep. No one was really wicked, though.

A couple of my friends did a few things like boxing with a proper helmet and gloves. They were always trying to get me to do it but I wouldn't. I didn't fancy it. One of them used to get punched without a mouthguard and braces on his teeth. He cut his mouth every single time. He was mad. He didn't make it on the tour either.

At the weekend, practice was optional. Most of the time I would train in the morning and then take the bus into the city, to the shops, the Hard Rock Café, the English-speaking cinema, the go kart track or the internet café. I loved it. I felt free and independent and, although the days were ridiculously long, the priorities were tennis first and school second which was the right thing for me. I still needed to study, but the most important thing to me was tennis. My priorities had been the same in Scotland, I just wasn't allowed to follow them.

The days were incredibly busy. I'd train on court from 9am to noon, do fitness from noon to 1pm; lunch 1pm–2pm; school 2pm–4pm; tennis 4.30pm–6pm; school 6pm–8pm. I'd certainly said goodbye to my younger self. I'd gone from training one and a half hours a day on three or four days a week, to four and a half hours a day of high intensity tennis in hot conditions abroad.

Inevitably there was trouble. I wasn't eating properly. I didn't really like the food there. I'd still eat, but for the daily energy I was using, I wasn't eating enough. Then I woke up one morning, in the early hours, feeling just terrible. My head was throbbing, I had a huge temperature and, having walked to the toilet, I fainted. I found myself lying on the ground in the cubicle, struggled to my feet and, still feeling terrible, fell again. I banged my back and for two days I felt awful. I think I was literally burned out. After that I realised I had to do things properly.

It may have helped that I've never smoked, and after two episodes in Barcelona, I never drank again either. I had a bad experience. I made myself look like a prat in front of my friends. The only reason I was drinking was to see what it was like to get drunk. I hate the taste of alcohol. I absolutely hate it. I don't even like champagne. I don't like wine. I think beer is disgusting and I haven't tried whisky.

It was just curiosity that made me drink on those couple of occasions. I think you can have enough fun without drinking and I prefer the taste of lemonade to beer. I was pretty sick after my drinking bouts, but the only reason I felt bad in the morning is because I knew I'd behaved like an idiot. I just thought: Why? What was the real point?

It is not as if Mum and Dad had talked to me or given me a lecture on the facts of life before I left. They didn't. When I lived at home, I didn't want to go out on the street, drink cheap alcohol and think it was cool to be hanging around. I was always told to look after myself, but we didn't have a huge chat about it. I called home every couple of days when I was away, but basically I enjoyed doing my own thing.

When I first went to the Academy I didn't feel I had any time to have a girlfriend, I wasn't interested at all, but after a year of being there – when I passed my exams and stopped doing school – then I started to have some time. I began to speak to the girls more and take a bit of an interest.

People used to say that I was shy. I didn't feel it. Maybe it is because until I know someone, I just don't like to say that much. If I had to meet a roomful of people, I wouldn't feel uncomfortable. It's fine. It's just that if I don't know someone and trust them, I have never seen the point of going up and speaking to them.

So there was this one girl from Germany at the Academy, we were friends pretty much the whole time I was there. I always liked her. Then a different girl came and I started spending time with her. Then the first one got jealous and decided to go out with me. It just sort of happened.

She was the one the newspapers descended on when I did well at Wimbledon. However, we hardly saw each other. We were both travelling and there was just no point in continuing. I saw her for ten days in three months.

I was quite lucky really. There was no one I was really infatuated with and couldn't stop thinking about. It never got in the way of my training and practice. I was never trying to sneak away from training to go and see someone. There was no one I liked that much.

Eventually, I moved out of the dormitories and went to live with a Romanian family who rented a couple of rooms in their flat to me and a couple of other guys. One of them, Matt Lowe, was my best friend at the time. We used to mess around quite a lot. The apartment was pretty high up and we would chuck wet paper towels out of the window. On a scale of one to

Asbo, I guess it was pretty minor, but even so it nearly got us into terrible trouble one day.

We were throwing the paper towels at a girl. She went away. We thought that was the end of it. Fifteen minutes later the same girl came back with five guys. We were completely panicking when they came into the apartment block and started banging on everyone's door. We didn't have a clue what to do. They knocked on our door. We tried not to move or breathe and didn't answer. Then some other resident shouted at the guys: 'Get the hell out of our block.' Finally they did, but not before the flat owner's son, who had been sleeping, got up and asked us what was going on. What could we say? Only 'Don't know!' with as much innocence as we could.

But, in general, we didn't commit any arrestable offences. Although I don't know for sure whether you can get arrested for dropping wet paper towels in Spain.

As for Spanish, the language, I didn't learn much. I only picked up little bits and pieces. The Academy was so international that all the coaches spoke English. I wasn't forced to use Spanish and that is the one regret I have from my time there – not learning to speak the language fluently. It is a shame because Mum is great at languages, having studied French, German and Latin. I should have tried to learn but I didn't.

I loved life in Spain. For a Scot, I didn't even suffer from sunburn. My nose got burnt but the rest of me was OK. Much more importantly, I made friends that I still have to this day, like Danny and a Peruvian guy called Carlos Mier who I didn't speak to for a year because he is the shyest person I've ever met and doesn't speak unless you speak to him first.

We got to know each other better when we all went on tour to South America at the beginning of 2003. It was five weeks in conditions I'd never faced before, moving from Colombia to Ecuador, Peru, Bolivia and Paraguay. It was so good for me because I'd spent ten days over Christmas training indoors in freezing Scottish weather only to fly to Colombia to play doubles and singles in 30-degree heat on clay courts. It taught me about the quick adjustments you need to make on the tennis tour.

I'd never played for such a long stretch before and some of the places were an eye-opener in terms of the poverty. It made us realise how lucky we were to be getting everything paid for. We also came to realise we were really naïve and had a lot to learn about travelling.

An American guy came up to us in Colombia. He seemed really friendly and asked us if we were tourists. We told him we were here to play tennis. 'Oh, that's great,' he said. 'I came over a week ago to play golf, but the guerrillas came and stole all my stuff, including my watch and my wallet.' He came out with this story and then asked us for money. He said he just needed enough for a place to stay that night. We said: 'No, sorry,' but some of us were feeling bad. We didn't really know what to make of it.

A couple of days later, this guy is in the lobby of our hotel and caught trying to steal the bags of some of the players who had just arrived. It made us realise we had to be careful. Most of us came back with our bags only three-quarters full after people had helped themselves to our clothes and other stuff. We were just fair game. It was a fun trip, I enjoyed it, but I realised I had to look out for myself.

On court, I did a reasonable job. In Colombia I won the tournament, the Pony Malta Cup, without dropping a set. I reached the third round in Ecuador. I was a quarter-finalist in

Peru, semi-finalist in Bolivia and quarter-finalist again in Paraguay. I was pretty sure I was making progress, but whether it was far or fast enough, I didn't really know.

Danny and I then hooked up in the doubles and went on our successful run at a string of tournaments in Italy. We won three or four titles, I won a singles. I reached round three of the French Open Juniors, losing in straight sets to Marcos Baghdatis, who was two years older than me and looked like a full-grown man with a beard. At Wimbledon I did badly, losing in the first round, but from there I won the Canadian Open Juniors against a string of older opponents, beating the Romanian Florin Mergea, the Wimbledon junior champion, 6–2 6–1 in the final. I was almost in the World Junior Top 10.

Naturally, it couldn't last. In my short career so far, the one thing you can say is that it is an absolute roller coaster ride. Up, down, good, bad, great, terrible. At least I've never wanted to get off, though in 2003, aged sixteen, I was close.

I said to the Academy physiotherapist one day that my knee was hurting me. He said: 'It's probably growing pains. It's just playing a lot of tennis on hard surfaces. Take a little bit of time off and make sure you ice it.' So I would do that, it would be OK and then it would come back. Worse than before.

I went to see the physio again. 'Try to keep everything loose and ice it,' he said. In other words: 'Yes, I know it's sore but it's not too bad.' I'm telling Leon, my coach: 'It's bad, it's hurting me,' but he's listening to me and listening to the physio as well, and eventually accepts that it's just growing pains.

So I carried on playing. I faced Baghdatis again at a tournament in Luxembourg, and lost a 3-hour match 7–6 6–7 7–5. My knee was incredibly sore afterwards but ten days later I turned up for a Spanish Futures event, the type of tournament where juniors come up against seniors who have already played on the tour. In other words: it's tough. My first match was against a 30-year-old professional who'd played at Wimbledon, Emilio Benfele Alvarez, and it was a really good win for me. I woke up the next day and I couldn't walk. My coach said: 'It's not too bad,' so I went on court, lost 6–0 6–0 and didn't play another match for seven months. That was probably the worst time of my life. I was young. I was doing well. I was enjoying playing. In juniors I was competitive with the top guys two years older than me. I was pretty much in the World Top 10, and, suddenly, all gone.

It seems ridiculous now that I didn't retire from that last match, but at the time I was sixteen and when I said it was sore, no one was believing me. I didn't have the confidence to go against them. Maybe it was growing pains, but I didn't think so. I went to see a physio, then a doctor and they both said the same: 'It's inflamed, just rest it. It will calm down.'

I was back home in Scotland by now and after a little while I tried to play again. It was hopeless. I remember that a newspaper photographer came to take a picture of me and Jamie and a couple of other guys on a court. He asked us to squat for the picture. I tried but my knee said 'No'. I wasn't even close to being able to do it. I was in agony, and this was ten days before I was supposed to be going to the Australian Open Juniors.

In the end, after more doctors, more physios, more opinions, I was desperate. The first time they said they couldn't find anything wrong, I was fine. The next time, I was upset. The third time, after I had had a scan and an X-ray, I was crying. The fourth time, I was completely dejected. I was angry and feeling so sorry for myself, but when you are that age you can't turn round to the doctor and say: 'What the hell are you talking about?' I'd do that now. I'd demand answers to questions and not go away until I had them.

'You're fine' is one of the hardest things to hear when you know you're not and the thing you love most has been taken away from you. All you're getting told by the experts is: 'Just come back in three or four weeks.' I felt they weren't taking me seriously. I was thinking: 'This is my career. You're not giving enough time to me to understand the problem.'

Eventually, I was told I had a bipartite patella, a pretty common condition that affects about seven in every 100 people. It means that your kneecap is not fully formed, with fibres and tissues making a kind of canal down the middle where everyone else has bone. My kneecap was basically on fire. That is not a technical description but that is exactly how it felt. Surgery wasn't an option as I was still growing, so I just had to be patient and do the rehab.

I went to the gym every single day and did upper body weights. I was miserable. It was horrible. I tried playing tennis, just going on court and hitting balls sitting in a wheelchair or standing on one leg, but it wasn't the same. When you sit in a chair, it feels so strange. Everything seems much bigger and the net feels ridiculously high.

It reminded me of a wheelchair player I'd met in Tarbes as a junior who had the hardest handshake I've ever felt in my life. That was just him saying hello. I thought: 'Wow. My hand is completely crushed.' It hurt like hell. Now I know why they have to be so strong. Having tried and abysmally failed to do what those guys do every day I have so much respect for them.

The injury seemed to go on and on. My mum has described the time as 'hell for everyone', but the knee finally responded to rest. By the following summer I was ready to play again, nervously, as a wild card on the grass at Surbiton. It was a nice easy warm-up for Wimbledon – I wish. In fact, I was playing Jimmy Wang, a 20-year-old former junior world number one, ranked about 200 on the senior tour. Within minutes I was two breaks up, leading 3–0 in the first set. I'm thinking 'Wow, I wasn't expecting that.' Then at 3–1 I slipped on the grass and hurt my hip. Game over.

I don't even want to think about how disgusted I was, but there are only two options: give up or keep going. I kept going, not least because I met a man who proved to be really good for me. Mum found this French physio, Jean-Pierre Bruyere, working part-time for the LTA, and I don't know how he was able to get me fit enough to play Roehampton, a tournament for juniors running up to the first week of Wimbledon, but he did. In ten days I was on court again, winning 6–1 6–1. In fact, I won my first three matches really, really easily and reached the final. There, I admit, I faced an obstacle in the shape of Gael Monfils, my long-time friend and rival, who was runaway world number one junior. He had already won the Australian and French Opens that year, and this was his warm-up for an assault on Wimbledon. I lost 7–5 6–4, having served for the first set. Normally I'd be furious with myself, but this time I was happy. I was so relieved, after all I'd been through, that I hadn't completely lost my game.

I owe a great deal to Jean-Pierre. He was one of the most caring people I'd ever met. After all those physios and doctors telling me: Don't worry about it, it's just growing pains, come back in three weeks, at last here was someone who believed me. He always told me: 'Don't let anyone mess with you. Take care of yourself. I want you to achieve your dreams. I don't want anyone to stop you by pushing you too hard when you're too young. It's your body, your life. If you're hurt – regardless of what anyone says – don't play.' You can see that I've carried that advice with me ever since. He was often pretty dramatic about things, but then he's French. I was fine about that. I understood him and knew he would occasionally go over the top in his analysis. If I said my back was hurting, he would say: 'OK, let's get an MRI scan.' Many physios would say: 'It's fine, don't worry.' Jean-Pierre would say: 'Maybe it's the start of a stress fracture. Let's be sure.' I was certainly grateful to be in good hands and he has helped me through many other injuries since.

I reached the third round of Wimbledon Juniors, losing to Woong-Sun Jun of Korea. I didn't play particularly well, but my body was still hurting from my efforts the week before after a seven-month lay-off. I'd lost strength and coordination, but slowly I could feel my game rebuilding again.

Maybe not so slowly. I took off with Leon to play four Futures tournaments, three in Spain and one in Italy. Basically I was a 17-year-old taking on the men. I won the first, made the semis of the second, the second round of the third and that's when I stopped working with Leon, my coach since I was eleven.

I can't remember what the row was about, but it was certainly something silly. I was at that age when I was starting to grow up and I didn't want to be treated like a kid. I was rebelling against being told what to do. We'd been together so long that Leon, though not quite a father-figure, had obviously been telling me off since I was a child. I respected him. He was a good friend and very caring, but maybe I was at the stage where I was starting to become a bit more independent which led to arguments.

Leon went home and Mum came to Italy instead. Somehow I managed to win the tournament, despite being 2–5 in the final set of one match and 3–5 down in the next. I was pleased. It gave me confidence, and I needed that badly. After the longest and most miserable lay-off of my life, I was setting off for the US Open Juniors – with no coach.

New York is unbelievable. I enjoy it. I love it. The noise, the pace, the energy, the size of it. I love the people. New Yorkers are perceived as arrogant and loud, but I think they're just being friendly. We were staying at the Grand Hyatt Hotel right above Central Station and the minute I walked in the lobby I was amazed by how enormous it was. There was a shop where you could get bagels and the people at reception were so great. Sometimes I had to get up and go out at 5am, and everyone in the hotel seemed upbeat even at that time in the morning. If you get up at 5am in Britain and go into a garage or something, everyone's miserable, but they seem happy to see you over there. It's been my favourite tournament ever since.

My room was huge. It had a massive bed, loads of pillows, a big TV with thirty channels. This was paradise. At Wimbledon, they put the juniors up in little rooms with one bed and one desk, miles away from the courts. There was absolutely no comparison. The US Open made the juniors feel they were part of the main tournament and I loved that most of all.

When I went to Flushing Meadows where the tournament is played, about a half-hour bus ride from the city, I just thought: 'Wow.' It was a completely different atmosphere to anything I'd ever experienced. There is no way that Wimbledon would let juniors mix with the stars, but in New York we were allowed in the main lounge area. Everywhere I looked there seemed to be one of the best players in the world. I met Guillermo Coria who was one of my favourite players at the time. I saw the Ryder Cup golfer Sergio Garcia on the putting machine. The fact they even have a putting machine in the lounge is fantastic. I beat Tim Henman on that, much to his annoyance, because he is a pretty low handicap golfer.

I owed a lot to Tim that week. He was great to me. He was on a run to the semi-finals in the main draw and so we spent quite a bit of time together. He didn't have to. I was just a Scottish kid in the juniors, but he found time to teach me backgammon – which I have repaid many times by beating him whenever we happen to meet. He tells it differently though!

The first match I ever watched there was a night match, Kim Clijsters against Justine Henin. The place was completely packed and with an atmosphere more like a football match with the noise, the lights and the tension. It didn't matter that I was so high in the stadium I could barely see the ball. It wasn't the sight that affected me. It was the feeling it gave me. I realised I wanted to win here one day more than any other tournament in the world.

I had no idea the dream would come true, at the junior level, that very week. I won my first three matches, two of them indoors because of rain, for the loss of only seven games. That felt good. Seeded three, I was living up to the numbers.

It didn't happen for everyone. Gael Monfils was vying to become the first boy to win the junior grand slam since Stefan Edberg in 1983. He had won at Wimbledon after beating me in the Roehampton final, but then suffered an injury. In New York he was on his way back, but it was going to be tough. It was big news when he lost in the third round to a Serbian called Viktor Troicki. It was even bigger news – on the junior tour anyway –

when he was seen smashing his rackets to pieces in frustration afterwards. For the rest of us, however, it meant that the field had just opened up. A grand slam title was waiting to be won.

I was feeling pretty confident going into my next match – and, typically, nearly lost it. I had to battle my way out of trouble after losing the first set 2–6 to Sam Querrey, a tall Californian, in the quarter-finals. After that sharp reminder that I had to play with my brain as well as my racket, I played better against Mikhail Zverev of Germany in the semis and won in straight sets. However, it was not so much the match I remember as the day. This was Saturday September 11, the third anniversary of the terrorist attack on New York. It was my first big press conference at a grand slam event, and I ended up being asked about world terrorism. I said that I hadn't realised what day it was until I turned on the TV in my hotel room that morning, and how sad it was, but when I saw people crying, I turned it off again because I didn't want to feel like that when I walked on court.

I seemed to be having one new experience after another. The next one would be the grand slam junior final against Sergiy Stakhovsky of the Ukraine. I was on form, prepared, supported . . . and petrified. I've never been as petrified since. My mum was there, my brother, my uncle had flown in from Dallas, some of the other British juniors like Jamie Baker and Tom Rushby, all supporting me, but as I walked to Court Ten with Jamie at my side, listening to my iPod, I was really, really nervous. I wanted to win so much, but I lacked the confidence that comes from having won a major junior title.

The night before, we were sitting in a café – me, my brother, Jamie, Tom, my mum and a couple of coaches – chatting about the celebrations if I won the next day. Maybe that had been slightly premature. I certainly wasn't thinking that the next couple of hours would be easy as I stepped on to Court Ten.

It was packed. My mum and my friends were there in the corner. There wasn't an empty seat to be seen. The atmosphere crackled. I stopped my music, unpacked my rackets, took a deep breath and prepared to return serve in the first game of the first set. I was well prepared for the match because we had taken a video analyst from the Scottish Institute of Sports with us to the tournament and she had videoed Stakhovsky's semi-final match. My mum and she had analysed it and I'd watched it to decide on my tactics. I knew he would serve and volley and I knew I had to find his feet – make him volley up, so I could attack him. My return has always been the best part of my game and a few points later, I'd relaxed. I had almost broken his serve. I broke his next service game, and despite my previous nerves, the match went smoothly from there. I played well. The guy hardly had a chance and I won 6–4 6–2. At match point for the second time, he hit a return and I knew immediately it was going out at the back.

I dropped my racket, took my cap off, and I just put my head in my hands. I didn't cry. It was such a release. I suddenly felt so relaxed, so confident, so assured. After all the nerves and sacrifices and the injury, I had won a grand slam. That was the moment when I felt I could be one of the best players in the world.

I would know real fame at Wimbledon in a few months' time, but this was my first taste of the madness. The morning after the victory, I did interview after interview by live links back to London. I had no idea what was going on. They gave me earpieces, pointed cameras at me and I didn't have a clue where to look. I'd had a little media training when I was injured, but nothing prepares you for this. My mum was there, organising all the interviews, but when it came to doing them I was on my own. I just said what I thought, which may or may not have been a good thing.

I remember telling someone that the moment after I'd won, I hit a ball into the crowd aimed right for my mum. I said I was trying to hit her because she had been making so much noise. I was only joking, but I think some people took me seriously.

That evening we flew back to Edinburgh, with me feeling better and more relaxed that I'd ever known. Then we walked through the arrivals door at the airport and I realised how much life had changed. Gran was there, Leon was there, even Abby my dog was there, but so were about ten photographers and television crews, all waiting for me. There were more photographers at my house when I got home. I thought it was a little bit over the top for a junior. I hadn't seen anything yet.

Chapter Four:
The 100 Club

I almost didn't make the 2004 Sports Personality of the Year show because I was stuck in a toilet. This is true. It was hardly the most glamorous start to my celebrity life. I was due to pick up the award for Young Personality of the Year – Wayne Rooney had won it the year before – and within about an hour of the show starting I was stuck in a hotel bathroom behind a door that was completely jammed. My friend was trying to prise it open from the other side with a two-pence piece. He couldn't do it. He called reception and a guy came up with a wrench and he couldn't do it either. Obviously we were laughing at the start but gradually it didn't seem so funny.

On top of that, we were already late. I had been playing in a Futures event final in Spain that afternoon. Within seconds of the match finishing – I won – I had to rush for the airport with two huge bags and jumped on a plane. It was a tiny local airport in the north of Spain and the tournament director had to phone to ask them to hold the flight for me. I only just made it and when I got to Heathrow I somehow managed to come out of Terminal 1 instead of 2 where my mum and an old pal, Matt Brown, were waiting for me. By the time I found them and was escorted back into Terminal 2 by airport security to reclaim my bags, it was already 5pm and we had to be at the BBC Centre for 7pm. We took a cab to the hotel, grabbed something to eat and went up to the room to get ready.

I went for a quick shower, put my suit on – no cufflinks! Had to call down to the concierge and borrow a pair. Went back into the bathroom for a final brush of my teeth and couldn't get out! I was stuck in there for about twenty minutes, sweating buckets, before the guy from reception went away, came back with a knife and finally opened the door. I flew out, leapt in a cab and made it just in time.

It was pretty cool but also quite nerve-racking to receive my award from Boris Becker. I tried to remember all the advice I'd been given, like 'Don't chew gum!' because that had been Wayne Rooney's problem the year before. I had to do this speech in front of all the best sports people in Britain and I was really young at the time. So I played it straight, no jokes, and it went pretty well. Or so I'm told.

Afterwards I met Chris Eubank who was wearing a top hat and carrying a cane. Being a massive boxing fan, I was loving that. I met Sir Clive Woodward. Kelly Holmes was there. I remember laughing at Matt snapping everyone and anyone with his throw-away camera! The best thing, though, was being out of the toilet. It occurred to me that I was probably the only winner there who had just been sprung from a toilet but I didn't mention that at the time.

Maybe that wasn't the ideal way to turn the year, but at least I was now a tennis player ranked 411 in the world, with a couple of sponsorship deals, thanks to the US Open Junior win, and every intention of going up the rankings by a long way. I actually said in an interview with the BBC that by the end of

Apparently I couldn't wait to get on my feet, so they strung me up

I could scowl even back then!

Family holiday in France with friends. Dad in green, Mum in grey, Jamie in navy and me, aged three, in my Scotland goalie top

Looking good in my kilt aged four
at Aunt Lynne's wedding

On holiday in France with Jamie.
I'm told I made this face every time
someone aimed a camera at me

At Dunblane Sports Club with Jamie when
I was six. Check out the Agassi denim shorts
with the pink lycra underneath!

Primary One at Dunblane Primary School

Trying my hand at cricket aged six
wearing my Hibs goalie top

Chilling with Nina, my gran's dog

Watching Jamie
play football
aged seven

At the Hibs Kids
Fun Day at Easter
Road (aged five)
with striker
Gareth Evans

Glad my backhand
footwork has
improved since
I was eight

Gladiators Day at
Gleneagles Hotel.
Note I was knocking
Jamie off the blocks!!

With mum and Jamie at
the tennis club aged nine

(*Below left*) About to take
off on another overseas
trip aged eleven

(*Below right*) Looking
good in my new Adidas
tracksuit aged eleven

Me and my gran with my Orange
Bowl Trophy in December 1999.
She never did give it back!

Orange Bowl Champion

With my coach Leon Smith

Grinding it out at the National 14U
Championships in Nottingham, 1999

(*Inset*) School photo –
First year at Dunblane High

My eleventh birthday bowling party with Jamie and some pals,
followed by McDonald's. Pretty sure I won

2005 I wanted to be in the Top 100. A few people said: 'He should keep his mouth shut. He's got a long way to go.' Perhaps that was a bit precocious. I wasn't the world's best junior, I had never played in an ATP event, I had won four Futures events (the lowest tier of senior tennis) but had not even reached the quarter-finals of a Challenger (the next tier up) since 2003. Put it this way, Roger Federer was not exactly quaking at the thought of meeting me.

I could not possibly have known that by the end of the year I would play Federer in my first ATP event final, beat Tim Henman in Switzerland, cause 'P-Andymonium' at Wimbledon and become the youngest Briton ever to play in the Davis Cup. I could not even have imagined that, because the start of 2005 was horrible.

My coach, Pato Alvarez who worked at the Sanchez-Casal Academy, had this plan. He was sure I could reach the World Top 50 pretty quickly and he wanted me to play in the qualifying events for a few Challengers in South America to get there. He kept saying, 'You have to learn how to play at the next level, the Futures level is very, very bad.' That meant winning matches and I was losing them instead. I was playing badly. I had a growth spurt which caused problems with my back. It was a horrible run and I was losing early in loads of tournaments. I struggled for two months, finding the step up to Challengers, even qualifying for Challengers, really difficult.

In the middle of this, I suddenly received a wild card for my first full ATP event, the tournament in Barcelona. I think Emilio Sanchez has contacts with the tournament and he probably swung it for me. I should have been intimidated, yet for some reason, I managed to feel quite confident. I don't really understand why except it felt like playing on home ground with all my friends from the Academy coming to watch. Obviously I was really nervous, but I was able to practise with the Spanish players, including Juan Carlos Ferrero, who were already on the tour. It was the first time I had been able to hit with players of that level for three or four days in a row. Instead of making me more worried, it actually boosted my confidence. This was my chance to play in front of a decent crowd for a decent amount of money against decent opposition. My first opponent was Jan Hernych, a 25-year-old Czech player who was ranked 67 in the world. I suppose I should have been intimidated, but my mum sent me a scouting report the night before telling me how he played, and saying that my gran was a better volleyer than him.

I was so close to winning that match. I should have won. I had chance after chance. I had something like 18 break points but only converted about 3. I was a break up in the third set but eventually lost 3–6 6–4 6–4. Looking back, I think I played pretty well, but at the time I was furious. I came off the court snarling: 'That was a terrible, terrible performance from me.' I felt I'd let him off the hook, having twice been within a point of a 4–1 lead in the final set. I had expected to win. I didn't think he was anything special as a player, despite being seven years older than me and ranked over 300 places higher. I was totally frustrated.

Later, when I calmed down and looked back on that day, I could see that the match had helped me a good deal. I had played in an ATP tournament and I had not felt out of place. I knew from that moment on that I could definitely reach the World Top 100. That had been my dream. Now it was my goal.

But first I had to resolve an ongoing problem with Pato as

my coach. It had degenerated into a difficult relationship. When I met him at the Academy, he struck me as a really friendly, nice guy. He used to bring us sliced oranges that we would eat by the side of the court while we were training. He was famous for having coached about forty guys who reached the Top 50, including Ilie Nastase, and he is credited with being one of the main reasons behind the turn around in Spanish tennis in the last twenty years. They called him 'El Guru del Tennis'.

There is no doubt he was hugely knowledgeable and I know I learned loads from him, but by now he was a 69-year-old man and I was a 17-year-old boy and maybe the numbers just didn't add up. It was a bit like being with a grandparent. Also, I wasn't always travelling individually with him. Usually, I was with a small group of players – three or four of us would go to tournaments together – and I was at the stage where I felt I needed a little bit more individual coaching. I wasn't particularly happy. I seemed to need someone to pick me up more. And, I'd been in Spain going on for three years. The training was great, but it was becoming very repetitive. Barcelona had been good for me, but it was time to leave.

I looked at myself pretty ruthlessly. I basically had no variation in my game. I was playing the same way as all the other guys around my ranking. I wasn't as fit, nor as experienced as them and, mentally, I wasn't as strong. I was losing a lot of matches. I needed a change and wanted to play my own game.

At first, the separation was uncomfortable. I remember spending my eighteenth birthday at a Challenger in Germany on my own. It was probably the first birthday in my life when I hadn't seen anyone from my family. I was struggling, but I didn't give up and it wasn't long before I managed to turn it around.

My mum came over to be with me when I played in the French Open Juniors in Paris, my first grand slam since becoming the US Junior Champion. I was ambitious for the tournament. I wanted to prove I could perform on clay as well as hard courts. I felt well and determined. Then I got food poisoning the night before the tournament started. I was running to the toilet every twenty minutes before my game against Piero Luisi of Venezuela in the first round but, fortunately, the problem eased and when I beat the highly-rated Argentinian Juan-Martin Del Potro in straight sets in the quarters, I felt pretty happy. I even gave a press conference afterwards and we had a laugh about a streak of blood on the court that I left from scraping my knuckles. I thought it added to the scene of battle.

If tennis teaches you anything, it is that your mood can change overnight. My semi-final was against Croatia's Marin Cilic, who went on to be the number two junior in the world, and suddenly everything was rubbish again. It had been raining and our match was switched to one of the smaller show courts where the wind was swirling and making it difficult to get into a rhythm. I was furious at blowing a lead to lose the first set and smashed a couple of rackets on the court. The frustration was getting to me so badly that at one point I just yelled: 'What are you *doing*, Andy?'

I tried not to make any excuses afterwards. I had been playing doubles with my friend Andrew Kennaugh late into the night before, which might have affected me, but I was still furious with myself. Then I tried to be more rational. Losing here was just giving me more time to get used to grass. I felt I could do well at Queen's, then Nottingham and maybe even at Wimbledon. It didn't daunt me. I don't know why I thought that. I just did.

I went into Queen's Club unknown, unseeded, and pretty anonymous except to my family and my dog. I came out of Wimbledon four weeks later and everyone seemed to know who I was. I felt exactly the same person, but the way I was treated was suddenly very different. Just to prove it, the ATP tournament at Newport, Rhode Island, offered me a wild card as a kick-start to my American hard-court tour. Of course, I said yes, and – not for the first time – I then found myself in trouble.

The tournament is really nice but the grass courts there are terrible. Everyone knows that. Unfortunately, not everyone says so in their press conference after the game. I did. I said they were the worst tennis courts I'd ever played on, which probably wasn't the most tactful thing to say after the tournament had been kind enough to give me a wild card. But, it was what I felt.

It was a fair indication of how much they cared about the surface when the tournament director and the players joined in a massive game of whiffleball, like baseball only with a lighter ball, on the courts during the player party. We were sliding into bases and everything. Can you imagine the groundsman at Wimbledon letting you do a thing like that? It was pretty funny, in a way.

Something always seems to happen to me at Newport. The following year, I received a point penalty for losing my temper during a match. That's the only point penalty I've ever had. Back in 2005, though, I scuffed my way into the second round and then came up against a Frenchman called Antony Dupuis who I should have beaten comfortably even though he was ranked 111. But it had rained. The courts were so soft and the bounces were so low, I couldn't find any rhythm. I was struggling big time and getting very frustrated. Having done quite well at Wimbledon this was ugly tennis.

My language was OK but I thumped a ball into the crowd and hit my racket into the court where it made a huge mark because the surface was so soft. Whenever the press compile lists of my 'bad moments', Newport 2005 and 2006 often get a mention. In 2007, I had to miss the tournament due to my wrist injury and I expect the organisers were really relieved.

That was just the beginning of the American adventure. I looked ahead at six more tournaments, plus the US Open where I would be playing the senior event for the first time. Mark Petchey and I were road buddies, now that he'd been confirmed as my coach. I hoped I could afford him. Money is not the reason you play tennis, but it certainly helped when my prize money began to outstrip my expenses for the first time. I used to be afraid of checking out of hotels in case my prize money didn't cover it. Budgets were really tight. At least eating cheap food wasn't a problem because I didn't know what expensive restaurant food tasted like. When I reached the semi-finals of the French Open Juniors, it was mostly on a diet of baguettes and chocolate spread.

I don't know how many thousands of miles we did on our American tour, but the next stop was Aptos, California right across the country. Tony Pickard would have been pleased. At last I was back on the Challenger circuit. All the press had gone and now I was back playing again where I deserved to be in front of fifteen, maybe twenty, people. I wasn't even living in a hotel. Mark and I were staying with a family, and their dog, and we had one room, with a dartboard. We played a lot of darts that week.

I played quite a bit of tennis too, winning my first Challenger when I had never previously been beyond the quarter-finals. The prize money was over $10,000. That was a handy amount to put away. Next up was Indianapolis, a $500,000 ATP event that I entered with a wild card. I won a round there which did my confidence good (prize money $5,225) and then we went on to a little $75,000 tournament in Granby, Canada (where I won $1,460), followed by a flight across the continent to Vancouver for a $100,000 Challenger in one of the nicest cities I have ever been to.

I really enjoyed that tournament, but after the quarter-finals Mark had to leave me to go to a wedding back in Britain. I was there on my own and feeling devastated. I suppose I was still quite young to be by myself abroad trying to organise everything, including courts, practise, flights and hotels. I lost 6–7 in the final set of the semi-final ($2,920) and then I had to fly six hours on my own to New York.

Mark joined me again and we went to Binghampton, about a three-hour drive north of Manhattan, which was probably one of the worst tournaments I have ever played. The courts are like the ones you would find in a public park. The referee's office was a Portakabin. There was no food and you couldn't shower unless you were willing to use the facility in a caravan.

I must admit I do remember having a laugh when we got there, mainly because I was – I still am – pretty immature for my age. When Mark was driving the car, I used to honk the horn when we came to a standstill. He used to (kind of) laugh about it as well. But on the way to Binghampton, we found ourselves in a pretty rough place near a trailer park. I couldn't resist. I honked the horn for a pretty long time and Mark hit me and yelled: 'Don't do that. You could get us both killed.' It was the first time he'd told me off for being an idiot. I found it quite funny, but it was also rather awkward. He was like a father figure to me, but also a friend, and it was sometimes difficult to know how to behave with one another. Obviously it didn't upset me too much because I won Binghampton ($7,200) and then set off south to Cincinnati, another ATP event that had given me a wild card.

All this criss-crossing America was tiring but I was enjoying it too. I was getting stronger and fitter all the time, but the improvements went beyond physical. I had a moment on a tiny little propeller plane to Cincinnati after Binghampton that I will always remember as it suddenly occurred to me how close I was to the World Top 100, having played six weeks over there and risen to a ranking of about 130. 'I'm so close now,' I thought. 'I've got a really good chance of doing it.'

It was realising a dream. I wasn't there yet, but I knew it was going to happen soon. Small planes like that are not normally the most comfortable experience, but it didn't even register. I was thinking about what I'd put into my career, the sacrifices I'd made and that's when I realised it was starting to pay off. I'm not a crier, but I was quite emotional on that plane. When you put four or five years of your life into something at that age, it is a big deal. Only as recently as April I'd been playing rubbish and not enjoying it. This was August and it had all started to click. I sat there feeling really satisfied. Mark was sleeping opposite me – there was only one seat on each side of the aisle. I didn't wake him up. It was a moment for me alone.

Cincinnati might have brought me back to earth, but instead

I had another amazing experience. I won a first round against Taylor Dent (who must have been pretty sick of me by then because I'd won our match at Queen's only two months before) and then faced the highest-ranked player I'd so far come up against, the fantastically talented Marat Safin, who had won the Australian Open that year.

I hardly believed I was on the court with him. This was the first grand slam champion I had ever played and I had a huge amount of respect for him. Taking him to three sets was a pretty good effort in the circumstances. The final score was 6–4 1–6 6–1. My shoulder hurt, but my confidence wasn't dented at all.

By now I'd played seven weeks in a row and if the All England Club had been willing to negotiate a main-draw wild card for me at the US Open by swapping one for Wimbledon the following year, I could have avoided playing in the qualifiers for the main draw. But they weren't. I was tired and annoyed. All the other grand slams offer a few wild cards into their own tournament to get their own country's best players into the others' – it is like a deal that suits everyone – but Wimbledon refused, so I had to play three matches of qualifying. Tired and cross or not, I qualified.

My first-round match against the Romanian Andrei Pavel remains one of the most satisfying victories of my life. Remember that when I left Britain there were people telling me I wasn't fit enough, wasn't strong enough and I wouldn't last a five-set match. This grand slam challenge was a five-set match, against a player who was thirty-one years old with loads of experience and I was just coming off a run of seven straight tournaments with a sore shoulder. What happened next made the front pages – but not in a good way.

In the middle of the match I drank too much of my energy drink in one go and threw up all over the court. Twice. I don't mind drama in my matches but this was over the top. At first, I just felt I was going to burp but somehow that turned into me being sick all over Pavel's bag. (We had a bit of a joke about it afterwards. At least, I did.) I sat down and when I went to stand up again, the same thing happened. The crowd were groaning, especially the second time. I think it's quite funny but I've never wanted to see any of the videos.

It was one of those matches that, for a lot of reasons, I will never, ever forget. I don't know how long I was on court. The official statistics say 192 minutes, but they must be wrong. It felt nearer five hours to me. I had agreed with my critics who said I needed to get stronger and here was the proof I was going in the right direction. I won 6–3 3–6 3–6 6–1 6–4 and I was *so* pleased. It was a huge match for me.

At the moment of victory, there had been so many things going through my head. I was thinking about what some British coaches had said to Mark when they found out he was going to work with me: 'You're not going to coach him are you? Be careful. He's pretty weak.' It had been so long since Britain had produced someone with a chance of being a decent player, not counting Tim, and yet here they were still being negative even though they didn't know me, they hadn't seen me practise, didn't know the sacrifices I had made and how hard I'd worked in Spain.

There was the usual British atmosphere of bitching behind people's backs. The coaches blaming the players, the players blaming the coaches. It could be a terrible atmosphere. I admit I'm making a generalisation, but it seemed to me that the majority of players and coaches were like that in Britain around that time. The match against Pavel was my vindication. At the end, I just put my finger to my lips and went: 'Ssssshhhh!' That was my way of saying, 'OK, you can all stop now. I'm not in bad shape for my age. I can get way better as a tennis player. Just give me some time.' I didn't have a career-threatening problem. I was young. That's all. I kept the thought to myself. I didn't even say anything controversial in the post-match press conference. I didn't have to say it out loud. There was just a feeling of inner warmth and satisfaction.

Tennis doesn't let you sit around feeling warm for very long. I lost another five-setter in the next round against Arnaud Clement in four hours and two minutes and an attack of cramp ended the tournament for me. That brought another volley of criticism about my fitness. I didn't let it undermine my confidence. Within a month, I was playing Roger Federer.

I was called up for the Davis Cup tie in Switzerland, only my second appearance since my debut against Israel in March, when David Sherwood and I played out of our skins to beat Erlich and Ram, their Top 10 doubles partnership, in four sets. That had easily been the highlight of my tennis career to that point – maybe it was the trigger to everything that happened next – and it had led us here, to Geneva, to come face-to-face with the greatest player in the world who had just won the US Open.

I was excited but also a little confused when Jeremy Bates, the Davis Cup captain, decided not to play Greg Rusedski on day one. I don't know why he put Alan Mackin, then ranked 262 in the world, up against Federer, and I suppose it wasn't a surprise that he was beaten 6–0 6–0 6–2. In the next rubber I played Stanislas Wawrinka with the full intention of beating him, even though he was in the World Top 60. That plan went wrong when I was 1–5 down in the first set. I won the next set in a tie-break, but lost the decider 6–4.

At least I had the honour of playing Federer in the doubles. That is not overstating how it felt to me, even though Greg and I lost in four sets. After the match I actually told Roger it was 'an honour' to play him and he told the press later that he reckoned he would have some battles with me in the future. He just didn't know how soon.

We both flew out of Geneva together for the next ATP tournament in Bangkok. Other than that, our situations were not quite identical. He was already a grand slam champion six times over. I arrived in Thailand ranked 109 in the world, having never proceeded beyond the third round of any ATP tour event. What happened next remains very special to me. I would call it the most significant moment of my year. Even better than reaching the third round of Wimbledon, this was the time and place that I finally achieved my main ambition to break into the World Top 100. I won a £400 bet too – a few of us had agreed that we each had to give £100 to the player who made the Top 100 first – but the money was secondary to the feeling.

To reach the landmark I had to beat the Swede Robin Soderling, and he is one of the best indoor players in the world. We don't get on either. He doesn't like me and I don't talk to him much. So there was quite a bit of tension in the match and although I won in straight sets, both of them went to a tie-break. When it was over my feeling of relief and happiness was amazing. I sent Mum a text just saying: 'I did it.'

From there the week just kept getting better. In the next round I beat Robby Ginepri and then I faced Paradorn

Srichaphan, ranked 57th at the time, in the semi-finals. He is absolutely massive in Thailand, one of the most famous people in his country, second only to the king, I'm told, and travels on a diplomatic passport. Being British, I know I have a partisan crowd on my side, but Paradorn has about four billion Asians on his.

I lost the first-set tie-break and started smashing my racket. This probably was not a good sign, but I decided to be more aggressive in the second set and Paradorn seemed to tire. To the huge disappointment of the crowd, I came back to take the match in three sets and so take my first crack at Roger Federer in a singles match that also happened to be my first ATP final.

I'd played him in singles before . . . but only on my tennis computer game. When I actually stood on the court with him and started warming up, I felt a little bit strange. It just didn't feel normal. I don't really know how to explain it. I stood there on the same court as Roger Federer and it was almost as though I was looking down on myself from above. It didn't actually feel as though I was on the court. It was something I had imagined so many times in my head that I wasn't sure whether it was real or not. It was like being parachuted into a scene you've imagined a hundred times before. You're obviously there, but you don't feel like it. That is probably why I can't really remember much about the match. As I've told you, I can remember pretty much every point of every match I play, I know my stats, but I can hardly remember a single point of this one. I wasn't really focused on what I was doing. It just didn't feel like reality.

This shouldn't make me sound like a complete freak. Quite a few players have told me that when they played Pete Sampras or Andre Agassi for the first time, it was a little bit weird. The stars are so famous, their mannerisms are so recognisable, that it hardly makes sense to be playing them. Obviously Federer didn't have too many mannerisms. He doesn't need them. He just walks backwards and forwards across the back of the court and looks really relaxed. But it was still a cool experience to me and will always remain pretty special.

I lost the match 6–3 7–5, having gone down 3–0 at the start of the match. In the second set I had some chances. Yeah, I got beaten in straight sets but I didn't feel I was completely outplayed. It was a learning experience, making the world number one do some running left and right. I wasn't blown away. It gave me some confidence.

We did the trophy ceremony together and while the press were taking pictures we had a little chat. He is a really nice guy. I was pretty relaxed by now. I no longer felt as if I was a character in my own video game. I'd taken eight games off Federer and lived with him for a while. I was in the World Top 100. I was on my way.

Unfortunately, I was on my way to an industrial estate in Belgium as well. My reward for reaching the final in Bangkok was a night flight out of Thailand to London followed by three and a half hours on a Eurostar train to a Challenger in Mons. It was as far removed from the bright lights as you could be, but I had committed to play and there was no question of pulling out. That triggers an automatic fine. So I hauled myself through three rounds, before having to retire midway through the match against Xavier Malisse with a hamstring injury.

The year could have ended there and still been outrageously good. I'd made all the progress I'd asked of myself, but there was one more surprise. I was in Switzerland for the ATP event in Basle. Federer had pulled out and the tournament offered me a wild card, not perhaps as a direct replacement, but, whatever the reason, I was glad to be there. They invited me to join the draw, when the player match-ups are pulled out of a hat. One of my favourite players, Guillermo Coria, had been invited too and I was joking with him that it was a total certainty that I would play Tim Henman in the first round. Sure enough, the tournament director drew Tim's name out of the hat and then said to me 'Who do you think will play him?' There was a long pause. The name came out. Of course, it was me.

Tim was a great player, he had been ranked 4th in the world and had played in six grand slam semi-finals. He was also my friend, he was my mentor, and I looked up to him. We had practised together many times and I had never beaten him. I knew this was going to be a tough game for me mentally. He wasn't just an opponent. He was the man who had been generous to me with his time and his advice. He often talked to me about my game and what I could do to improve. Now I was playing him. It was a very strange feeling.

I saw him briefly before the match but it was quite awkward. I just tried to concentrate on how I was going to play. My game stacks up quite well against his. He likes to come to the net and I like to pass. I felt very, very confident going in, but it was very close. I served for the match in the second set and then became a bit nervous which dragged us both into the third set, which I finally won 7–6.

That was a big win for me mentally. To beat him in a match as close as that when I could easily have crumbled was huge for my confidence. At the end he just said to me: 'Good job.' I didn't really say anything. I would *never* do or say anything to Tim to offend him. It is not the nicest moment when you shake hands with one of your friends after losing. Well, one of your friends is not so bad, but when it is someone who you know respects you and looks up to you as much I did to him, it must be a little bit strange. Maybe I was more sensitive about it than he was.

The press wrote about it afterwards as though some kind of baton had been passed between us. The end of an era, and that kind of thing. It wasn't that at all. It was me winning a tennis match and, to be honest, Tim having a bad back. Not for the first time, the media had gone slightly over the top.

After that match Sean Connery phoned me again. I can't remember exactly what he said. I suppose he might have been pleased that I'd finished the year pretty strongly. I was too. That Christmas I went home to Scotland as the 64th best tennis player in the world.

Chapter Five:
The Brit Awards

My mum is to blame for the state of British tennis. I think it was the tennis correspondent of the *Guardian* that came up with that joke. He said she should have had more children. But when you looked at where we stood in the world at the start of 2008, maybe he had a point. My brother Jamie was still the reigning Wimbledon mixed doubles champion, my win at the Qatar Open had taken me to number nine in the world, but while there were twelve Spaniards, fourteen Frenchmen, eleven Argentinians, eight Germans, six Russians, four Croatians, three Serbians, three Swedes, three Australians, three Chileans, two Swiss and two Belgians among the Top 100, from Britain there was just one. Me. Same as Latvia. Same as Cyprus. Tim Henman still had enough ranking points to be number four in Britain, but he'd been retired six months.

Of course it was an indictment of a system that's been wrong for years. Between the ages of thirteen and eighteen I saw at first hand what it was like. That is when I was most actively involved in British junior tennis, even though I was living away in Spain for some of the time. I often practised with British players, before and during competitions. You could just see the sort of stuff they got up to.

There are *some* players that work hard. Jamie Baker, my fellow Scot, is one of them and he's moved away to Saddlebrook in America now, just like I went to train in Spain. In Britain, there is something wrong with the mentality. There's just so much jealousy and negativity at most of the tournaments.

I used to go away on trips as a junior with one of the British teams for up to five weeks at a time and the other British guys were wanting me to lose. That's when you know something's wrong. These guys are supposed to be your friends, but nobody wants anyone to do better than they do themselves. It's good to be competitive, but why couldn't they just try to raise their own level or believe in themselves instead of wishing someone else would lose in the first round, so that they weren't the worst player there.

I've been there when British players are talking behind the back of another British player. There is way too much jealousy. It is so, so annoying. There is no need for it, especially at that age when everyone is trying to get better. It's not about just winning at that stage. It is about developing – but many of the players, parents and coaches seem to think that winning is the only thing. You just have to see what some of the kids and parents are like at some tournaments, and you would understand.

If I was sitting watching a match alongside the court, you would see me clap and shout and get pumped up on their behalf, but there were loads of examples of fellow British players sitting watching my matches, emotionless.

I've never seen a punch-up, but I have seen parents arguing

when their kids are playing. It was completely different in Spain. When I was playing Futures over there, the players didn't come with their parents. They didn't even have coaches with them half the time. They were just playing a tennis match. There were no other people involved.

There was no cheating or people 'forgetting' the scores, as I have experienced in Britain. Some kids had a habit of pretending they didn't remember the score because the rule is that if you don't have an umpire on the court – and many junior matches do not – you go back to the last score both players can agree on. Essentially you get cheats 'forgetting' that they have just lost a game. Funnily enough, the last thing they can remember is a score of 15-all. It happened to me all the time at that age.

We have such a closed mind compared to the rest of the world. Everyone seemed to think that being the best in Britain was great. I was always asked: 'What's it like to be number one in Britain?' I used to say: 'I don't mind.' I meant it. I didn't mind. It's a worldwide tour and I would much rather be 11th in the world than number one in Britain. You don't hear Rafa Nadal celebrating the fact that he's number one in Spain. He wants to be known as number two in the world. We live on a world circuit. That is how we are judged. I don't understand the whole British mentality. Why do they think it's a big deal to be British number one, when it's so completely irrelevant?

I can't work out exactly what is wrong with us. Perhaps it is as simple as money. Between the ages of thirteen and sixteen in Britain, you do get given a lot, but I think you have to be hard on players at that age. Maybe the people around them aren't hard enough. I don't think they understand how much effort the Spanish players put in, for instance, and when a Spanish guy turns eighteen, his funding stops. That's it. That is the cut-off. They make it on their own or they don't. It makes them work hard and look after themselves. However, when you're funded all the way through your career, then maybe sub-consciously you relax.

I know people could accuse me of being hypocritical when saying that, because one of my coaches, Brad Gilbert, was subsidised by the LTA when I was on the tour. But when I went to train in Spain as a teenager, my mum and dad had to find the money from all kinds of sources and I genuinely think it made me work harder, knowing the sacrifices they were making for me. I definitely did not have money on a plate during my junior career.

Obviously there isn't just one way of getting to the top. Borg did it differently from Becker, who did it differently from Agassi who was different from Sampras, and Federer was completely different again. There isn't just one way of doing it – but whichever way you choose to do it, players have to be made to work *hard*. If a player isn't told 'Go to the gym,' they're not going to go.

To me, the most important days in tennis are weekends. That's when semi-finals and finals are played. We don't have a nine-to-five job. We're not getting paid for five days a week. I can understand someone taking Sunday off, if they have worked really hard all week, but not the whole weekend.

I'm away a lot of the time, but I turn up at the National Training Centre in Roehampton, the multi-million pound headquarters of British tennis, and *no one* is there. I'm often looking for a partner to hit with and I have to call one of the coaches to try and find someone. He will call around three or four players and the response I have got from them range from:

'No, I don't normally practise at weekends' or 'I'm feeling a little bit sick today.' Last time it happened, I eventually found one guy, James Ward, who had already left the Centre because he couldn't find anyone to hit with either. He was on a train home, but he turned round and came back to practise with me. I really appreciated that. Maybe it's just a coincidence that he has spent much of his time training at an academy in Spain.

As for the others, there are fifty-two weekends in a year and if you are missing most of them, plus taking time off over Christmas, that's a lot of potential practice days lost. I would say that a large number of British players only practise half the days of the year.

At the Sanchez-Casal Academy during the time I was there, it was fine to take Sundays off. If you were absolutely knackered by the Saturday – and we were – it was sensible to have one day of rest. In Britain, however, I don't see the players doing what we did in Spain: the four-and-a-half hours on court every day, the four hours of school, the hour of fitness. I don't see it at all. Sometimes I turn up at Roehampton and it's like a ghost town.

I don't really know why the coaches don't enforce a greater work ethic, but if they're only paid for five days a week – and quite a few of the Belgian coaches go back home on a Friday evening and come back Monday morning – I can see their point of view. But I just don't get why nobody is going to the gym at weekends, or doing a recovery job. The LTA have built the facilities, but the players don't make the best use of them. When I go to the gym there never seems to be anyone in there. Basically, I have the equipment to myself, which is great for me, but what a waste. Only a couple of times have I ever walked in and found four or five other people there. There is something wrong with the mentality and work ethic of most of the British players.

There doesn't seem to be anyone who's brutally honest about it either. I think the best way is to confront it, especially when it has been so bad for so long. Someone in authority at British tennis should come out and say: 'Look, we're doing really badly. We're not good enough. We must make some changes.' But everyone is being really unrealistic with goals, announcing things like: 'We're going to get eight players in the Top 100 by 2008, and then it changed to seven players in the Top 100 by 2010.'

Which players are they then?

The new regime at the Lawn Tennis Association has definitely tried to improve things and get great coaches involved – that's without a doubt – people like Brad Gilbert and Paul Annacone. They are excellent and will do a good job – but, at the same time, would Sir Alex Ferguson ever work with Plymouth Argyle? You've got the best coaches in the world, who have helped Andre Agassi, Andy Roddick and Pete Sampras between them, but they are working with players who don't really deserve it.

These world-class coaches have gone from working with world-class players to teaching someone how to play tennis. That is not what they have done before. As a coach to Agassi or Sampras, they were not teaching them the game – it is pretty obvious that that had been sorted already – they were teaching tactics and helping with the mental approach. In my view, the current regime are putting the wrong people together.

The LTA have obviously spent a lot of money on their coaches, but the first thing the players need is to get into much better shape: to train harder and get in the gym more. I appreciate the irony of me saying this, when I was criticised so heavily for being unfit, but I always understood I needed to be fitter and I made the commitment to improve.

To my mind, the LTA should not spend so much money on a number of the world's greatest coaches. That does not mean I am ungrateful for my time with Brad, but I think British tennis at this stage needs good, experienced, committed, less-expensive coaches plus experienced fitness coaches and physiotherapists who understand the demands of the game. To me, that is more of a priority than the tennis. The players have to understand what hard work is. They need someone who's not going to take any shit from them and if they say they're tired – tough. They still have to work hard.

I don't know if it's going to get any better under the new LTA regime. I hope so but it's one of those cases where you have to wait and see. I'm not an expert on running a national federation, but I have my ideas and I can pass on my experience of what I saw when I was younger. I don't think it's changed a whole lot since then. The results would suggest not.

The other issue in British tennis is how much people like to put you down. When I started to do well as a junior, British coaches like Alan Jones – who worked with the number one British woman Elena Baltacha – and Tony Pickard and a few others criticised me in public. I just don't understand the attitude. It is as though success is a bad thing.

When you go over to the United States, it is completely different. Over there, everyone is pumped up for the young players. You hear people within the sport saying: 'Have you seen this kid play?' and they say it with pride, not criticism. Last time I was there, the talk was about a young American kid called Donald Young, who turned professional and then lost thirteen ATP matches in a row. They didn't rip into him. They still said they believed in him. By 2008, he had broken into the World Top 100.

I think a lot of British tennis is influenced by the media. The people who run tennis have rarely confronted things head on. From my point of view, they seem to mismanage the news that sneaks into the papers. If it is something negative, they get all defensive about it. Why can't they be honest and less frightened of the media? Sometimes they get themselves into the ludicrous position of saying how great everything is.

Meanwhile, within tennis, there is just so much bad-mouthing going on. Within days of me taking David Nalbandian to five sets at Wimbledon, there was virtually a queue of former Davis Cup captains waiting to criticise me.

In a newspaper article, David Lloyd said: 'Murray is an 18-year-old who played pretty good on grass. That's as far as you can go. You can't say he is going to win a grand slam. But because we are so desperate, he already has a noose around his neck. We have to be careful with him. It is hard to live with that expectation and hype.'

He was basically saying that I wasn't that great and don't rush me, which is fine. I didn't disagree with that.

Then Tony Pickard said: 'He is off now to play some Challengers in the US, and if he can win a couple that would set the fire, it would mean he has taken away an awful lot from Wimbledon. But he has never won a match at Challenger level yet, and that worries the hell out of me.'

He shouldn't have worried so much. I had won quite a few matches at Challenger level. I'd reached a quarter-final actually. So he was wrong about that. But the rest of the things he said didn't quite make sense. David Lloyd was saying don't rush me. Tony Pickard was saying that I needed to win matches straight away: so, rush me. Which is it? Rush me or don't rush me?

It just all seemed so negative. I can understand what they were saying. I wasn't in the Top 10 yet – not even close – and I needed to work to get there, but they were giving these views straight after my first Wimbledon, aged eighteen, where I'd won two matches in straight sets – one of them against a Top 20 player – and lost in five sets to a former finalist. It would have been nice if they could have been a bit more positive or maybe even waited to criticise me. After all I was completely new to this but within the next six weeks, won two Challengers in America.

Pickard also complained that I'd taken what he called 'the glamour trip to Newport', instead of stepping down immediately in class – but if you are eighteen years old and offered a wild card into an ATP tournament, what the hell are you going to say? 'No, sorry, I'm going to play a Futures tournament, just to keep me grounded.' Then they would have accused me of lacking ambition.

Lloyd even had a go at Jimmy Connors for saying something nice about me at Wimbledon. I would have thought that a compliment from one of the greatest players ever was a good thing. Everyone in tennis has a lot of respect for his judgement as a match commentator, but when he was nice about me some people disagreed. Lloyd said he shouldn't have praised me so much because I was that 'kid who didn't try in the fifth set against David Nalbandian.'

Why couldn't the critics just have sat back and said: 'It's been a great run, hopefully he can build on it for the rest of the year'? That's all you need to say. But that tells you everything you need to know about the mentality of British tennis. Those guys are two of the most experienced coaches in Britain and they are coming out with stuff like that. Obviously, there are so many different ways of making it to the top. No one is going to be right all the time. Whatever they said, I had to do it my way.

It was the same for Tim Henman. He did it his way too. Not everybody liked that. He was horribly and unfairly criticised for it, but I know that as his successor, I owe him a great debt. He gave people hope in British tennis when, before he came along, there was just disaster.

I didn't meet him properly until I was sixteen. I'd obviously watched him and supported him while I was growing up, so when I did meet him, it was strange. You can imagine what I was expecting. Everyone knows that Tim comes over as a pretty serious guy on the court. He doesn't show too much emotion, except those little fist-pumps. He seems very reserved. So when I joined the Davis Cup squad in Luxembourg in April 2004 I thought I would be totally intimidated by him.

I couldn't have been more wrong. He was friendly and funny, always making jokes and wanting to play games – any game from Top Trumps to throwing a piece of screwed up paper into a bin, or seeing how many times you could keep a tennis ball bouncing on your head. I was at the age I wanted to do all those things as well. It was as though the 13-year age gap just didn't exist.

I was a 16-year-old kid who couldn't even play because of my knee injury and I would have understood if he was almost a little bit rude to me. But he wasn't and he could not have been more the opposite. I obviously couldn't practise, but I watched all the time and picked up balls by the side of the court. Tim was never less than great to me.

He does a good job of covering up his real personality. It was his way of dealing with the fame and you have to have a lot of respect for that. He didn't want to have to deal with the hassle of being asked about controversial subjects. I should know. Controversial subjects tend to involve fellow players or someone you are going to be seeing for the rest of your career. He understood that controversy puts you in an uncomfortable position. He did a really good job of making his life easier.

He was also a great guy to have around the locker room of any tournament. He always spoke to everyone. After thirteen years on the tour, there are almost bound to be guys you have arguments or problems with, but I don't know anyone who dislikes him. There was just the one time when David Nalbandian said something after their match in Madrid and, apart from that, I have never heard any other player say anything. Nalbandian was raging that Tim was pretending to be something he wasn't. The quote was: 'All this selling himself as a gentleman is not true. He is the worst rubbish there is.' It was so obviously against everyone else's opinion that Nalbandian was probably just upset because he lost.

I don't think Tim ever really cared about his press. He had a really successful career. He played at the top level of his sport for thirteen years. He is now the father of three daughters and I am sure he is going to enjoy settling down with them and his wife. I am positive he has no regrets about the way he dealt with the press, even if they regret he wasn't more colourful. He never had any big issues with them, he never threw them any bones to chew over. He just tried to be positive in his press conferences. I completely understand. It gives you time to concentrate on your tennis.

It is part of the job, the press conference, but it can be tough to conduct one after every single match. In the end, it becomes a routine. If I've won I say: 'I played well. I executed my game plan well.' If I've lost, I say: 'I didn't play well.' That is, more or less, it. We probably have to do about 110 press conferences a year and who can blame someone for sparing themselves the trouble of being interesting.

Anyway, I think it is unfair of the media to comment on how somebody deals with them. They don't know what it is like to be on the receiving end of some of the articles that get written. I don't think it was right of the press to criticise Tim's dealings with them, especially someone under as much pressure as he was. They didn't see it from his point of view. Tim has done a lot for British tennis, no question. It is not his fault that there aren't enough British kids playing tennis. That is the responsibility of the governing body. His responsibility was to win matches. It was irrelevant whether his personality was best suited to young children.

He was even accused of coming from a background of middle-class privilege, but that is how he was brought up. Was he supposed to act as if he was working class? It is not comfortable trying to change your personality, pretend to be someone you are not. Tim was always the person he was, in terms of being middle class. He just didn't show the real and funny side of his personality. I don't blame him. I have seen first hand that you can get yourself into trouble when you do.

He was never completely perfect. He swore on court, although he didn't make it as visible as some players. He loved winning, he hated losing, but instead of getting really pumped up or obviously down, he just showed the same emotional level all through the match. Who is to criticise that? Some of the greatest players of all time were the same. Björn Borg was one and Roger Federer, to an extent, is another. I can't be like that, but there is nothing wrong with it as an approach.

Tim and I have spent a decent amount of time together ever since. After Wimbledon in 2005, when I was embarking on the tour in America for the first time and didn't know any of the players, he took me out for dinner. He also played backgammon with me and tried to make me feel comfortable. It could have been really horrible for me as the new boy. He always made an effort, despite the fact that I was a potential rival. That is why Jamie and I, and so many other guys on the tour, have so much respect for him. He was always, always helpful to us. He's a great person.

He always said I was hopeless at backgammon and I needed a lot more practice, so when my eighteenth birthday was approaching, he had his chance. He was out shopping when he saw a great backgammon set for sale in a London store and went in to buy it for me. But when they told him it cost about £400, he thought better of it. 'I like Andy,' he told my mum, 'but not that much.'

Even though he's clearly a bit tight when it comes to my birthdays, I regard him as a friend. When Greg Rusedski was a star in ITV's *Dancing on Ice*, Tim and I were texting each other all the time with our comments. Some of Tim's were pretty funny. I imagine he would no more go on one of those reality programmes than I ever would, but that doesn't mean Tim is not a fun guy to be around.

It annoys me that some people saw him as a loser. That is the press. If you don't really follow the sport and just flip through a newspaper, you would have seen headlines like: 'Henman Loses' or 'Henman Fails Again.' That was not the real story. Headlines rarely are.

Tim was a god at Wimbledon. He had unbelievable support and has a fantastic record. He didn't win a grand slam, that is true, but he came along at the wrong time. During the years he played Wimbledon, Sampras was all-dominant through the nineties, followed by Federer who recently won five years in a row. There wasn't much room for Henman to be the champion.

I don't think you can see it as failure when you spend your career at the highest level. If a journalist was the fourth-best journalist in the world or a lawyer the fourth-best legal mind in the world, they would be considered pretty damn good. Then they would have to maintain it for ten years to be up there with Tim. To do what he did in such an unbelievably hard field is fantastic. To be at the top for so long in any area, let alone sport, is something to be proud of. Tim was not a failure.

I know people will say: 'But he didn't win a grand slam.' But would he exchange his whole career – the four Wimbledon semi-finals and four quarter-finals – with Thomas Johansson, who won the Australian Open in 2002 but only spent a couple of years in the Top 10? I don't think so.

If you haven't played this sport at the highest level you cannot appreciate how hard it is to win a grand slam, especially with guys like Sampras and Federer around. What you do on court isn't always controlled by you. I could play brilliantly, then someone like Goran Ivanisevic would come along and fire down forty aces. You can't control that. That's the tough thing about this individual sport. You can do all the right things and then someone comes along who plays a little bit better on the day.

I'm not disputing that everyone really wants to win a grand

slam, I would *love* to win a grand slam, but it doesn't mean that your whole career, everything you have worked for, is ruined because you don't win one.

It might surprise some people that Tim and I were good friends, given the difference in our characters. I seem to have generated more controversies in three years than he did in his whole career, but we still had more in common than people think, though not, I admit, in the disciplinary record.

As a British player, I was accused of triggering the country's first fine for player misconduct in the 106-year history of the Davis Cup, when I swore at a match official in Glasgow during the tie against Serbia and Montenegro in 2006. It caused a massive fuss, but it was ridiculous. That was another one of those things that the press jumped all over.

I know players who have said way worse things than I did to umpires. In this case, the man was the youngest umpire in the history of the Davis Cup. I suppose that might seem pretty rich coming from someone who was a teenager at the time, but I felt he gave such a poor performance that I told him what I thought of him. I said: 'You're fucking useless.' That is terrible. I should never have said it. In the history of sport I think worse things have been said, but still, I am not saying it was right. I'd just lost a match and I was annoyed. I played rubbish. I was angry. It was wrong of me. However, the press were trying to suggest I had said something far worse. Then they started investigating what the maximum fine could be and speculating that maybe Great Britain could be thrown out of the competition for two years. They wanted to make the story as extreme as possible.

In the end, after the referee had sent in his report, we received the smallest possible fine, just over £1,000, about the same amount as you receive for a warning on the ATP tour. It was ludicrous. I didn't feel guilty afterwards, I was just amazed that something could be so blown out of all proportion. Obviously what I said was wrong, but I've sat in press conferences when one of the journalists has sworn while he was asking me a question.

We were talking about the sudden possibility of me qualifying for the end-of-the-season Masters Cup in 2007, and the reporter said something like: 'Did you think to yourself: "Oh shit! Now I've got a good chance of qualifying"'

I said: 'Hold on a sec, you can't swear when you're asking me a question. Imagine what you would say if I said that to you.' He just laughed it off, and to be honest, I found it quite funny too. You've got to have a sense of humour about these things, but I just thought I'd point out the hypocrisy.

I had pretty decent support from my colleagues at the time. Greg Rusedksi admitted: 'At Wimbledon I've used every bad word in the book. We have to remember he's only eighteen years old but he's moving in the right direction.' John Lloyd, who went on to become my Davis Cup captain, gave some pretty good advice: 'If he's going to swear he should learn where the microphones are.'

The truth is, I don't swear *that* much. When I'm with a group of people I don't swear *that* often. Anyway, a lot of people swear. Everybody swears sometimes, but just because you do it when you're on TV seems to make it worse somehow. When you're playing a tennis match, you don't think the cameras are on you. You are just in the zone and you say things you probably shouldn't.

I know it's not a good example to set to kids. I hope I can stop doing it. However, I remember when I was playing football when I was young, the parents were swearing, the players were swearing, it went on all the time. It is pretty much similar in most sports. I'm never going to be on court not saying a word. Sometimes you need to let off steam.

It has never really caused me too much trouble, apart from that Davis Cup fine. The worst time I remember was when I was younger, playing in a team competition in the Czech Republic and I swore then on court. Gran had come over to watch me and she didn't speak to me after my match because I had behaved badly. Actually she didn't speak to me for quite a while. She was *very* angry.

People have this impression that I'm some sort of foul-mouthed brat because I have so much attention paid to me if I shout on the court. I admit I do swear sometimes towards the people I know sitting in the players' box, including my coach and sometimes my mum. If you're getting mad, you're pretty uncomfortable and when you see someone in the crowd supporting you, you are basically looking for a bit of comfort from them. Just because I'm swearing in someone's direction doesn't mean that I'm swearing *at* them.

My old coach, Leon Smith, understood. He said he didn't mind when I shouted at him because he knew it was my way of getting my temper out. He used to think I did it because I had a close relationship with him and so he was the first person I turned to when I was feeling frustrated. He thought it was a positive thing, a trust thing. It was obviously better to shout at him than at the umpire or the crowd.

There were some negative comments about the way I seemed to be swearing at Brad Gilbert when he was my coach. I know it's not right, and after a few months of doing it, I tried to stop, but Brad said he understood. He did similar things in his playing days. He used to speak to the crowd a lot during matches. It wasn't an issue between us. He said he understood that I was not so much angry with him as raging at myself.

I am not stupid enough to wonder why my temper is a story. It seems ridiculously exaggerated to me, but I suppose the media will highlight anything that is different. Maybe I'll grow out of it. I think I am calmer and more mature on court these days. However, I have to accept there will always be attention on me that other players don't get. Wherever and whenever I play, there will always be a high level of press interest, not because I'm bad-tempered, not because I swear, but because – as Tim discovered – I'm British and the media in this country have a peculiar fascination with one of us winning Wimbledon one day.

Tim Henman

I remember when word first reached me about 'this kid with an unbelievable feel for the game . . . always seems to play the right shot at the right time . . . but he's a bit temperamental on court.' That should remind us of someone. All those characteristics are still there.

The first time I ever really met Andy was when he came to Luxembourg as a hitting partner to the Davis Cup team in 2004. It was funny because I knew I was one of his heroes when he was growing up, but it wasn't obvious from the way he behaved. I think I had been much more unsubtle when I met my own hero, Stefan Edberg, who used to live and train in London. The first time I ever hit with him I'm sure I was just staring at him and making a fool of myself.

With Andy, even though he was struggling with the knee injury, you could tell he was listening, taking things on board. I think he's very perceptive and a quick learner. Off the court, however, we played stupid games for much of the time. My sense of humour can be quite childish and I'm very good at silly things like juggling rackets or mobile phones, or lobbing screwed up balls of paper into bins. I've always been into games and jokes, and I'm sure I played a few practical jokes on Andy.

There was the time, at the end of 2006, when I was under some pressure to return to the Davis Cup team. The matter came up for general discussion and Andy being Andy, when asked by the press, said he thought it might be better to play someone younger, for the future of British tennis. I sent him a message saying: 'Thanks for the vote of confidence. Good luck in April' (when the next round of the Davis Cup would be played). He tried to call me so many times because he thought I was seriously pissed off. Every time I saw his number I ignored it. He sent messages saying: 'I don't know if you're really cross or joking, but I'm really sorry . . .' After about three days, I felt a bit guilty, so I called him up, laughing, and said: 'Don't worry, I was joking.'

That's what I'm like with people I know and, I suppose, trust. It's different to when I'm in a press interview room with my guard up. There have perhaps been two different people throughout my playing career. Me with friends, and me with the media. I think, that's why Andy was surprised to meet a completely different character to the one he was expecting. It is more a true reflection of who I really am, but my defence mechanism blocked it from the outside world. I know my apparent character hasn't always appealed to everyone.

I was aware how difficult it might be for Andy to make the step up from juniors to seniors. Every time you go up a level, from satellites to Challengers, main tour to grand slams, it can be a somewhat intimidating environment, and I tried to put myself in Andy's shoes. I will go out of my way to help people I care about. He was a young British guy who I had heard a good deal about and I definitely wanted to make him as comfortable as I could. If that's what he says too, I'm glad he feels that way.

His progress was pretty rapid, and I was obviously keeping an eye on his results. Queen's 2005 was a big breakthrough and we nearly ended up playing each other there. That would have been one for the media. I was due to be his next opponent if he had beaten

Thomas Johansson instead of hurting his ankle and then getting attacked by cramp. He was still very raw, but he was also playing to a really high level. I had a feeling it wouldn't be long before he was appearing more regularly in the same tournaments as me.

I was right. The next tournament was Wimbledon and while I was knocked out in the second round (for the first time in a decade) by Dmitry Tursunov, Andy went on to the third round where he played David Nalbandian. I remember texting him to wish him luck. I can't recall what I said. Probably: 'Keep your head down and enjoy it.' He did. I could see he was streets ahead of me when I was the same age. I had lost 6–2 6–1 in the first round of the Wimbledon Juniors when I was seventeen. That put his progress in perspective, especially as your first senior Wimbledon provides an intense spotlight. You're growing up in front of everybody's eyes. That isn't necessarily easy and your mistakes can be magnified. You just have to try and embrace it as much as you can and he did. That's why I think he has a really mature head on his shoulders.

He wasn't a lost soul in the Wimbledon locker room. Far from it. He believed he was meant to be there. I'm sure he felt nervous coming into the first round with the likes of Federer and Nadal, not to mention the senior players like McEnroe and Becker, but he had this inner belief that he was where he belonged, so he might as well get used to it. It comes across to me that he's always believed he's going to be a great player. This is just part of his journey. His career has not necessarily taken him by surprise. If you've always had those dreams and aspirations, you might surprise a few people around you, but you yourself think: 'This is what I've been waiting for.'

Our next grand slam together was the US Open a couple of months later, where I went one worse and lost in the first round. Andy says I lost to him on the golf game in the players' lounge as well, but I don't have a clear memory of that. I do recall there was this Sega tennis computer game and I was one of the players you could choose to be. Ironically, I was hopeless at it. I was never really into computer games, but Andy was phenomenal on it. I'd go and watch him when he played. He usually chose to be me and then played the most ridiculous shots (way beyond my game). That is the other side to him. He's still a kid. He's as happy as can be playing on those games, and yet an hour later he could be on the stadium court in real life, playing one of the best players in the world. It was pretty amusing.

I spent quite a lot of time with him and it never occurred to me that I was being nice to a rival. I've always had great friendships with various players, like Pete Sampras, Todd Martin, Roger Federer, and it has never bothered me in the slightest when I had to play them. I played Federer thirteen times in my career (7–6 to him) and it wasn't because we were friends that I lost those seven times.

This is where the men's tour deals with some things a bit better than the women's tour. You can go out on the court and do everything you can to beat your opponent, and when it's finished you can shake hands and go and have a beer. On the women's tour it seems that the rivalry lasts a bit longer. They're not able to separate the two things so easily. I got on really well with Andy. I wanted to try and help him, to pass on a few things I'd learned over the years, but it was never going to detract from how hard I was going to try when I did finally play against him.

That collision turned out to be much sooner than I thought. It was four months after his Wimbledon debut, the first round of the Basle tournament – just another match on the circuit, but at the same time very much *not* just another match. The British media always made sure any clash between us countrymen took on much greater significance than it deserved. Whenever I played Greg Rusedski the match was always blown out of all proportion. I desperately wanted to win but luckily I always felt totally comfortable and confident going in against him. I must admit when I played Andy, it was different.

His game doesn't really suit me. The last thing a serve-volleyer needs is someone who can hit inspired passing shots from the baseline. Andy is more a counter-puncher, and I felt I was over-pressing because of his style of play. At Wimbledon, I never felt any great burden of expectation – and I think that's credit to me – but when I played Andy I did feel the pressure. For some reason I put extra pressure on myself which was stupid. I already had a good player in front of me, I didn't need to make it any harder.

It was an uncomfortable match, mentally and physically, and he should have beaten me quite easily. In the end it went to three sets and was settled in the final set tie-break. I did discover the next day that I had fractured my rib, but, much as I would like to say it affected the match, I had no idea at the time and felt 100 per cent fit. Funnily enough, I knew Andy was upset afterwards. I could see he had tears in his eyes and was pretty affected by it. Disappointed as I was, I took that as a real sign of his respect for me. It was noted. You remember that sort of thing. When I retired I suddenly heard what my peers thought of me. As much as you can be moved when Barry Flatman of the *Sunday Times* writes something nice about you, what means most to an athlete is the good opinion of your peers.

Obviously my defeat was treated as highly significant at the time and I asked the press afterwards what exactly it was I had just handed to Andy: 'Is it a baton, is it a torch, is it a flag, is it a crown? Whatever it is, he's welcome to it.' I meant it. With his game, it wasn't going to be long before he overtook me. It wasn't upsetting. He was the future. I'd been in that position for such a long time. There had been my rivalry with Greg in which I had mainly had the upper hand, but this was a young guy coming up, ready to overtake and he deserved it. Rankings don't lie. You don't buy your ranking points, you earn them.

We played four times before I retired. He won the first three, but I pulled one back in our final match in Bangkok in 2006. I played a lot better to win 6–4 6–2 and this time he wasn't so calm. He was losing his temper and getting mad with his coach, Brad Gilbert, on the side of the court. Those were all good signs to me.

It was a fine win for me because I beat a good player but, once again, there was that extra edge that comes from being fellow-Brits. It is ridiculous really. When two Argentinians play one another, or two Frenchmen, or two Spaniards – which they do, week-in, week-out – nobody takes any special notice. Our culture doesn't play by the same rules. Two Brits going head-to-head always causes a stir. I understand why. It's about scarcity value. There are so few players at the top level, these matches are always going to have an extra dimension.

In the short time we were on tour together, I actually like to think I helped make Andy a better player. Did it help him beat me eventually? It may well have done, but I don't view it like that. It was a role I enjoyed. We talked a lot about things like schedules and, of course, the press. I remember having dinner with him in Cincinnati in 2005, during his first few months on the tour, and not being afraid to give him my advice about things like that. With his temperament and his personality you could see that it was going to be much more confrontational with the press than it ever was with me. That can work both ways. It certainly would make the media's job fairly entertaining and, at times, it can motivate you as a player. At other times, it might get in your way a little bit. But you learn as you go along.

You'll never change him. That's why he's so good. He's got that competitive nature and he expresses it fairly freely, but obviously he needs to channel it. I would say my main concern regarding the press is that lots of opinions are going to be expressed about Andy and sometimes he's going to get a little bit affected by them, not to mention a little frustrated. In my opinion, that's not going to do him any favours. He shouldn't be influenced. He sometimes gets a bit caught up in it. That's just a distraction and he's got enough to concentrate on already. He might be completely right, but he's never going to be able to correct the media. If he's confrontational, he's fighting a battle he definitely can't win. If that's the reality of it – and it is – you're better focusing your attentions elsewhere. I think you've got to have a thick skin and get on with it.

I learned from my mistake at Wimbledon when we were talking about equal prize money in the late 1990s. I tried to give an educated answer in a press conference, and because I was on the Player Council at the time I had all the facts and figures. I finished off by saying that if the women wanted more money, I thought they were being a little bit greedy. That, to me, was the end of it.

Then I came into Wimbledon the next day and there were probably eight or nine cameras crews jostling to talk to me, saying: 'Do you stand by what you said about equal prize money?' I said, genuinely bemused: 'What did I say?' For the next forty-eight hours it was a complete distraction. That's why you end up playing a straight bat. The next time I was asked about women's prize money, I said something like: 'It's nothing to do with me. I'm just here to concentrate on my tennis.' Now I was labelled the boring idiot. Talk about a rock and hard place.

When Andy tells people I'm quite a comedian, I can imagine them being completely unable to believe it. That's why I say I'm two people. I ask myself about that sometimes, but, even with hindsight, if you asked me would I do anything differently, I wouldn't. I don't let everyone in. That's just my way. When I'm around my close friends, they do see a different person. I'm fine with that. I'm totally comfortable that I chose to do things that way because maintaining an element of privacy has always been important to me. That's not right for everyone but that's the way I am. If the world thought I was boring rather than funny, then that doesn't bother me. I'm not in a popularity contest and nor is Andy.

I've always been honest to myself. I haven't tried to put on any false fronts and play a game I'm not interested in. Andy isn't a million miles away from that either. He's more expressive on court with his emotions, but he's pretty reserved off the court. He needs to trust people first and it doesn't take much in our position for your lack of trust to increase when you've been burned a couple of times.

I was there when he earned his reputation for being anti-English and it was a complete joke. In both senses. It was during an interview with a journalist at Wimbledon 2006 when England were preparing to play Paraguay in the World Cup, and the whole thing was just good banter. We were laughing and giggling. I was teasing him about the Scots not being there, and when the journalist asked Andy who he would be supporting, Andy said: 'Anyone that England's playing.' Before you know it, someone's picked it up as though he was being serious and that kind of thing is a pain in the arse. It's a joke. Why can't people take a joke?

I don't need to tell you that that sort of thing is where the press can shoot themselves in the foot, because all of a sudden a player like Andy isn't going to give as much, especially when things like that keep happening. He'd been through it before in Adelaide that year when he said after a match that he and his opponent had been serving 'like women'. He meant they had both dropped their serves a good deal, which happens in women's tennis. It was a joke, no more than that, and suddenly they're having phone-ins on BBC Radio.

In 2008, he was taking flak again for pulling out of the Davis Cup tie to Argentina. That was a little bit different because I thought it was just badly handled. If Andy's knee was bad, then his knee was bad and that should have been the end of the argument. However, at the time, his brother didn't know anything about that and that was rough.

At a slightly different level, when Federer and Nadal pull out, they say straight out: 'I'm not playing' and that's their prerogative. That's not to say I necessarily agree with their decision – I played for twelve years before I pulled out because my body was falling apart – but it is still *their* decision to make. They say: 'No, it doesn't fit into my schedule' and that's that. Andy's entitled to say that too. If, for whatever reason, he doesn't want to play, he should say so and let the right people know in time. I thought the way the whole story unfolded became a bit messy.

You do have to remember, though, that he's twenty. I was in exactly same boat regarding public relations at his age. Would a better relationship with the press have made me a better tennis player? No, so I wasn't interested. Could it have made my life a little bit easier? Yes, I think it could. But you don't see that at twenty. You're not interested. That's why I think it's important for the people with experience around you to guide you. They don't have to change him, but a little guidance at this stage can go a long way. I'm talking with hindsight, though. At the time, you go with what you think is best. It's only later, maybe ten years down the line, you think: 'Maybe I could have developed things differently,' but you just don't know it at the time. Isn't that life?

Likewise, Andy would be naïve and silly to think he knows everything about tennis already. I look at his game and I see some things he is doing so well now and I think: 'Brad Gilbert told you that twelve months ago.' I look at his serve. He's standing up to the line, cracking it into both corners and that's a huge weapon. Brad was keen on that, but for whatever reason it took its time to get through. That's the reality of dealing with a strong-willed kid.

I remember myself at his stage. It's very difficult when you've gone from being 800 in the world to 400 to 150 to 29 to 17 and then people come along and tell you to do things differently. You think: 'Hang on a minute, I'm not bad the way I am.' You look at your progress and say: 'If it ain't broke don't fix it.' Andy's listening to people telling him what to do and he's saying to himself: 'I rate myself. I think I'm pretty good and those results aren't bad either.'

It's tough for a coach. Dealing with your own children is hard enough, but dealing with someone who is not only young but also one of the best players in the world is never going to be easy. Maybe that's why I won't go into coaching. Maybe. But never say never.

I wasn't surprised when he split with Brad. It was a huge clash of personalities. It was unfortunate the way their relationship was managed because Brad is one of the best coaches in the world, no doubt of that. His knowledge of the game is second-to-none, but his personality is sometimes not that easy to gel with. The fact they were spending so much time together – breakfast, lunch, dinner 24/7 – was difficult. It's hard enough with your wife, let alone your coach. When you've got personalities that are different, there was never going to be a dull moment – but to focus on the positive, look what they did together. In eighteen months Andy's game came a long way, he had a string of great results and he reached the Top 10.

It has all happened so fast and he hasn't even learned to play backgammon properly yet. He's rubbish at it *and* he's a little slow in paying his debts. It's true, the tale he tells about the backgammon set I wouldn't buy him for his birthday. I'd seen it – a small wooden travel board – in a shop and I was going to put a card in with it saying: 'Get some practice. You need it!' But when I went in to buy it, I was told it cost £400. I thought: there's no way I'm spending that on him, I'll get a plastic one. I don't mind spending £400 on the right person, but not some whippersnapper.

But I have to admit his potential as a tennis player is enormous. The way I look at it now, Federer, Nadal and Djokovic are the top three players in the world, but then there's the chasing group and Andy pretty much heads that. It makes me laugh when people say accusingly that he hasn't yet won a grand slam. How many has he played? He'd been in eight up until the start of 2008. Look at Federer and how long it took him. He played seven before he reached his first quarter-final. He played sixteen before he had his first win at Wimbledon in 2003.

Patience is a word that people are not very keen on, but I don't have any worries about Andy's future possibilities. He beat Federer in Dubai in early 2008 and a reflection of how well he served is that he did not face even one break point. That tells you that you're serving pretty damn well. He's so good when he's proactive like that rather than reactive. He can react as well, because he's a very good athlete, but if the ball's there to be hit, hit it. He is doing it more. The modern player, someone like Jo-Wilfried Tsonga who beat him in Australia, possesses the fire-power to hit you off the court so you can't keep running and running. It's hard if you haven't got the artillery to compete, but Andy's got it. He's got all the shots. So why not use them? I have no doubt that with (his) time and (our) patience, he'll learn to use his game to maximum potential.

I'll watch him with interest. You won't catch me at the French and US Opens, but I am sure I will be at Wimbledon in future to see him. I'll sit in a comfortable seat on the Centre Court and just be grateful it isn't me out there any more. I had no idea how nice it would be to get away from it all. In all those years I played Wimbledon I never felt there was a burden on my shoulders, but after my last professional match, the Davis Cup tie against Croatia at Wimbledon, I went for a long walk with our dogs, Bonnie and Bumble, and I felt a weight had been lifted from me after all. I was so relaxed. I'd never known life without it before. It was the absence of weight I was feeling.

I cannot tell you how much I have enjoyed life after tennis, being at home with my family, playing golf, having a few holidays, without looking over my shoulder at the next training session. Everyone said: 'Oh, just wait, you're going to get itchy feet,' but I have to report it's not happened so far. Maybe it will, but all I feel now is this real sense of freedom. It might be normal to most people, but I'd had such a structured life – tournament, practice, dinner, match, hotel, flight for thirteen years – it was unknown to me.

So that's why I was so happy to hand over the baton/flag/crown, whatever it was, and he can count on my whole family to be some of his best supporters. My oldest daughter, Rosie, knows who Andy Murray is. She remembers when he twisted his ankle at Queen's. She was very upset at the time for him and whenever she sees him now, she says: 'That's Andy Murray. How's his ankle?'

If Andy ever does win Wimbledon, it won't be a bitter-sweet moment for me. Good luck to him. I've had my time. If he wins a grand slam, it won't make me a worse tennis player. There are a few guys I would rather didn't win because I don't like them, but I'll always support him. We still text message each other all the time, especially when Greg Rusedski was performing during the winter of 2007 in ITV's *Dancing On Ice*. Andy and I are pretty united in our certainty that we would never, ever appear on a programme like that. Put it this way, there's as much chance of me writing an autobiography as doing that.

There is no final piece of advice I'd offer Andy, unless he asked me to. It is his life, his career. Anyway, how can you improve on what I've already told him. 'Keep your head down and enjoy it!'

Chapter Six:
The Year of Living Controversially

It was probably a bad idea when I opened my mouth after a tennis match and said: 'I think we both played like women.' I just didn't realise how bad at the time. This was the start of 2006, my first full season on the tour, and I was excited by the possibility of building on the achievements of the previous year. I was not far off the Top 60 in the world, the Australian Open was coming up and I was playing a warm-up tournament in Auckland, with a first-round match against Kenneth Carlsen of Denmark.

I'd never experienced a match like it. I haven't since. It was unbelievably windy and we just couldn't hold serve. There were seven, maybe eight, consecutive breaks before I won 7–5 6–2. Immediately afterwards, I was asked if I would do an on-court interview and I didn't think anything of it. 'What was going on with all those breaks of serve?' the interviewer asked me and out it just came: 'Yeah, it was tough, really windy. I think we both played like women in the first set.'

It was one of those comments you just throw out there. The crowd went: 'Ooooohhha-ha-ha', the sound of mock-shock turning into a laugh. I finished the interview and was applauded off the court. It was all fine.

The next thing I know, I am being woken up the next morning with phone calls from radio stations demanding to know if I'm sexist. People were now reporting that I'd been booed off the court when it couldn't have been more the opposite. The crowd had been laughing with me and they certainly clapped me off. There were guys from the British press there who saw and heard the whole thing. They knew what had really happened and yet the reports continued to say that I'd been booed. It was lies, complete lies.

I couldn't believe it. I'm not sexist. I just made a little joke. It wasn't meant to offend anyone. And, anyway, it was a fact. Girls do get their serves broken more than guys. I wasn't saying it was a bad tennis match. I was saying we both had our serves broken a good deal, which happens in women's tennis because they cannot serve as hard as the men.

It wasn't in the same league as Richard Krajicek, the Dutchman who won Wimbledon in 1996 and scandalised women's tennis by saying: 'Eighty per cent of the Top 100 women are fat pigs who don't deserve equal pay.' He corrected himself later after an outcry: 'What I meant to say was 75 per cent.'

I was beginning to learn that telling one of my little jokes didn't always have the right effect. For some reason, the world thought it was a big deal. I didn't know what to do. Perhaps I was too young at eighteen to understand what was happening. I couldn't really work it out. I thought what I'd said was quite funny and yet some sections of the media thought that made me a sexist. How can I be a sexist with a mum and a gran like mine?

I suppose I was learning all the time about the way fame works. Everything is fine for the first few months when you burst on to the scene. Then it suddenly twists and people are trying to find an angle on whatever you say. Your opinion starts to matter on things, even if you're a teenager playing tennis matches with no idea of any other agenda. A couple of things can be said and blown out of all proportion. Suddenly, you're portrayed as a really controversial person, just because you tried to have a little bit of fun.

Maybe not surprisingly, I lost in the next round against Mario Ancic and then my coach and I moved on to Australia. I didn't arrive in the best of moods. I was still upset and mystified by the way I'd been treated in Auckland and the next thing to happen was a press conference to discuss the Open draw. Not much could go wrong there, I thought. I hadn't played a match yet. I was wrong again.

In the first round I had drawn Juan Ignacio Chela, the Argentinian ranked eleven places higher than me, but all anyone wanted to talk about was Lleyton Hewitt, the local hero, who I might have to play in the second round.

Hewitt was a fantastic player and former Wimbledon and US Champion, but I couldn't understand why I was being asked about something that clearly might not – and did not – happen. 'So it's Lleyton in the second round?' 'So how do you feel about playing Lleyton in a night match?' everyone seemed to be asking. I felt like saying: 'What are you talking about? Chela is an unbelievably good player. I'm not even expected to win that match and you're all talking to me about Hewitt!' I think I did say something like that. My mood was now even worse.

Then I went out and got killed by Chela. I played really

badly and lost 6–1 6–3 6–3. Looking back, I am not at all surprised. I was still worked up about all the sexism business in Auckland. I didn't know if I could trust the press any more and then I felt they had unreasonably expected me to win against a player as good as Chela.

It wasn't their fault I lost the match and if you look back at what I said during my post-match press conference, I didn't say it was their fault. What I did try to express was the difficulty I had with unreasonable expectations. I said: 'If you guys expect me to play well every single match and every single tournament, then it's not going to happen. You guys are expecting me to win matches like this. The guy's ranked nearly twenty places in front of me. He is a much better player than me. It is difficult for me to go out there and try to perform to the best that I can when I'm expected to win all these matches.'

It wasn't a rant. It was a plea for a little understanding. Someone pointed out that I'd had nothing but good press since I had arrived on the circuit. I thought about all the criticisms about my fitness after Wimbledon, all the coaches who had queued up to say I wasn't so good after all and the recent fuss in Auckland, and found I couldn't really agree.

'Well, if you think that, then I'm obviously going to disagree on something,' I said. 'If you guys don't think you're putting pressure on me, then that's fine. I'll forget about it.'

I received some bad press after that, but I think they understood me a little more. I do not look down on other players. I do not get ahead of myself. I've noticed I don't get asked about future opponents any more until I've actually won my matches. With hindsight, it was probably wrong, what I did. I shouldn't have said all that. But it was honest. That is how I was feeling at the time, especially after the injustice of the things that had been written in Auckland.

None of the press ever apologised to me for the lies that were written about that incident. That didn't seem right to me somehow. If I do something wrong I hold my hand up and say: 'Look, I'm sorry. I was wrong to have said it is difficult to play when there is so much expectation on me.'

It was such a shame, in a way. To me, at eighteen, it was hard to discover in Auckland that if you try to be yourself, show a bit of personality and make a little joke, some people will try and make you look like an idiot for it.

That was when I stopped speaking to the press as freely. When I first did press conferences, I used to enjoy them. Later, I felt they could be a trap. There are not many other walks of life where you are expected to sit in a room full of people immediately after some major event in your career, sometimes a miserable one, and answer any question on any subject. Lawyers don't have to do it after a bad loss in court. Journalists don't have to do it when they get sued. Basically, no one is put through the same thing. Even footballers are protected by their managers, and if they do meet the press it is usually just to answer one quick question and then they're free to go. Tennis players do it after every single match. I reckon in any one year, I have to give a hundred press conferences.

I now realise you have to be so prepared. The only thing I can do if I want to make a little joke, is crack that joke *about* the journalist who is asking the question, which the other journalists might find funny. Then it's all kept between four walls.

Tim Henman led the way. I absolutely understand why he behaved like he did with the press. It was a wise move. It's just so much hassle if you make a flippant comment and it gets blown into a huge story. It's not fair. That might seem a slightly childish thing to say, but if people had to watch their own innocent remark being turned into a global news story, they might be a little bit more understanding.

It is a bit of a shame that I have to sound more boring than I really am, but if it saves me hassle that's fine. Sport is not a popularity contest and if it means that I can concentrate more easily on playing well, rather than constantly explaining myself, I'll do it. Once a story is written you can't change it. Better not to give them the story in the first place.

I don't want to sound as though I don't realise the media have a job to do. I do get on well with quite a few of the British tennis writers. It just seems to me that some of them take their job to a different level, and that they have no sensitivity as to how it hurts people. It would definitely affect me – if I was going to tear someone to pieces in the course of my work, I would feel horrendous. I wouldn't be able to look them in the eye. I'd never speak to them and I'd go out of my way to avoid them through sheer embarrassment. However, what seems to happen is that they write their piece without any warning and when they see you the next day, they say: 'Hi, how are you?' as though nothing at all has happened. Perhaps I am being naïve, but that doesn't seem right to me.

I suppose this horrible start to the year could have derailed me for quite some time. Instead, something that went way beyond my immediate ambitions caught me by surprise. I think it caught everyone by surprise: my coach Mark Petchey wasn't even there.

Just a couple of days before I was due to go to San José for the start of the American hard-court season, Mark said he couldn't come with me to California. So at the last minute I asked my girlfriend, Kim, if she could come instead – and that explains the famous 'kiss' pictures that were splashed all over the newspapers when, still aged eighteen, I won my first ATP title. At least it was a good story this time.

The tournament was being held at the home of the San José Sharks ice-hockey team. I remember it because, just as you walked on to the court, there was a big sign that read: 'Hard Work Beats Talent When Talent Doesn't Work Hard.' It was a lesson I had long-since absorbed and one you can never afford to forget.

I didn't play like the guy who would win the tournament in the first couple of games of my first-round match against the American, Mardy Fish. I went 0–2 down really quickly. I was a little bit uptight because Mark wasn't there. But from then on I started to play really well and winning 6–2 6–2 made me feel so much more relaxed. Now, everything seemed to suit me. I often played late matches well into the night which meant having room service with Kim and a late wake-up call. I am more of a night than a morning person. I felt wonderfully chilled all week.

The exception came in the quarter-final when I played Robin Soderling again, the Swede I had beaten at Wimbledon and later in Bangkok in that landmark match when I finally reached the World Top 100. You couldn't call it a grudge match, but we don't really get on very well and things became argumentative. Both of us received a warning from the umpire and it was a little bit ugly for a while.

I should have lost, that is for sure. I was down 4–6 and then 1–3 and as I was fighting to turn things around we had this massive row about a line call. He hit a ball down the line and the line judge mistakenly called it out. Then the umpire over-ruled and we had to replay the point. I could see why Soderling was angry because his shot was on the line, but I had been in a really good position to play a passing shot, so I was a little bit annoyed as well.

He went up to the net to argue with the umpire: 'How could she call that ball out!' I walked up to the umpire and complained that it was a tough place to over-rule because it was on the back edge of the baseline. Soderling turned on me: 'What the fuck are you complaining about?' That started the row, and it was the best thing that could have happened to me. I was really fired up and then channelled the adrenaline to mount a comeback. I am sure that's why I went on to win the match. That was a satisfying victory.

In the semi-final, I was playing Andy Roddick, who was ranked third in the world at this stage. By coincidence I had practised with him for the first time in my life the day before the match. I had never seen his famous serve first-hand before. I wasn't terrified because my return is the best part of my game. It took me a little while to get used to it but I learned how to handle it pretty well. The method wasn't complicated: just take the sting out of it and put the ball back in the court.

I wasn't nervous. Why should I be? He was third in the world, I was ranked 50-something. I wasn't expected to win. Five or six games into the match, I felt just like I had against Nalbandian at Wimbledon the year before. 'OK. I know how to win this match,' said a voice in my head. Against Nalbandian my body didn't hold up. This time it did. I won 7–5 7–5 and did not once lose my serve. I think Roddick was shell-shocked. Put it this way, he broke a racket in the locker room after the match.

This was my first win against a Top 10 player and now I was playing in my first ATP final, against Hewitt, the opponent-that-never-was in Australia. He wasn't as huge as Roger Federer or Tim Henman in my mind, but I still felt a little strange to be playing him and I started off pretty badly. It wasn't that I thought I didn't deserve to be there, but there was still something of a fantasy about the whole situation. I lost the first set 2–6 in about twenty-five minutes and he must have thought the rest of the match would follow that easily.

I knew what I was doing wrong. I was rushing, which is the worst thing you can do against a player like him because he makes so few mistakes. I was trying to finish the points quickly and moving so fast between them that I wasn't really thinking about what I was doing. I had to put a stop to that. I took a toilet break at the end of the set and forced myself to settle down. It worked better than I could have dreamed. I won the next set 6–1 and nine games later found myself holding a match point on his serve.

We became involved in a rally. The first few shots were fine but so much was riding on the outcome that as the rally extended to seven, eight, nine, ten strokes, I became more and more nervous, my arm felt more and more heavy and, inevitably, he saved the match point. Then he aced me. I thought: 'Oh, God, typical.' He held his serve. It's 5–5.

Then I hold my serve and create another match point during his next service game. Same thing happens. Another ace. That sparks the thought: 'What can I do?' which is not a good one to have at this stage because we are about to enter the tie-break. I am still nervous but maybe he is too because he makes a big mistake on his forehand which gives me a 4 points to 2 lead. The seventh point tends to be huge in a tie-break, and winning that point gives me a great advantage. Two points later I'm 6 points to 3 up, match point again. Another rally. I hit a backhand down the line, he scurries across, picks it up, but I'm there to crack a backhand cross-court winner that he can't reach. My brain is trying to grasp what is going on here. I am a champion.

Then I didn't really know what to do. This had never happened to me before. I'd just won my first ATP title in a final set tie-break against a guy I used to really love watching when I was growing up, and it was pretty awesome. My coach wasn't there, but my girlfriend was, so I climbed up to the players' box and kissed her. Twice.

That night I couldn't sleep at all, for the adrenaline still streaming round my system. The next day I took Kim shopping and she bought a pair of sunglasses and a bag, which may not seem a huge thing to do as a celebration but we couldn't think of anything else. I didn't buy myself anything. I was happy enough with the result.

But tennis never lets you stay satisfied for long. It would be an understatement to say that the whole American stretch did not go so well after that. It was terrible. From the end of February when I played in Las Vegas to the start of Wimbledon four months later, I won precisely *five* matches. I lost in so many first rounds that it was almost a waste unpacking my bags. Many were close matches that ran to three sets, but that wasn't much of a consolation.

What was wrong with me? I had no idea. The sad details are that at Indian Wells at the beginning of March I lost to Nikolay Davydenko 1–6 6–3 3–6 in the second round. Two weeks later I'm losing to Stanislas Wawrinka 5–7 6–3 4–6 in the first round at Miami. Maybe I'll have better luck on the clay courts in Europe. Apparently not. I lost to Jean-Rene Lisnard, the local boy, in Monte Carlo 6–4 6–7 5–7. A week later David Ferrer put me out of Barcelona in the second round 6–4 6–7 1–6. In Rome I lost in straight sets to another local boy, Filippo Volandri. At Roland Garros, my first appearance in the main draw of the French Open ended with me losing to Gael Monfils, my old friend from France, in five sets. The pattern was pretty clear. I was making a lot of home crowds very happy by losing to their favourite players, but I was beginning to take it personally.

I had finally split up with Mark Petchey just before Monte Carlo, so I was travelling without a coach, just my physio and sometimes my agent, and I was finding it all a struggle mentally. I desperately wanted to start doing more winning and find again the feeling that I had had in San Jose. I wasn't mentally breaking down but was really depressed and definitely not enjoying life. I talked to my agent and my mum about it. Then Mum started travelling with me again, and when I managed to win a couple of matches at Nottingham the week before Wimbledon, it all seemed to turn around.

Maybe that place has a special effect on me but as I walked on to the Centre Court at Wimbledon for the first time in 2006, I suddenly felt confident again. I don't know the reason. Perhaps it was the support from the crowd who were fantastic. Whatever it was, I played well enough to beat Nicolas Massu of Chile, ranked eleven places higher than me, in straight sets, and if you watch the video you can see how much it meant to me because at the moment of victory I let out a huge roar of relief.

My next match – also on the Centre Court – was against the Frenchman Julien Benneteau. I should have won in straight sets but the onset of darkness seemed to disrupt me. I wanted to finish the match. I was up two sets but I was rushing as I saw the light slipping away. It meant I was playing my opponent and the darkness at the same time, and I ended up throwing away the third set. Then the umpire suspended the match for bad light and I had to spend all night annoyed with myself.

My nerves were bad the following day so that I was almost ridiculously careful. I hardly missed a ball but I was hitting it really softly, just putting it back into court, hoping he would miss. Luckily he did and I was in the third round, but I knew I should have played more aggressively.

And that is when the whole Paraguay thing happened, the next hugely over-blown controversy of 2006. Let me say, here and now, that I am Scottish. I am also British. I am *not* anti-English. I never was. I'm patriotic and proud to be Scottish, but my girlfriend is English, my gran who I love to bits is English and half her family is English. My fitness trainer's English, my physio's English, some of my best friends are English. I have a flat in London, I supported Tim Henman all through his career, I love watching Ricky Hatton and Amir Khan, two English boxers, I practise in England with English players, I play Davis Cup for Britain – but I love being Scottish. There's nothing wrong with that.

OK. What happened was a little joke – again – that went wrong. It was the time of the 2006 World Cup and England were due to play Paraguay. Tim Henman and I were being interviewed together for a newspaper article on behalf of our sponsors Robinsons, and before we started the journalist asked Tim about England's chances in the World Cup and asked me who I would be supporting. He was making the point that Scotland weren't there. I got the joke. I just laughed.

We did the interview and the last question was: 'Who will you be supporting at the World Cup?' Remembering our previous banter, I just said: 'Whoever England are playing, ha ha.' I had a smile on my face. It was obvious I was joking and just entering into the spirit of our previous conversation.

It wasn't reported like that. The gist of the headlines was that I hated the English. They made up stories about me buying a Paraguay shirt. I never said that. It was a complete lie. The whole thing was absolute nonsense.

I had already dealt with this nationality issue a little at the French Open Junior semi-finals the year before. It was one of the first big press conferences I had ever done and I was being asked about all sorts of things including the fact I was Scottish, not English. It was fine. It made an interesting conversation. Bud Collins, the famous American commentator, asked me – probably for fun – what the difference was.

I said obviously there was a difference because they're two different countries, and I'm from Scotland not England. That's just a fact. I said it was like calling someone from France 'German'. It's just wrong. Is Bud Collins a Canadian? If someone walked up to an English person and asked them if they were Scottish, they would say 'No.' That wouldn't make them anti-Scottish. That's just pointing out where you're from. It isn't my fault that I have to do this from time to time because the majority of the world thinks England is the only country in Britain.

I don't really worry about who won the Battle of Bannockburn, although Robert the Bruce and his boys won it easily I think. Being Scottish is just a fact, not a racist state of mind.

So that is the context of what happened at Wimbledon. One

minute everything was fine, the next I'm this Scot who hates the English. I remember walking through the crowd on my way back from practice when I overheard a woman talking on her mobile phone. 'That Scottish wanker's just walked by,' she said and I was quite shocked. That's when I realised how big this thing had become. I purposely hadn't been reading the newspapers and I had been trying not to pay any attention to it, but that was when I realised that some people had taken great offence.

I probably shouldn't have said it. But, again, it was a *joke*. If anyone understood all the circumstances, they would have realised that. I walked on to court to play Andy Roddick that day in the third round still feeling quite awkward about the whole experience. A few months earlier in Australia I had played dreadfully because of the storm I had caused by accident. This time I was stronger. My game didn't implode.

It was a strange atmosphere to begin with because we had already been watching the beginning of England's quarter-final against Portugal, having beaten Paraguay in the previous round. (So my non-existent Paraguay support hadn't brought them much luck.) Wayne Rooney had been sent off and you could tell that loads of people on Centre Court were half listening to the match on their radios. Even so, Andy and I did our best to distract them because we played a close, intense match where both of us had chances.

I don't remember that much about it, but I know that we were really pumped up and exchanging words across the net. I get on well with him usually and I had practised with him before Wimbledon started, but he was giving me a little bit of shit on court. That's fine. That's what happens in sport. It is the same as football, the guys are trying to wind the other guys up, as Portugal's Ronaldo had just proved in his confrontation with Rooney that ended with Wayne getting a red card. Players try and disrupt their opponent's game plan and that is all Andy was doing.

I managed to win in straight sets 7–6 6–4 6–4. It was a huge win for me and one of the first questions Gary Richardson, the BBC journalist, asked me in his interview after the match was: 'You probably know that England have just lost, what do you think of that?' I said something like: 'Look, it's a shame. It would have been great for British sport if England had won the World Cup.'

After a match like that the last thing I wanted to do was discuss why I'd made a joke out of something and it had been – I keep saying this – blown out of all proportion, but I knew I had to do something. In the end, I just wanted to clear it up by saying the right thing and getting it over with. I don't know whether my tactful answer made any difference to what people thought about me. I just remember being quite annoyed about the whole fuss.

I had never won through to the second week of a grand slam before, and at this point I didn't know what to do. I was nineteen years old, I didn't have a coach and I couldn't decide when or how to practise on the Sunday off. As a result, I felt a little bit flat when I played my old rival from junior days, Marcos Baghdatis, on a sweltering Centre Court and lost in straight sets.

Maybe it was a good thing. I had played so well against Roddick, but you could play seven matches over fourteen days at a grand slam and I needed to learn how to pace myself. You don't want to be too distant and relaxed. You don't want to be over-anxious and impatient either. I don't think I had the balance quite right yet.

Jimmy Connors said afterwards that I needed to do a 'gut check', not just with tennis but with my attitude, so that I was able to 'embrace the pressure'. That is, more or less, what I said too. I needed to get stronger, physically and mentally, and my game needed to improve, but I wasn't down-hearted. I still thought that by twenty-one or twenty-two, I could be playing my best tennis at grand slams.

Clearly, I needed a coach again, and not long afterwards a deal was done that allowed me to work with Brad Gilbert, the former Top 10 player who had coached Andre Agassi and Roddick and was reckoned to be one of the best in the world. The Lawn Tennis Association had hired him to work with a number of the British players, but it was accepted that he would be travelling a fair amount of the time with me. The papers debated whether he was worth the money, a reputed £750,000, but that was nothing to do with me. I was just glad, having been coachless since the spring, to have someone so knowledgeable in my corner. It seemed to work OK – within about a month I had beaten Roger Federer.

Directly after Wimbledon I made the so-called 'glamour trip' to Newport again and this time made the semi-finals. I did moan about the courts, but not in my press conference. I was learning. From there I had to come back for the Davis Cup against Israel at Eastbourne, which was where I discovered I would be linking up with Brad. We started working together in Washington DC, where I immediately made the final and then moved on to Toronto where I reached the semi-finals, having beaten Tim Henman again in the second round.

Strangely, a week later in Cincinnati, I played Tim yet again.

The match went to three sets but produced the same result. I won. That was three times in a row now in less than a year and my reward was to play Federer, the runaway number one in the world who had just won his fourth Wimbledon in a row. Maybe that wasn't much of a reward after all.

I went into the contest well aware that there was no pressure on me. No one expected me to win, not against a man who was on a 55-match winning streak and who had only been beaten by one guy, Rafa Nadal, all year. The chances of him losing to a 19-year-old kid ranked 21 in the world, who had never been beyond the fourth round of a grand slam had to look pretty slim.

We both began pretty badly, trading breaks of serve. My first service percentage was disgusting, somewhere around 33. I was feeling strangely tired because I was so uptight inside. I was seriously worked up about playing him and it seemed to be draining the energy out of me. Despite that and my inefficient serving, Federer didn't seem his usual dominant self either. It was I who reached set point in the first set and, perhaps to some surprise, I sealed it with an ace.

The second set produced a slightly higher standard of tennis, but I was suffering from the same physical problem. I was so tired I couldn't feel my legs. They seemed so dead and so heavy. I think part of the problem was the fact that I had been failing to serve out my last few matches. I would be in a really dominant position and then allow my opponent back into the match. It happened against David Ferrer when I was leading 6–2 5–0 in Toronto – the final score was 6–2 7–6. It happened again when I was leading 6–2 5–3 against Tim. That kind of thing preys on your mind. You can't stop thinking about it and it affects your game with doubt.

Against Federer, I refused to let myself think like that. Instead I was thinking: 'Just forget about it. You can do this You can do this.' I wasn't panicking like I was in the other matches. I held it all together and on my second match point, Federer came into the net and I hit a backhand pass down the line to beat him. The relief was astounding. I just slumped back in my courtside chair and put a towel over my head in a daze. It felt as if I'd won the whole tournament, not just a match in round two.

It gives you such a shot of belief, a result like that. It told me that one day I could win a grand slam. There was now a voice in my head saying: OK, you've now got a good chance of being one of the best players in the world. Beating Federer was always something I had wanted to do, but until you actually win against a guy like him, it's tough to imagine it happening.

I didn't see much of him immediately afterwards. He left there pretty quickly. It can't have been very enjoyable for him. He doesn't normally get into a bad mood on court, but during the match he received a warning for hitting a ball over a fence. Maybe he was tired. At the end of the match, he just shook my hand and said something like 'Good job'. Nothing too deep, but it sounded pretty good to me.

Jamie

I can remember running round with Andy when we were little kids at the tennis courts in Dunblane. My mum was coaching somebody and we were at the back of the courts, chasing after tennis balls and probably getting hit by some as well. When we got bored with that we would go over to the park, kick a football and chase the ducks while one of the other mums looked after us. We were quite close in age so we did pretty much everything together and got on pretty well. We argued as all brothers do, but mostly it was all in good fun.

At home we'd make up games all the time and they were always competitive. Sponge ball football in the hallway was a favourite or indoor short tennis in the living room with all our trophies lined up as the net. We'd put the bigger ones at the end for the net post and the smaller ones in the middle. It was a bit silly but we loved it. I can't remember breaking any ornaments, but when we were five or six we once played basketball using a closed window as the hoop, so the first time we threw a shot we smashed the window. That was very, very stupid. My mum wasn't too pleased but my dad just sighed and said: 'We'd better get another window.'

As boys, we were similar in many ways but different too. Andy was quite fiery and stubborn; I was more easy-going. He didn't like being told what to do and he didn't always listen to what you had to say. He doesn't even now. He liked to figure things out for himself – he still does – and that can be a bit frustrating at times.

When we were kids, he'd often refuse to play what I wanted and we'd end up arguing. I guess we had disagreements over silly things. But we didn't fight. We maybe threw a punch or a kick, but we wouldn't be scrapping it out over ten rounds.

I am the elder brother, so I would tend to win at games the majority of the time. I usually beat him at tennis until we were about twelve and thirteen – then Andy improved a lot and started to beat me. He was so competitive, he wanted to win at everything, even Snap. I admit, I used to let him win sometimes. I liked winning, but not to the point he did. I wouldn't get mad if I was losing at Monopoly or Cluedo or whatever, but he did. So, anything for a quiet life, I thought. It was better to see him with a smile on his face than throwing a tantrum – it was just less hassle.

We shared a room until we were about ten. I was much tidier. I didn't like mess. Even if I was a bit untidy, it was controlled mess. My clothes would be folded up on the floor as opposed to Andy's dirty clothes in a heap. We had bunk beds and loads of posters all round. Mine were Manchester United, his were Liverpool. Then we became fans of WWF wrestling. I was a Hulk Hogan fan, and Andy loved The Rock. Of course, we tried the moves ourselves. We made a couple of belts out of cardboard and put duvets on the floor for a stage. But I only ever let him win the women's belts, if I was feeling generous.

We were always competing at something. Neither of us were happy just sitting around in the house playing computer games all day, although we had Game Boys and Nintendo. We'd much rather be out playing football, tennis, squash or golf. I played quite a bit of golf up to the age of seventeen and got down to a handicap of three before tennis took over. Maybe it runs in the family: my uncle Keith, Mum's brother, is a professional in America.

Andy and I never did anything really naughty growing up. We never got into trouble at school and never experimented with smoking or underage drinking but we were once in a bit of trouble for chucking eggs with some friends at Halloween. We would wind each other up a lot, but the only time I really hit him was when we were on a minibus coming back from the Solihull tournament. He had beaten me in the final and was going on and on about it. He had his hand on the armrest and I punched him right on the nail of a finger. There was a bit of blood and my mum had to stop the bus to sort us out. I didn't think it was that bad but the nail went black and blue and eventually fell off. He even had to get a tetanus shot the next day. He still talks about it and shows off the scar. I do regret it, but everyone has their breaking point.

I don't remember Mum telling me off really badly afterwards. I am sure she was annoyed but she was also understanding. She was – and is – a great mum to have. Dad is great as well. Even though they separated when we were teenagers, I've always thought we had a really good childhood and were brought up pretty well.

Looking back, it's strange that I wanted so much to go away from home when I was twelve. I loved being at home but I had this fierce ambition to board away from home because I wanted to be a tennis player and I thought that's what I'd have to do. I ended up at the LTA Tennis Academy in Cambridge. It was a rushed decision because I'd been told that my original choice, Bisham Abbey, was to be closed down, just four weeks before I was due to go. Everything had been arranged for Bisham Abbey and I was going to be looked after by Pat Cash's old coach, Ian Barclay. I'd known since the February that I would start in August and my bags had been packed for months! I was really excited and when things changed suddenly, I still wanted to go somewhere. The new regional centre at Cambridge was the option given to me by the LTA and it was a mistake. I was twelve years old and I didn't like it at all. My tennis suffered and I was often miserable on the phone home to my mum. My friends were at the same training academy, but I was a little younger than them so I was sent to a different boarding school. It would have been logical to come home sooner as I was so unhappy, but I wanted to try and stick it out – maybe I thought it was the brave thing to do. I stayed eight months in the end and then enough was enough.

Going away for that time meant that Andy and I didn't really see much of each other and my experience definitely put him off leaving home for his tennis. Three years later when he was fifteen, he went away to Spain, and though I was still competing we were nearly always at different tournaments. Even though we're very close in age – only fifteen months between us – it is really only in the past two years on the tour that we've been able to hang out together.

Things haven't changed that much since we were kids. We're pretty similar and we get on really well but we still argue about all sorts of things. I think that's normal. Andy still doesn't like being told what to do. Sometimes I get a bit annoyed with that. But he's his own person. I don't interfere with his decisions because he won't necessarily like what I say. It's not worth arguing. I think I'm more laid back than he is. Even if I'm doing something I don't want to, I still put on a smiley face and do it, whereas I think Andy is more likely to look completely fed-up.

I am very proud of what he is achieving in the game. He deserves it because he has put in the work. He's overcome so many ups and downs. I am sure in the next five to ten years he'll become a great player. I don't think there's any doubt about that. I guess he's inspired me to try to reach the level he is playing at. Obviously I'm not up to his standard, but in the doubles, with my partner Max Mirnyi, I am still playing on the ATP tour week-in, week-out. I'm loving it. I'm living the life I always wanted to lead.

Chapter Seven:
Can I Also Ask You This?

In 2007 I stopped talking to the BBC. There were a number of things that contributed to the silence, but the main reason was an interview that I did with one of their journalists at a smaller tournament in Metz. He said he was interviewing me about one thing, but it seemed to me more like a covert operation to get me to talk about something else entirely. Something that then dropped me into a whole heap of trouble.

Some people, I understand, would just let this sort of thing go. I am one of those who can't do that. If I think something is wrong or unfair, I will say so. It makes my life harder in many ways, but I have never changed. It is just the way I am.

The situation arose out of nowhere. I was playing in one of the smaller ATP tournaments in Metz in France, my first visit back to Europe following the wrist injury that wrecked half my year. I was playing in the singles and also in the doubles with my brother, trying to get back to match sharpness after such a long lay-off. I wasn't anticipating any press interviews. It wasn't the kind of tournament that the world's media would find of great interest.

On this particular day, I was in a bad mood. My brother and

I had just lost in the doubles and I didn't play that well either. I was just about to jump into my car and go back to the hotel when the press woman in charge of the event ran up to say: 'Someone from the BBC is here, just wondering whether you could do five minutes with him.' I said I didn't really want to.

'Well, they've requested it. I'm sorry. It's just a general chat about the tournament.'

I had no reason to be suspicious because normally Patricio would red flag a situation that could be awkward. But this time he had no idea it was happening. The ATP did not send him their usual email about interview requests at tournaments probably because it was one of the smaller ones on the tour. Then a guy came up to introduce himself. I'd never met him and I had no clue who he was. It turned out to be Brian Alexander, a BBC journalist who had been trying to talk to me for ages – so Patricio told me later – because he was doing some sort of investigative programme into the state of British tennis. Patricio had said no, explaining that I wanted to concentrate 100 per cent on recovery from the wrist injury. This guy didn't seem too happy about it. He sent an email back just saying, 'would 15 minutes with me seriously delay his recovery process?!'

So the man said to me: 'I don't believe we've met. Nice to finally meet you. I just want to talk to you about some of the smaller tournaments on the ATP tour and what life is like away from the glitz and glamour of the grand slams. Is that OK?' I said it was fine. No alarm bells were going off. It sounded perfectly OK to me. I swallowed my tiredness and disappointment about losing the match and tried to be as decent as I could.

The interview began without any problem. He asked me

about the atmosphere in Metz, what it was like to play in somewhere like an old school hall. He asked me about the Davis Cup and whether it was important to me. I explained how much I enjoyed it, although the scheduling could put a huge strain on the body. Then he said: 'Can I also ask you this. There's obviously been some negative stuff about tennis recently. About betting and suspicious betting on odd matches. Are you shocked about that?'

I answered truthfully, that I really wasn't surprised. I said it because I'd been reading in newspapers that four different players had said they had been offered money to throw tennis matches. Arvind Parmar, the British player, was one; the Belgian Gilles Elseneer was another. Gilles said that he had been offered £70,000 to lose a match at Wimbledon two years before. Dick Norman had also said he had been offered a bribe to lose a Challenger match. A few guys had come out and talked about it.

That is why I said I wasn't surprised. I also said that it wasn't acceptable and that it was difficult to prove whether someone was trying or not in a tennis match because they can do their best until the last couple of games of each set and then make mistakes or serve double faults. It is virtually impossible to prove. I said it was disappointing for the other players, but 'everyone knows it goes on'.

I wasn't properly prepared to have a serious conversation about something as sensitive as gambling in sport. In trying to be helpful, I had blurted something out without really thinking about it. I didn't mean to imply I knew matches were being fixed, only that approaches were being made to certain players.

For the record:

He then asked me two follow-up questions on the same

subject. I should have realised what was going on – that this was the whole purpose of the interview – but it was late, I wasn't thinking straight and maybe I was a bit naïve. We were talking about the fact that you couldn't stop people betting on tennis and therefore it was difficult to stop potential problems with players being offered money to lose.

He said: 'You don't sound surprised then. You actually feel this is locker-room talk. You and fellow players know this kind of thing is going on?'

I said: 'Yeah, I speak to a lot of guys, especially experienced ones who have been around a long time. They obviously know that it happens. A lot of guys have been approached about it. I've seen articles saying guys even at Wimbledon are doing it, so . . . everyone knows it goes on . . .'

Those were the words that came back to haunt me: 'Everyone knows it goes on.' A few days later, Patricio called me and said: 'Have you been talking about betting? Because there is a guy doing a show on Radio Five called *The Usual Suspects* and it's about betting in tennis.' I said: 'Yeah, but I only answered a couple of questions.' I didn't think I had said anything that other people weren't saying. Tim Henman had been on television saying that he thought betting on matches was a growing trend because of the internet, and tennis would have to be vigilant against it. John McEnroe had even talked about it as a 'cheap way to make a buck'. So there were lots of opinions out there and I didn't think I had said anything different.

Then the programme was aired and it was something like: 'We're talking about corruption in tennis. This is what Andy Murray thinks about it.' Then it was my words: 'Yeah . . . everyone knows it goes on.' They made it sound as though I was saying tennis was a corrupt sport.

The BBC website made the situation even worse. On there I was quoted as saying: 'Everyone knows corruption goes on.'

Many things seemed to happen very quickly after that. It caused headlines around the world, the ATP told me I shouldn't be saying such things; and some of my fellow professionals like Rafa Nadal and the Russian Nikolay Davydenko, who was being investigated following unusual betting patterns on a match he lost in Poland, had a public go at me. I just didn't think it was fair for a number of reasons.

The ATP ought to have found out what the BBC were looking for when I was asked to do that interview. They are the ones that asked me to do it, as one of our media obligations. If they had said: 'No, sorry, he can't do the interview' or even if during the interview, the representative from the ATP had cut in and said: 'Sorry, you said you were here to talk about the tournament, not ask questions about betting' they might have solved the problem before it started. It was obviously a touchy subject and the ATP woman was standing right next to me at the time.

The context of this is important. It is a fact that tennis players are not allowed to bet on matches, their own or anyone else's. Neither are people in their entourages. There was an Italian player called Alessio di Mauro who was suspended for nine months and fined £29,000 for being found guilty of betting on matches – not his own – but I thought the punishment was a little bit harsh given that the reports said he only bet a few lire. The real fear for tennis was a different one: that players expected to win matches would be bribed to deliberately lose them, so that criminal gamblers could back the longer-odds opposition knowing they were likely to win.

So it was a real, live, dangerous issue. There was an investigation going on into that Davydenko match against the lower ranked Vassallo Arguello in Poland when Davydenko pulled out in the third set with an injury and I think the ATP staff might reasonably have intervened when they sensed what the interviewer was after. Of course, you can blame me too. Maybe I should have taken the responsibility myself – I do try as I get older to do that – but I was taken by surprise, and I had believed this guy when he told me he just wanted to ask about the atmosphere at minor tournaments. At no point did he tell me he was gathering material for an investigative radio programme on match-fixing. If I had known that I wouldn't have done the interview. I thought it was pretty poor.

It turned out that he had spoken to five or six other players at Metz, all about betting. It was clearly his mission, but he didn't mention that to me. In the programme that went out, they just ran part of my answers and none of his questions so the context was completely lost. Obviously we protested and the head of BBC radio sport wrote a letter to me in part-apology.

The issue of betting is still there. I haven't said any more about it than most people. Since that interview, Michael Llodra, Arnaud Clement and Dmitry Tursunov have all come out and said that people have approached them to throw matches. It happens. We know that the approaches happen. But I don't know anything else. They have been holding investigations, but no one's been found guilty of trying to fix their own matches.

It is not fair to say that tennis is corrupt and make it sound as if those words are coming from me. I never once said that tennis was corrupt. It is *my* sport. I couldn't give 110 per cent every match, or even play it at all, if that were the case. I have to believe in its essential honesty. I have never been offered money myself and when I spoke I was going by what other people had been saying.

I had a great deal of negative press afterwards. Nadal, obviously, had read all about it. He said I had gone 'overboard'. Davydenko clearly didn't like getting asked about the subject in press conferences. 'If Murray says that he knows, that means he gambles himself. This is outrageous. How does he know what I was trying to do? I was so upset with the whole thing I started crying.'

Both of them had received a message that I believe had been badly distorted by the BBC's reporting. You don't want that sort of issue with players. You spend thirty weeks of the year with them. It's not the most comfortable thing if you're trying to avoid them.

As far as Davydenko was concerned, it probably sounded as if I was directing some sort of blame at him or saying he was guilty. It was bad enough for him to be caught up in the whole betting controversy, but it must have been pretty tough to take when he was told that one of his fellow players was saying he was guilty. I guess what he said in regards to me was a reaction to that.

After I played him in Doha, I apologised to him for what had happened. I never did have any kind of row with him because we don't normally speak on the tour. I don't know him that well. He doesn't speak very good English and my Russian isn't that great.

As usual, I have learned from the mistake, but even now if someone came to me and said: 'What do you think about betting in tennis?' I am not sure what I am supposed to do. Should I lie and say nothing? Should I say: 'No comment', which basically makes it sound as though I think something dodgy is going on. Or should I tell the truth? That is what I did. I told the truth, which is what I was always taught growing up. I didn't point the finger at any player. I just told the truth as I saw it and then watched it get splashed round the world as a headline.

So that is why I decided I wouldn't speak to the BBC. I felt an important trust had been broken. It wasn't the only problem I had with them either. I was on the shortlist for the 2007 BBC Sports Personality of the Year Award and one of the things they do on their website is a little 'Did You Know?' section about all the contenders. Amir Khan's said: 'Did you know Amir has a cousin who plays for the England cricket team?' Mine said: 'Did you know that Andy Murray was called 'Lazy English' when he trained in Spain?' That would be fine if it was true, but I never, ever heard anyone call me that. I was baffled. I asked all my friends who were at the Academy with me and none of them had heard that expression either. It came from nowhere and no one had bothered to check whether it was actually true. Perhaps you shouldn't worry about what people call you, but I had worked so very, very hard in Spain that it seemed to me unjust.

Then there was Jamie winning the mixed doubles at Wimbledon. Radio Five had asked me if I would come and speak to them on the air after the match and I said sure. I went along and did the interview, but as Jamie lifted the trophy, I couldn't speak. I was crying. So Jonathan Overend, the Radio Five tennis correspondent, cut in with the description: 'Jamie Murray lifts the Wimbledon trophy . . .' etc.

Then this woman says to me on air: 'Andy, just before you go – you must be jealous of Jamie. I'm an older sister and I love it when I get one over on my little sister.' I looked at her in disbelief. My expression must have said: 'What the hell are you doing?' I didn't say anything. There was just a moment of silence. I definitely wasn't jealous of Jamie, I was thrilled for him. If I had been jealous I doubt I would have been in tears. If you listen back to the interview, you can hear in my voice that I can hardly speak without my voice cracking.

I'm thinking: 'My brother's just won Wimbledon and you're freakin' asking me if I'm jealous of him!' I took my headset off and moved away. People were saying: 'Oh, I'm sorry' as I left because they knew it was out of order. I asked who the woman was, but I still don't know her name. All I know is that she wasn't part of the sports team.

In the end, I put all these things together and decided it wasn't worth speaking to the BBC any more.

Some people might think this is all very petty – the media have a job to do and I should get over it – but I don't think it's a bad thing to ask people who can influence millions of listeners, viewers and readers to get their facts right, and present them honestly, especially if it makes my life and work really difficult when they get it wrong.

The fall-out from the betting story went on for a while. When I turned up for my next tournament in Madrid, I had to speak to a couple of people from the ATP. Obviously, I had nothing to tell them, only the stuff they had been reading themselves in the papers. They told me that I had to be careful about what I was saying because it was a pretty rough time for the sport, but no one lectured me.

Then I met someone who is working for the ATP's new anti-corruption unit. He asked me about five questions, such as did I know of anyone who had bet on a tennis match, had I seen anyone betting at matches? The answer to everything was no. I don't know of anyone betting on matches and I don't know of anyone throwing matches. I asked him a couple of questions in return. He said they were investigating over a hundred matches, mainly with strange betting patterns attached to them, but so far they haven't found anyone guilty.

The trouble with these strange betting patterns is that a lot of them could be completely innocent. If you're a gambling man, sitting in the stadium watching two players, one ranked 20 and one ranked 90, and suddenly the guy ranked 20 clutches his hamstring and calls a trainer, it might be a smart move to bet on the lower-ranked guy. Good luck to you. It doesn't mean that in every – or in any case – a player has been bribed to lose a match against a lower-ranked player. As I said all along, it is a very, very difficult thing to prove.

I know the episode didn't exactly heighten my popularity, either with some of the players or with the public, but I survived. The one thing I always say to everyone around me is that it doesn't matter what people say because they don't know me. The majority of critics don't know how difficult it is to achieve anything in sport and, in this country, the press seem to like it when someone fails. That's what makes a story. It is rare to go to the front or back page of a newspaper and read a positive story. I'm not playing tennis to be popular. That's not why I do it. I've got the same friends I had when I was fifteen. I'm still the same person to my family and that is important.

I never thought for one minute that going on the tour would change me, and it hasn't. In the first three years on the senior tour I played 45 tournaments in 35 cities in 18 different countries. I've thrown coins in the Trevi Fountain in Rome and seen the whole of New York from the top of the Empire State

Building – that was awesome – but being on tour has never struck me as glamorous or amazing. I've been doing it, in the juniors, since I was thirteen. It is a way of life. I guess I am used to it.

I can't say I've seen much of most of the countries because between playing and practising, there just isn't time. Even in Rome, I've never bothered to go to the Colosseum because there is such a long queue and I don't really have the time to wait.

Most of the time of a professional tennis player is divided between the court, the locker room, the hotel and the airport. Most of that is spent alone or with your coach, but the locker room is where you get to know the other guys a little. For me, the best thing about men's tennis is the characters. There are so many different ones on the tour these days.

Roger Federer is the ultimate in being cool and calm on court, Rafa Nadal who is always bouncing around and absolutely ripped, Andy Roddick, the all American boy, super-confident, serves at 145mph and appeared in the US sitcom, *Sabrina the Teenage Witch*. I am just never going to do that kind of thing, by the way.

Then you've got guys like Janko Tipsarevic from Serbia, who is really clever and studies Nietzsche and reads Dostoevsky. He has a tattoo on his arm that says: 'Beauty Will Save The World'. If I was ever going to have a tattoo, it would probably repeat something said by Muhammad Ali but I don't think it's going to happen. Tattoos aren't that great. My dad's dad had one and said it was fine until he was about thirty-five and then it started to get wrinkled.

Not that I give tremendous thought to tattoos. The main, the only, professional focus is winning. Not just playing but winning. By the start of 2008 I had been on the tour nearly three years and I just sensed that when Federer lost to Novak Djokovic in the Australian Open, it started to open up more possibilities for us all. Perhaps I went some way to proving it a month later by beating Federer in the first round in Dubai, although he later came out and announced he had been suffering from glandular fever. So it was premature to say there had been a shift from the old guard to the new, but it made me think that men's tennis was in a really good state.

We had someone, Federer, trying to win the most grand slams ever as well as being one of the greatest players of all time. We had someone else, Nadal, who I would call the best clay-court player in history. And then Djokovic had just won his first grand slam to freshen up the story. In previous years, it had been a case of the favourites versus the outsiders. Now the players below the top two in the world were no longer huge outsiders. There were a few of us in that mix: Djokovic, obviously, Gasquet, Berdych, Blake, me. There were chances for quite a few on a given day. I reckoned by now I was in that few.

I've known Djokovic for years because we grew up playing in the juniors together. I still speak to him and get on with him now we are on the tour together, but you get to the stage where you don't want to be too close. I reckon for the next five or six years I'm going to be playing him in the semis and finals of major tournaments and I want to beat him. It's easier to do if we're not close friends.

Many people like his personality, including his famous impressions of other players. He does great take-offs of players' serves. The best ones are Roddick and Sharapova, and Nadal tugging at his shorts. I don't think he does me though. He's been accused of arrogance on one or two occasions, but I wouldn't want to say anything bad about him. Given that we're rivals, we get on fine.

He does speak his mind. That is probably a good thing. I remember him having a go at Nadal once by saying Rafa took too long a break between points by walking too slowly, dragging time out, bouncing the ball. It's true. I was timing the break between points when Nadal was playing Jo-Wilfried Tsonga in the Australian Open 2008 (Tsonga had put me out of the tournament in the first round, so I had some spare time on my hands). You are allowed 25 seconds to prepare to serve and Nadal was taking 37 seconds, while bouncing the ball over twenty times.

The top players obviously do get away with too much even though the rules are there. You can't be too strict. I'd say 28 seconds would be fine, like driving at 73mph on the motorway, but once the time goes beyond that, they're breaking the rules. The rules aren't there to be broken. They should be stuck to. The umpires should tell the players to get a move on.

I don't know exactly why they don't, but a player should get a warning if it happens repeatedly. They shouldn't get away with stuff like that. It's not fair on the other player. That is one of the little things I would change on the tour. Then again, I would change pretty big things too.

If you were starting from scratch you would redesign the men's tour completely. As things stand, it doesn't seem right that we only spend four weeks playing on grass and yet we can spend up to four-and-a-half months playing on clay. The Masters Series tournaments – the biggest tournaments on the tour, the next stage down from the grand slams – are all bunched together when they should be more spread out, and they also need to do something about the Davis Cup. It's at the wrong time, in the middle of the tour. You go to a different surface in a different time zone and you're going to get injured doing that. If affects your preparation for the next two or three tournaments as well because you can't just turn up on the day in the Davis Cup and start playing. You need to get used to the surface and then you switch straight back to another one. It's too hard. They need to do something about that.

We must respect traditions, but innovations can be good too. Most of us thought the glamour ball girls in Madrid were fine. It certainly brought a bit of attention to tennis when football usually gets all the headlines. They're not the best ball kids I've ever had, but it's fun. At most tournaments, the ball kids play at the club or love tennis, whereas the models haven't played much tennis. They don't throw the balls very well and they can't catch them very well either, but they're not terrible. They are easy on the eye, although some players get a bit distracted. I guess it's better than having a 14-year-old spotty boy throwing balls at you.

That doesn't mean I want to get swept up in the Hollywood side of tennis. That is not the way I am. Quite a few players know actors or have dated actresses and models. Tommy Haas is friends with Arnold Schwarzenegger and dated a Hollywood actress, so did Andy Roddick, and Robby Ginepri went out with Minnie Driver. I don't really know a lot about this, but there is a cross-over between tennis and celebrity at some level. It doesn't interest me, but I think my brother might be tempted to enjoy it.

I suppose when you think of some of the players on the tour over the years – McEnroe, Borg, Connors, Becker, Sampras, Agassi – these are some of the biggest names in sport. Their fame goes beyond sport and it is natural that people would want to be around them. It is pretty obvious that Federer is established as a global superstar, doing adverts with Tiger Woods and Thierry Henry, but I don't think for one second that any of the top players are stupid enough to get distracted by it because this is a really short career. You can be famous at any age, but if you haven't won a grand slam by the time you're thirty, the chances these days are that you never will.

That cuts down the fun in the locker room. There is nothing like the pranks and banter that go on in football or rugby, but that is because we are not part of a team. Even so, crazy things can happen occasionally. The Frenchman, Michael Llodra, caused a few headlines at Key Biscayne in 2005 when Ivan Ljubicic, the Croatian player, found him hiding naked in his locker. Not surprisingly, Ljubicic asked him: 'What the hell are you doing here?' Michael explained that as Ivan had been playing so well lately, he had been trying to absorb some of his positive energy.

I wasn't there, this happened a little bit before my time, but I remember thinking that I would have found it funny if it happened to me. I *think* I would have found it funny. Maybe I would have found it a bit worrying too. At least it proves that when people moan that there are no personalities in tennis any more, it isn't completely true.

One of my favourite players when I was growing up, apart from Agassi, was Guillermo Coria, the Argentine player. He didn't have Agassi's personality but he had a great game to watch. Following him gave me my introduction to another controversy in our sport – performance-enhancing drugs – because he was suspended for a while in 2001 for testing positive for steroids. I didn't really understand it at the time, I was only about thirteen years old, but clearly drugs have been an issue in our sport for a while.

There was a time when it looked as if a whole batch of supplements issued by the ATP themselves were contaminated with nandrolone and Greg Rusedski was one of the guys who had to fight to clear his name.

In the end, not many players have ever been found guilty. Coria's original ban of two years was reduced to seven months and he sued the multi-vitamin company that supplied his supplements.

I am really conscious about everything that goes into my body. That is why I don't take any vitamins or protein shakes, because of the potential for contamination. I am scared. If you fail a drugs test, your respect in people's eyes is just gone. When you are a clean athlete, even if they don't like you as a person, they can still respect what you do on the tennis court. But if you are seen to be taking drugs to enhance your performance, then that is really tough to come back from. I'd rather just eat a lot of healthy food and work hard. The only thing that I take that is not completely natural is the energy drink I have on court. Of course, you never know if something like that could be contaminated either. You just have to try and give yourself the least chance of that happening by taking as few supplements as you can. I have heard that apparently 10 per cent of the products on the shelves could make you fail a drugs test. Maybe that is a scare story. I don't know for sure, but I would rather not risk it and find out.

We get tested so often throughout the season and in the off-season that I think it would be difficult to get away with much. When I was in Miami training during the 2007–8 winter break, I was tested three times – twice for urine, one blood – and that reassured me. I like the fact they test us all year round. Obviously, there have been bans for some players but I still believe I am competing in a relatively clean sport.

Other players have other opinions. I know that Lleyton Hewitt once said: 'I'd like to think that tennis is clean but I can't say 100 per cent. Sometimes you are not so sure. I know I'm clean but sometimes guys look stronger in the fifth set than they did in the first. You have to worry about that.' That is his opinion. I don't really worry that much. The testing makes me feel more comfortable about it.

I get criticised a lot for being too skinny. I've been called a 'scruffy Hugh Grant', which actually isn't that bad because he's quite good looking. I had a reputation for being unfit when I first came on the tour and maybe some people thought I would bulk up quicker if I took steroids, but that's obscene. I would never do that. I have worked really hard for my muscle with my fitness trainers in the gym and I would never take a short cut. It is not something that would make me happy. Imagine winning Wimbledon and then looking at yourself in the mirror and seeing a cheat in the reflection. It would feel awful.

Look at Marion Jones, one of the best athletes the Olympics has ever seen. She lied to the whole world by denying she took drugs and now she is locked away from her family in prison. Her Olympic medals are all gone, her reputation is shot. Drugs are just a short cut to the end of your career.

I don't even eat bananas. Not because I am scared of contamination but because I don't rate them. I think it's a myth that they're good for you as an energy-giver. Players do sit there and eat them at changeovers, but it can't be to give them energy because they take ages to digest and because other things are way better. Maybe it is just because they are easy to eat compared with chewy bars that get stuck in your teeth. And you thought we just worried about our foreheads.

To be honest, I think bananas are pathetic fruit. They don't look great for a start. They're not straight and I don't like the black bit at the bottom. All right, they're not terrible but they're such an average fruit. I'm more a peaches and plums sort of guy. And apples . . .

Apples are miles better. A good Granny Smith, a soft pear. A banana isn't even juicy. You bite into a pineapple and you get this great burst of juice. There's no juice in a banana. And it squashes easily. If you put one in your bag and someone kicks it, it spatters about all over the place and then sticks to everything. At least with an apple, all that happens to it is a bruise. You can still eat it. But if a banana gets squashed – there's no coming back from that.

They call me opinionated. I guess they're right. Even about bananas.

Chapter Eight:
We Are in Hell Right Now

Just when you think it is all going fine . . . The first three months of 2007 seemed pretty good to me. I reached the final in Doha, played the greatest game of my life so far against Rafa Nadal in the Australian Open, won San José for the second time in two years and topped it all by reaching two straight semi-finals at the master series events in America. On the 13th of April 2007, two years after turning pro, I entered the World Top 10 for the first time. Another goal achieved. Maybe I should have noticed the omen.

A month later, actually on the day of my twentieth birthday with my mum and gran over from Scotland to watch me, I hit a forehand against Filippo Volandri in a first-round match in Hamburg and felt a horrible pain. Game over, tournament over, summer over. I didn't play another match until August. A scan had shown up a small tear in the tendon of my right wrist and that injury wrecked a huge chunk of the season including Roland Garros, Queen's and Wimbledon. It was such a difficult and annoying time, not just for me but also for the people around me.

It was all the more frustrating because the year had begun

with so much promise. I had been working with Brad Gilbert for about five months by now and my first tournament in Doha convinced me we were on the right track. Having beaten Davydenko in straight sets in the semi-final, I lost to Ljubicic 4–6 4–6 in the final. I hadn't played as well in the final as I did in the semi, but since he was ranked 5th and I was ranked 17th, I couldn't be too disappointed. It was a statement of intent. I was playing well and next up was the Australian Open.

The previous year had been my horrible debut when I lost in the first round, after the row in New Zealand about sexism, and I felt really determined to do better in Melbourne this time. I do really like Australia and I love the crowd at Melbourne Park. It is a great place: the people are unbelievably friendly and they certainly love their sport. The Australian Open is, far and away, the most relaxed grand slam, and it is easier to get around there than my other favourite tournament, the US Open in New York, where the traffic is a shambles. In fact, the only thing wrong with Australia, as far as I'm concerned, is that it's rather far away.

But that didn't bother me as the tournament progressed. I was feeling quite at home, especially after my first-round win over Alberto Martin of Spain, which was on the Vodafone arena with the roof closed because of the heat. It was the closest I've ever been to a 'triple bagel', winning a match love, love and love. He managed to win the eighteenth game to make the final score 6–0 6–0 6–1. I was a bit annoyed because you probably only get one chance to win a match like that in your lifetime, but even I realised it wasn't worth getting too upset when you win a match that easily.

The next two matches, against another Spaniard, Fernando Verdasco, and Juan Ignacio Chela of Argentina, were tougher but I still won in straight sets to make the last sixteen. My opponent was the world number two and French Open champion Rafa Nadal, who I hadn't played since junior days. He was a year older than me, quite a few pounds heavier and one of the most aggressively physical players who has ever played the game. This was only the second time in my life I'd reached the fourth round of a grand slam. It was going to be the perfect examination of how far I'd come as a player.

At nearly 2am on the stadium court in Australia, after five sets of tennis against one of the best players in the world, I knew how far I'd come. It was the greatest game I had played so far. Both of us maintained such a high standard of tennis all the way through, and there were so many twists and turns in the course of the match that it would have to go down as a near-classic. It had everything, including an underdog (me) and a great set of fans who stayed to the end, and a little group of Scottish supporters who gave me a standing ovation in the fifth set when I won my one and only game.

It was the first time in my career that I had come off a match as brutal as that without losing due to a physical issue. I hadn't been blown away despite the awesome force that Nadal can produce. I held my own against him. I'd worked really hard in the off-season in Florida to get ready for this and I was still fighting to the very last point of the match. Maybe I only lost because he had more experience of playing big matches. While I'd only reached the fourth round of Wimbledon before, Nadal had already won two French Opens (he was on his way to three) and played in a Wimbledon final.

In the fifth set I had six break points on his first two service games. Had I converted them, I'd have led 3–0 instead of finding myself 0–3 down. It was that close. But finding myself down to someone as seriously good and fit as him, it was just too tough to come back. If I'd made a better start to the fifth set, I think I would have won.

Mentally, I wasn't crushed. For me, the worst thing in tennis is not losing matches. What I hate most is underperforming. If you're playing well and losing, it is easier to focus on the next point and believe you can win in the end. If you are playing poorly, it is much harder to believe you can get back into the match. I know how close I came to winning that match. Tennis is a game of inches. You can hit ten unforced errors, but on another day, if the wind blows a little harder, you can hit exactly the same shots and they will be ten outright winners. The better player usually wins, but these little things can still swing the momentum.

I wasn't sick with annoyance when the match was over. Everyone was gutted for me. Kim was there, so were Mum and Brad, and they all said: 'You did great. You deserved to win. Bad luck, you'll get him next time.' But I just wanted to spend some time on my own. I took a car back to the hotel and went for a run, up and down one of the streets, at 3am. I was sorting out my head. I was, for sure, disappointed that I didn't win but that was the match where I realised the standard of tennis I could produce. I was proud of the way I'd fought and I'm sure everyone watching enjoyed it.

You take away a load of confidence from a match like that and I proved that in the very next tournament by winning San José for the second year running. I think the first time was the more special of the two, but this one was still pretty cool. Maybe I had fond memories of 2006 because Kim had been with me – and Brad, with respect, wasn't quite as good looking. (I certainly didn't want to kiss him when I won.) But it was a good effort to win the final again with almost a mirror-image score, 7–6 in the third set. This time the opposition was Ivo Karlovic, the gigantic big-server from Croatia we call 'Lurch' (but not necessarily to his face), who at 6'10" is the tallest player in the history of the men's tour. Brad used to say that facing him is like having someone serve out of a tree at you! I lost the first set in a tie-break but after that I worked him out better. I knew I'd have a chance because my return of serve is the best part of my game. Even so, you have about a millisecond to see the ball coming at you. Sometimes you barely see it at all.

To reach the final, I'd beaten Andy Roddick again in the semis and he might have been getting a bit sick of me by now. We'd played three times already and I led 2–1 after my third-round victory at Wimbledon the year before. Now here we were again. The first set was really tense and I came through a first-set tie-break 12–10 before closing out the second set 6–4.

I had a lot of close matches that week and came through all of them. Brad was a firm believer in fighting through matches even when you are not playing your best tennis, and his philosophy seemed to be working for me. In the second round against Kristian Pless of Denmark, ranked 83, I won the first set easily and then blew the next in the tie-break before coming back to take the third set 6–4. Against Hyung-Taik Lee, the Korean, in the quarters the match came down to a final-set tie-break. It was a struggle, but it was a positive sign that I was mentally strong enough to keep winning the tough ones.

The greatest comeback I'd ever made was the year before, just after Wimbledon, when I was playing horrendously in the first round of Newport against a Brazilian ranked 139 in the world, Ricardo Mello. I was down 5–2 and two breaks in the final set. This was the match when I earned a point penalty for the only time in my career on the tour, mainly because the courts were so terrible. I saved five or six match points, I can't quite remember, and then went on to win 7–6. Memories like that can really be good for you if you find yourself in the same situation again. I was learning all the time.

The upbeat feeling around San José got even better when my brother Jamie won his first doubles title there. I couldn't really watch it, even though I was there, because I was pretty nervous. It is always much more nerve-racking watching Jamie than it is playing my own matches. I don't get that nervous when I play, but I've struggled to watch him from a really young age. I don't know why. I suppose I've always wanted him to do really well. There is nothing else I get nervous about in this profession.

For most of the final I was hiding in the locker room occasionally watching on the television screen. Only when he was so close to winning that it was impossible for him to lose, did I run outside and watch in person. It was great. We had cause for a double celebration but we didn't have time. We had to catch the night flight to Memphis and, anyway, neither of us likes champagne.

Brad's old pupil, Roddick, had his revenge in Memphis but at least I reached the semi-finals. I was ranked 13 in decent shape and going into the back-to-back Masters Series events, the biggest in tennis outside the grand slams, the Masters Cup and Davis Cup. The best players turn up for Indian Wells and Miami because the prize money, the ranking points and the competition are all good, but I still fancied my chances.

When I beat Nikolay Davydenko in the fourth round in straight sets, I liked my chances even more, but during the quarter-final against Tommy Haas of Germany I managed to twist my ankle pretty badly in an awkward fall. It was the same ankle I had hurt at Queen's in 2005 and ever since then I have worn an ankle brace when I play. I think it saved me from doing some serious damage. I was able to win the match in the final-set tie-break but the ankle certainly wasn't feeling too good when I got up the next morning. I thought about pulling out of the semi-final against Novak Djokovic but I was so looking forward to the match that I wanted to give it a shot.

We were both nineteen years old and I was ranked one place behind him at 14. It could have been one almighty battle, but my best effort on a bad ankle wasn't good enough. I lost 2–6 3–6 and, although it may sound crazy to say it, I actually left the tournament feeling pretty good. It was the first time I had beaten so many top players in a Masters Series event and my confidence was growing all the time.

Two weeks later I was in the Miami semi-final playing Djokovic again, the perfect opportunity to reverse the score. It didn't work out that way. This was the worst match I'd played since joining the tour and I had no idea after the first three games that it was going to run away from me so horribly. We both held serve and I was 0–40 up on his next service game. After that I just made loads of unforced errors, he hardly made any and I didn't win another game. The scoreline 6–1 6–0 was fully justified by the way I played.

What went wrong? I don't know. Some people thought maybe that Djokovic was turning into my bogey player, someone I would always struggle to beat. He had beaten me once before at the Masters in Madrid in 2006 and was now leading our head-to-head encounters 3–0. But that is not the way my mind works. I just played a couple of bad matches against him. I don't believe in bogey players. He's someone I will play many times in my career, hopefully, and I don't plan to see him win every match.

The switch to the European clay-court season from American cement, not always a successful transition for me, instantly brought me problems. I was playing in a doubles match in Monte Carlo with Jamie when my back suddenly went into spasm. I had noticed it was a little stiff before we went on court but I didn't think it was anything serious. It was an evening game, noticeably cold for Monte Carlo, and I just couldn't get out of my chair after the first set.

Part of me really wanted to carry on. I never like letting Jamie down in the doubles and we had already lost the close first set 7–6. My mind was willing, eager to carry on, but my body was stuck in that chair. I had to pull out of the match, and the singles, and then take a little time off to recuperate.

I came back in time to play Rome, but only for one match because I lost in the first round against Gilles Simon of France. It was the first time I'd lost a three-setter all year but I wasn't really surprised given my lack of practice time going into the tournament. A week later I was in Hamburg, with no clue, no sign that half my season was about to be ruined by one shot. My first-round match against Filippo Volandri coincided with my twentieth birthday and my mum and gran came out with a home-made cake to help me celebrate.

Volandri was a tough opponent. He had beaten Federer the week before in Rome but I was playing really well and was up 5–1 in the first set when – *crack* – my right wrist just went. I don't know how else to describe it. I'd never had pain like that before in my life, it was just agony. I called the physio on to the court straight away while Brad was telling me that I should just get it strapped up and carry on. In retrospect, I saw his reaction as yet another sign of mutual misunderstanding. At the time, though, I was just in pain. I didn't know what to do. But the tournament physio had strapped the wrist really tightly and I tried to carry on. The next time I hit a forehand, the pain was even worse than before and there was no way I could carry on. I was really worried that by playing on I'd made the injury worse. I have had a few pains in my time but this was the worst I'd ever experienced by a long way.

So, I spent my birthday in an MRI clinic in my tennis kit with Patricio, having a scan for an injury and then waiting around for the results. I didn't need to be told it was serious. I knew something bad had happened because I couldn't open doors with my right arm. I couldn't even lift up a drink. It was just completely useless.

In the end, I think I was expecting worse news than we were actually given. I thought I had torn something really badly, ripped something off the bone, but I hadn't. I was lucky in a way. The German guy who ran the clinic explained to me that the tendon I'd damaged was like a tube and had split down the way, not across. That was good apparently. If the damage goes across, the tendon is snapped in two. Later they discovered it wasn't quite as they had first described, but I don't really know what it was. I just knew it hurt.

I could imagine the headlines about me being 'frail' again. Maybe those first impressions from Wimbledon 2005, when I suffered cramp, would stick with me. But I hoped people would understand this was an injury you could not control. If I hadn't been stretching properly and I'd hurt my hamstring or quad, you could say it was my fault. But a wrist injury can come from just one shot. Loads of tennis players get this sort

Taking a break from training in Stirling aged fifteen

With Jamie in Paris aged fourteen

With my gran aged fourteen

With my Scotland Junior Tennis Player of the Year award aged fourteen – I refused to get dressed up!

Playing in the ITF event at Craiglockhart in 2002 in the days when I used to get my hair cut regularly

My first French Open Junior Championships, just turned sixteen

My driving licence pic –
check out those eyebrows!

With pal Matt Brown and
boxer Chris Eubank at the
BBC SPOTY in 2004

Awards ceremony on Arthur Ashe stadium with my US Open Junior Trophy

My first Wimbledon

Loving my second round win over fourteenth seed Radek Stepanek – my first match on Centre Court

My first taste of autograph signing after beating George Bastl on court two

First appearance on the big screen at Henman Hill

Celebrating my first win, shaking hands with George Bastl on court two. So happy!

THE CHAMPIONSHIPS

Looking through the bars outside the All England Club during a photo shoot with Tim Henman in 2006. Hair's starting to get big!

San Jose –
first ATP title.
Loving it!

With British player
James Auckland
in Las Vegas

of damage – I know it's happened to Marat Safin and Mardy Fish. But I was also aware that quite a few come back too soon and then it takes its toll in the long run. I knew I was going to have to be patient, even though patience is not my strongest point.

So we were pretty glum when we went out for dinner to celebrate my birthday: Patricio, Mum, Gran, Brad, Kim and me. However, something happened that cheered me up a good deal. Eating in the same restaurant was Wladimir Klitschko, one of the recent heavyweight boxing champions of the world, who lives in Germany.

I didn't like interrupting his dinner but boxing is my favourite sport. You don't get the chance to meet one of the world's heavyweight champions every day, so I went over to him and someone introduced me. He didn't know who I was but I didn't mind. I might be well known in Britain, but I am sure he's much more famous than me in the sports world.

He was really nice and friendly, and incredibly massive. He must be about 6′7″ tall and his back looked about two or three times the size of mine. His hands were massive too – mine was lost in the handshake. I said, 'I'm sorry, I can't shake hands because of the split on my wrist.' He said, 'It's OK, we shake with the left because it comes right from the heart.' He was obviously a pretty intimidating guy and I'm just glad he doesn't play tennis. No disrespect to my family, but that made my birthday a bit better.

Contrary to what people may think, I never did have words with Brad about his suggestion that I play on in Hamburg before he realised how serious the injury was. He wasn't to know how sore it was from the side of the court and it is typical of the way his mind works that he would be keen for me to tough it out if I could. But I wasn't going to be playing tennis for a while, so we parted company and I just went home to have another scan – I believe in getting second opinions. When that confirmed the first diagnosis, all I could do was try and wait for it to heal.

The worst thing to do in that situation is sit around and mope. Luckily I had no time for that because it's one of the biggest fallacies that you laze around doing nothing when you're injured. I was still going to the gym every day, running, doing leg weights, going through rehab. I was desperate to get better as quickly as possible. I even tried swinging a racket underwater in a swimming pool, so that I could help strengthen my wrist without impact. We tried loads of things that were outside the box. After four or five weeks I could start to knock a tennis ball around, but because the injury affected the way I generated topspin. I could only hit slice forehands. That shot improved beyond belief but unfortunately it's not one I hit very often.

All the time, there was this little rumour that sometimes flared up that I might never play again. People who'd only seen me getting cramp at Wimbledon and injuring my ankle at Queen's were getting the idea that I was fragile. To be honest, the thought of quitting never crossed my mind. Wrist problems are a hazard of the job but I never thought it would keep me out for ever. I did have a lot of people asking me whether the weight of my racket was the problem. I said it wasn't and that's true. It was just one of those freak things.

I worked really hard because I wanted to give myself the best chance of getting back in time for Wimbledon. There was a difference of opinion about that. Brad thought I was ready to play and everyone else said I shouldn't play. I spoke to three doctors, two physios, Mum, my agent, friends and everyone told me the same thing: 'It's not worth it.' I was criticised for leaving the decision to the last moment but the conflicting advice made it difficult to decide. Brad thought I could and I was so keen to try, even if everyone else was against it.

I was in a really bad mood the Tuesday before Wimbledon. Kim said to me: 'What's up with you?' because I was visibly so fed-up. I told her I sensed I would not be ready in time. 'I'm not going to be able to play. It's not getting better fast enough.' To be honest, I didn't quite understand why Brad thought I could play. I'd practised with Jamie Baker at the NTC the day before and I still couldn't hit topspin. I was hitting it with my whole arm, instead of the wrist. No one ever won Wimbledon hitting with an unnatural forehand like that. Even if I could win one match playing with slice forehand, I wasn't going to win three matches in a row, especially if any of them went to five sets. Imagine what would have happened if I'd gone on court and then pulled out after a few games. Everyone would have gone berserk.

I'd like to say it was a tough decision, but actually no it wasn't. It was tough in the sense that I had to miss Wimbledon. But it was right for me. I can't understand Brad's attitude. Maybe he believed the injury wasn't that bad. He spoke to the doctors, but the doctors were wrong according to him.

I was criticised for announcing at a press conference just a couple of days before Wimbledon: 'As of now, I plan to play.' It annoyed some Sunday paper journalists because they thought I wasn't telling the truth. But I was really trying to give myself the best opportunity to play – just in case. Following practise at the NTC that morning, where I didn't feel totally comfortable hitting over my forehand and Brad said I would be

OK to play, I left the NTC saying, 'Fine, I'll play.' My mum and Patricio followed me out and we all came back to my flat where we discussed it. I calmed down and wrote up a list of pros and cons and when you saw it in black-and-white like that, there was no argument. If Brad hadn't thought so strongly that I would be fit to play, I might have pulled out much sooner. Regardless of what people think about our relationship, if I hadn't respected him I would not have listened when he kept saying: 'You can play. You can play'. I tried my best but it wasn't to be. I pulled out just after lunch the day before the event started. I was desperate to play and I was more than entitled to wait until the last minute. But if this was to happen to me again, I'd pull out the week before and continue with rehab instead of giving hopeful, but misguided, press conferences.

Two-and-a-half months later, on the 5th of August – a full month after Wimbledon was over – I was back on court beating Robby Ginepri 6–4 6–4 in the Canadian Open. It sounds better than it was because I still wasn't hitting through my forehand. After playing on grass where the balls come in at a nice height, I was having to adjust to American hard courts where the ball bounces high and you have to use a lot of topspin to control your shot. That was the movement that hurt my wrist. It was fine when I had my whole body behind the ball, but when I was out of position it was still really sore.

It wasn't surprising. You don't go from being in unbelievable pain and not being able to open doors to suddenly hitting the ball perfectly again. There was a lingering problem, in my mind as well as with the wrist. Every time I wanted to generate topspin, I was scared to try. I hadn't practised it enough and I was scared.

The doctors were telling me this was normal. Your brain is trying to protect you from feeling that pain again. Some mornings when I woke up, my wrist would be sore and stiff and it would crack a good deal. It's pretty tough in those circumstances to go out and hit a tennis ball at 100mph. It was tough on the mind. I was walking out on court just hoping to get through matches, not going all out to win.

I had stuck in my mind all the instances of other players, like Safin, who had tried to come back from a wrist injury too soon and then ended up needing surgery and missing far more time than he had already taken. A wrist injury is one of the toughest in tennis because you need to use your wrist on every shot. If you injure your shoulder that's better, because it is going to ache only when you serve.

I wasn't sure whether I had come back too soon in the States. My mind was badly affected, and on the court the matches went from bad to worse. After the fortunate win against Ginepri, I found myself floundering against Fabio Fognini, a guy from Italy not even ranked in the World Top 100. I didn't just lose, I lost easily 2–6 2–6. My relationship with Brad was deteriorating because I didn't think he was really listening to me. He felt I was just being depressed and negative. Maybe I was, but I had a pretty genuine reason to feel like that.

When you think it can't get any worse, it does. The next week I was slaughtered 1–6 2–6 in the first round of Cincinnati by Marcos Baghdatis. I couldn't go on like this. I phoned home and spoke to my mum and we made the decision that I should just cut short the American trip, come back to London and see a sports psychologist that she had found for me who had worked with the West Ham United football team. It was Brad, actually, who suggested I speak to someone professional who might be able to relieve the mental pressure I was feeling. But he seemed to think I had more deep-rooted problems and that worried me. I asked my close friends what they thought. They all said that off the court I was just as chilled as ever.

I had two or three sessions with this guy Roberto Forzoni, who had worked with a number of Britain's Commonwealth boxers as well as a few West Ham players such as Dean Ashton. He believes in motivational videos, reminders of things you do well to act as inspiration or maybe a distraction from your problems. He was also a big fan of the 'inches' speech that Al Pacino delivers as a basketball coach in the film *Any Given Sunday*. It sounded pretty appropriate to me.

We are in hell right now, gentlemen, believe me and we can stay here and get the shit kicked out of us or we can fight our way back into the light. We can climb out of hell one inch at a time . . .

I can't remember it all, but that was the gist of it. I don't even remember exactly what Rob and I talked about but I know it wasn't about my wrist. Maybe that was the secret. We were discussing other things like how I was going to win matches, how I saw myself as a player, what my goals were – positive things. For a long time, I had been dwelling on my injury and for months every single person I saw asked me: 'How's your wrist? How's your wrist? How's your wrist? Are you going to be OK for Wimbledon?' On and on and on. It was all people could talk about and all the time I just wanted *not* to talk about it.

When I went back over for the US Open, Rob came with me to watch and I started to play better tennis again. Even so, I was hitting the ball with only 50 per cent power. It was just taking me a long time to get over it. I had to go through a process first. I had to build up strength in the wrist physically and faith in it mentally until I was sure it was absolutely secure.

I went into New York, my favourite tournament, with a different mentality. Usually I am desperate to win but that wasn't my priority any more. I just wanted to get through it as best I could. I needed to do as well as I could without any more injury scares. The first round against the Uruguayan, Pablo Cuevas, ranked 129, went fine and I won pretty easily in straight sets. Then the real test came in the wily and experienced shape of Jonas Bjorkman, the 35-year-old Swede who had played a lot of doubles tennis with my brother's new partner, Max Mirnyi. It wasn't a comforting thought that he'd played fifty-four of the last fifty-five grand slams going into our match.

I was going to be tested but I wasn't scared any more. It was nice to be back on court again, competing with the top players. I was still not that comfortable on my topspin forehand and I was missing a lot of balls, but I was still in there fighting. I won a tough five-setter 5–7 6–3 6–1 4–6 6–1 and it was the first time since Hamburg that I'd managed to string two victories together. The relief didn't last that long. I lost in the next round to Hyung-Taik Lee, but all things considered, and throwing in a visit to the top of the Empire State Building which was awesome, I think I turned a corner.

I came home for the Davis Cup tie against Croatia and won another five-setter against Marin Cilic. Progress was good and I went off to Metz after playing the dead rubber (the one Jamie had given me a hard time about) to get a bit more match practice. It was while I was there that the BBC interview about gambling and match-fixing in tennis occurred. The controversy had yet to break when I played Tommy Robredo in the final and lost, having won the first set 6–0. I was playing really well and I should have won the tournament, but I came away pleased more than disappointed.

I played two rounds in Moscow and then came home for a week when the whole gambling issue erupted. The headlines were completely untrue. 'Tennis Is Fixed, says British No 1 Murray' and 'Murray Taking Flak For Fix Claim'. I could have done without it. Nikolay Davydenko, the Russian player under investigation after retiring from a match at the Polish Open, came out and said: 'If Murray says that he knows, that means he gambles himself because people who start talking out loud have their fears disappeared.' I wasn't quite sure what that meant but I could tell he wasn't happy. Even Rafael Nadal said he thought I'd gone overboard. 'I don't think anything like that happens. Everyone gives it 100 per cent and there are no fixed matches.'

For the record: I still have the feeling that if you are ranked 100 in the world and someone comes to you and says: 'Here, you can make $200,000 if you lose a match' then someone might be tempted. But so far no one's been banned for throwing matches or betting in large amounts. Players have come out and said they've been approached but all of them have turned the offers down. That is obviously good for the sport. We can't say that players are guilty of match-fixing unless someone is found guilty of doing it and that hasn't happened.

But we cannot ignore the problem either. At one of our ATP tennis meetings in Miami, in 2007, we had a visit from a guy from the American Mafia. He explained to us how wrong it would be to get involved with these people. If you do something for them once, they're not going to let you go. They'll approach you many more times and it's very tough to escape.

Obviously there were investigations going on then, otherwise there would have been no point in organising a visit from an ex-Mafia informant who'd spent time in jail. He said he'd turned his life around and warned us that anybody getting involved in this kind of business was in big trouble if they were caught. He was pretty authentic and looked the part because he wore sunglasses all the time. He made sense, and I thought it was a good idea for him to speak to us. Some of the other players didn't, they thought it was a bit extreme, but later events proved that there was a problem and something needed to be done to try and address it.

The controversy rumbled on. It was still with me when I arrived in Madrid but I had a good clear-the-air talk with Nadal, who understood how these things can happen in the media, and with that pressure off my shoulders I then played my best tennis of the year to beat Radek Stepanek in the first round, followed by Juan Ignacio Chela in the second. Both of them were fairly easy straight-set victories. I played so well against Stepanek that he never once reached deuce on my serve, and I would say it was probably one of my best matches since turning pro.

Maybe it was fate that my next opponent was Rafa Nadal, in front of his home crowd, playing only his second match since hobbling away from the fourth round of the US Open with knee problems. We hadn't met since that epic match in Melbourne, and this one followed the same up-and-down route. I slammed down a few aces, then lost my serve to love to go 6–5 down. I levelled when he failed to win a point on his next service game and then he won the first-set tie-break with a gigantic leap of celebration while 10,000 Spaniards went mad. He won the second set 6–4 but only after a battle.

It was another really great match between us and I wasn't too disappointed when I met Brad, my mum and Leon afterwards. I felt a little tired after playing three weeks in a row – Metz, Moscow and Madrid – but I wasn't even thinking about my wrist any longer. I was feeling more and more confident about how hard I could hit the ball again and moved on to St Petersburg with every hope of doing well.

This was only the seventh tournament I'd played since the injury, and winning it was a very good effort. I had an unbelievably tough draw as well. Playing two Russians in Russia is always going to be tough and after beating Dmitry Tursunov in the quarter-finals, I came back against Mikhail Youzhny after saving one match point. Later, my Mum said she cried with relief when I beat Fernando Verdasco 6–2 6–3 in the final because it meant I was back to my old self. I was playing well and winning again.

I am sure it is just a coincidence, but I've noticed that every time I've won a tournament there has hardly been any British press there. It's either been a long way from home, like San José, Qatar or St Petersburg, or else one of the smaller tournaments such as Marseilles. I am not reading anything into this. It is just something that struck me at the time.

I still had a chance of making the Masters Cup, the lucrative end-of-season tournament for the top eight players in the world, this year being played in Shanghai. I still had to keep winning and a couple of players in front of me had to lose, but I had my passport stamped with a Chinese visa just to be on the safe side. Six of the eight places were already taken but the chance to win $1 million was worth shooting for.

It came down to Paris: if I won Paris, I'd reach Shanghai, and it turned out to be eventful. First there was the car crash. It was funny that a couple of weeks before, when we were being driven round Moscow, I'd asked Brad if he'd ever had an accident in one of the tournament cars during his career, as some of the driving overseas is pretty suspect. He said he'd had a couple. I told him I'd never had one. 'Be careful what you say,' he'd said.

He was obviously right about that. We were on our way to the hotel in Paris in the pouring rain when our car braked suddenly and the guy behind absolutely nailed the back of the car. We were lucky we were in one of the big Mercedes people-carriers that they use at tournaments because we were basically fine. But the impact of the crash was really loud, and for a split second we had no idea what had happened. The front of the car behind us was pretty badly damaged.

Actually, it wasn't quite true to say I'd never been in a car crash, but it wasn't in a tournament car. It was in a New York taxi and I knew as soon as I got in the back that I had a dodgy driver because before I even shut my door he was trying to beat the red light in front of us. At the next set of lights, he stopped and another cab piled into the back of us, probably trying to run the red light himself. It was a pretty hard hit and as I didn't have my seat belt on, I went flying into the perspex window behind the driver and hit my head. I climbed groggily out of the car and the driver demanded five dollars for the fare. I couldn't believe it. I said: 'What? I've just got my head smashed!' I ended up paying though. The two drivers were really snapping at each other and I thought it was probably the safest thing to do. I may have been the only person ever in New York who's paid for a one-block ride and a crash.

This crash was obviously not the greatest start to a tournament I've ever had, and in the third round I was drawn against one of my favourite players to watch, and a Frenchman, the Tahiti-born Fabrice Santoro. They call him 'The Magician' because he has great hands and plays a wonderfully tricky game. At thirty-four, he was the oldest man in the World Top 50 but he had already beaten Djokovic in the previous round, who turned up for the match in a Zorro mask that he'd picked up in a restaurant the night before because it was Halloween. It didn't bring him much luck, but since he'd just had his wisdom teeth removed maybe he had an excuse.

I played very well to beat Santoro but ended up losing in the next round to another Frenchman, Richard Gasquet, who was also trying to get to Shanghai. I was disappointed and tired, not so much physically as mentally. The Brad thing was still going on. I wanted to win the match, but things were preying on my mind. We'd been together for five straight weeks in Europe and I wasn't enjoying it. I should have been loving life, getting so close to a place in the Master's Cup – and if I wasn't there had to be something major wrong. I knew it was time to address the problem.

Even so, being one match away from Shanghai was a good effort and I could go away on a two-week holiday to Miami with Kim feeling relatively pleased with myself. It was just typical that while I was supposed to be relaxing, I developed some sort of illness and ended up on a drip. Why isn't life ever simple?

Chapter Nine:
Repercussions

I can't say I hadn't been warned. I pulled out of the Davis Cup tie in Argentina at the start of 2008, and everyone around me had told me there would be 'repercussions'. I heard that word over and over again and they were right. There were repercussions – but not just in the way I anticipated. My decision made a number of people very unhappy. I was accused of being unpatriotic and selfish. I took a lot of heat, but the one person I didn't expect it from in public was my own brother.

The papers made it sound like a blood feud. 'Murray Boys at War Over Andy's Failure To Turn Up'. He was furious with me and the papers were full of quotes from him letting me know how he felt. 'It was very disappointing news, obviously,' he said at a press conference to the world's media just before the tie in Buenos Aires. 'It was a shock to me and I think for the team, it's also very disappointing. It's a shame that he decided that it was best for him not to come here. It kind of affects the way we feel about him.'

To be honest, I was shocked in return. I would never publicly criticise my brother. I don't think it's the right thing to do. I'd always be supportive towards him. That's why retaliation never crossed my mind.

To put the whole thing in context, you have to understand the Davis Cup. It is the only team competition in tennis and it has been around for over a hundred years. Britain was pretty good at it once. They won it nine times but, maybe not surprisingly when you know the history of British tennis, the last time was in 1936.

I'd played in seven Davis Cup ties and loved every one, but the timing of the ties always seemed to cause a problem. Many of the top players, like Roger Federer and Rafa Nadal, hardly played in them at all, but I had really tried to fit them into my schedule because I always enjoyed playing them. People also made it clear that it was important I played, not just for patriotic reasons, but for practical ones. With the retirement of Tim Henman and Greg Rusedski, there was no other British tennis player in the Top 150 apart from me.

The tie against Argentina was Britain's first appearance in the World Group for five years. We were already massive underdogs. Argentina had won their ten previous Davis Cup ties, nine of them by a score of 5–0. They were playing at home, in front of their own crowd, on their favourite surface, clay. The prospects did not look that great. Without me playing – I am not being immodest, it is just a fact – the chances for Britain were pretty well nil. They might have been nil with me playing as well. Clay is probably my least favourite surface.

By coincidence, I was at the National Tennis Centre the day the World Group draw was announced. I was just about to leave when I heard someone say: 'Did you see the draw? Argentina away!' They announced it with a groan, as much as to say we'd got no chance. I thought it was such a bad attitude, and typical. It doesn't fire up your enthusiasm to play. They could have said: 'What a match! What a great opportunity to beat Argentina!' They say the 'right' things in front of the cameras and radio microphones, but away from the public everyone was moaning that we had got no chance of winning.

So that was the background in the weeks leading up to the tie. The majority of the team had already gone to a clay-court training camp in Chile for a week at the start of February. I was due to join them a week or so later, after the Australian Open. In the end, Patricio called John Lloyd, the British Davis Cup captain, and told him I wouldn't be going. Obviously, it caused a huge fuss. Maybe I should have done a few things differently, but, even now, I don't regret the decision.

I'd had troubles with my right knee, the one with the bipartite patella, when I was warm-weather training in Florida in December. I told my trainer and physio that it was getting worse. We talked about it and I changed some exercises in my programme because it was getting too sore. Some people may doubt the truth of this and think the injury was just a convenient excuse, but the fact is that my kneecap being in two parts is a permanent condition, and the knee has to be protected sometimes. I remember only too well how completely miserable it was to miss half a season with a knee injury in 2004, and if I didn't protect it people would soon say I was being irresponsible.

It is true that my knee wasn't really bothering me in Australia, but I came back home after losing in the first round and on the very first morning of practice I had to stop because it was painful on certain movements. I saw the doctor at the National Tennis Centre, I got a scan done, and I paid over

£1,000 for a machine that would supposedly help to reduce the inflammation and help to knit the kneecap together. The instructions were to use it every day for 150 days. That ought to have been proof of a genuine problem, not some story I'd made up about an injury. The scan results came back and they confirmed what I felt. The inflammation was back.

At that point, I spoke to everyone around me. I wanted honest opinions from them. The physio who did my rehab when I first injured my knee in 2003 had said the worst possible thing I could do while the knee was inflamed, was to change surfaces. We – me, my current coach Miles Maclagan, my fitness trainers Matt Little and Jez Green – sat round a table at the National Training Centre and I said: 'Look guys, I'm thinking of not going to the Davis Cup, what do *you* think?'

Everyone reacted the same way. They said they understood how I felt, but it wouldn't be a good-idea because of the 'repercussions.' Repercussions. Repercussions. I knew what they meant. The rest of the team – my brother, Jamie Baker, Ross Hutchins and Alex Bogdanovic – were already in South America. I had known them all for years, I was friends with three of them and I was related to the other one. They were all expecting me to join them and they were going to feel let down, as would team captain John Lloyd, if I didn't go.

So I agreed with everyone round that table. Yes, there would be repercussions, but I asked them: 'Is that the most important thing? What is the most important thing to *me*?' They all agreed my health was the most important thing, bearing in mind that the next few months were going to be pretty stressful. I had a lot of ranking points to defend from last year and I was due to play in Marseilles immediately after the Davis

Cup, followed by Rotterdam, Dubai, a month in America and then the clay-court season in Europe.

They said: 'OK, we agree with you as far as that, but think of the repercussions. The press are going to have a field day.'

I said: 'Yep, I absolutely agree, but let's write down the positives and negatives.' The positives were easy to identify: keep the team happy, keep the press happy, keep the Lawn Tennis Association happy, keep whoever else happy. The negatives were easy too: miss Marseilles, risk the knee flaring up again, lose all my ranking points from winning in San José in 2007, ranking inevitably dropping. There was one common denominator. All the negatives affected me.

Even if I did play, Britain were not favourites to win. We had, I reckoned, about a 5 per cent chance of winning the tie. Argentina was on such a hot streak that they had whitewashed nine of their last ten opponents and beaten the other one 4–1. They were smashing everyone, and we had a much weaker team than the ones they had been beating 5–0. Maybe I wouldn't have won a match. They were some of the best clay-court players in the world, led by David Nalbandian, then world number nine. And on top of that I would be under pressure to fly between continents, with the time changes and different surfaces, and then win three matches.

So I thought it through and saw pretty clearly that all the positives were to keep other people happy. All the negatives were about what could actually happen to me. At the end of the meeting – and I discussed this with my mum and Patricio too – everyone said that as long as I was happy that I could handle the repercussions – them again – I should pull out. Definitely in terms of looking after my body and my tennis, they thought it was the right decision. So I made it.

Maybe it was a selfish decision, but when I'd played in the Davis Cup in the past I'd always given 110 per cent. I felt I'd done my bit and I know from experience that you can't please everybody all the time. If I'd aggravated my knee or if my ranking had dropped down to 20, people would have had a go at me for that. So it is ironic that by not going to the Davis Cup, by winning Marseilles and keeping my ranking up, people still had a go at me.

I felt like telling them it's not just my fault the team lost. I shouldn't be the only player that can win matches for Britain. It isn't just up to me. There are other players in the team who should be winning matches. It's tough if I am expected to win all three of mine every time. The one thing that was pretty hurtful during this whole episode was when people said I wasn't committed to my country, when everyone who knows me will tell you I'm one of the most patriotic people you will meet, for Scotland *and* Britain.

I'd competed for Britain in various European and world junior championships since I was about fourteen and always loved it. If you see the way I reacted when I won my first Davis Cup match in Israel in 2005, you wouldn't tell me I don't love playing for my country. It was one of the best experiences I've had in my entire career. Another Davis Cup tie in 2006 against Israel, this time at home, was the only occasion I'd come back from two sets to love down and won in five. The Cup really did mean something to me.

However it is not like other tournaments. Emotionally and mentally, playing Davis Cup is more tiring than anything else including the grand slams. Even when you are not playing matches, you are there supporting your team. I love being part of a team, but it is a completely different dynamic to being at a tournament on your own where you can dictate when you practise, when you rest, when you eat, and all the rest of it.

My experience was that playing Davis Cup left you pretty drained, mentally and physically, the following week. I'd never done well after a Davis Cup tie, except in 2005 when I went straight from playing Roger Federer in the doubles match against Switzerland to playing Roger Federer in the singles final at Bangkok. Every other time, something has gone wrong.

After the tie against Holland in 2007 which we played on an indoor hard court in Birmingham, I went straight to practise on clay for Monte Carlo and got injured. After the Ukraine match in 2006, which we played on clay outdoors I took three flights in twenty-three hours to get to Asia and lost in the first rounds of Tokyo and Bangkok. During our home match against Israel at Eastbourne in the summer of 2006, I hurt my neck diving for a ball and I had to miss the tournament the following week, and in Glasgow a few months earlier against Serbia and Montenegro, I was so sick I probably shouldn't have played, but I didn't want to let anyone down and then it took me ages to recover from it.

You would be pretty stupid not to look at these experiences and gather that there was a problem. I was looking at it from my perspective, I admit that, but if you want to win in sport you have to look out for yourself. Nobody else will. I was imagining what would happen if I had been asked to play all three days in Argentina, which was likely. I would have had to play two singles and a doubles, up to five sets each on clay, and then fly out on Sunday evening – if the match finished on time – from Buenos Aires to Marseilles.

It would have been unbelievably tough to have played Marseilles after three matches in the Davis Cup. I wouldn't have won, not after an overnight flight, losing four hours in the time change, playing a first round match on the Wednesday and then playing every single day if I wanted to reach the final.

In retrospect, maybe I should have called John Lloyd myself straight away when I made the decision. I spoke to Patricio and said I thought I should call him. He said he would buzz him as time was tight and I could speak to him the next day. I was hoping that when I spoke to John everything would have cooled down a little. I don't think that was cowardice, I think it was practical. I have often preferred to wait until people have calmed down before I talk through a problem. I didn't expect it to become such an issue.

I've always got on well with John, he's a really, really fun guy, but I knew how much everyone would have loved to win that tie. At least be competitive. I was well aware he was going to be disappointed.

Personally, I think the criticism about not phoning him first was exaggerated. It wasn't as though my decision was a secret. I'd spoken about my knee problem to Ross Hutchins, I'd spoken to the team doctor who had arranged the scans and I'd spoken to the team physio who was treating my knee and who was also out there with the team. It isn't as though I went into hiding. I'd spoken to quite a few people who were in the perfect position to explain the situation to John.

I can see that people might think it was me avoiding responsibility. I can only say that that wasn't my intention. If anyone thinks I am a coward about things, they obviously don't know me. Since the age of fourteen I have been making way harder decisions about people who are much closer to me than John. That is, when I broke up with my first coach, Leon. Then I spoke to him face-to-face because I thought that was the better way to handle it. When I stopped working with Mark Petchey, I handled that face-to-face too and that was really tough because we had been really close.

So that is my side of the story. I'd given everything when I played Davis Cup, and for the one match I didn't play – because I was trying to protect myself from injury and from losing my ranking – I was highly criticised. I think I made the right decision for me. I stand by it. Some people will disagree. They think it is black-and-white: you should play for your country – but they aren't putting themselves in my shoes.

Jamie was obviously angry. If I look at it from his point of view, I can understand that maybe I should have phoned him and explained myself better. But when you know that it would be one of those phone calls where you get someone shouting 'You're an idiot' down the phone, it makes you think twice.

I called my mum when I first heard what Jamie had said to the press. I told her I thought it was a bit of a mistake, especially as I have really tried to support him throughout his career. When I was asked advice about him by the Davis Cup coach and captain, I was really positive. The things he said became more hurtful because I had backed him to play in Tim Henman's last match, the doubles against Croatia in the Davis Cup at Wimbledon the year before.

That was the tie when I was asked to play a dead rubber on the Sunday even though we were leading Croatia 3–0 in the best-of-five match series. John Lloyd asked me because a big crowd was expected. The LTA backed him up and reminded me that TV would cover the match if I was playing.

I said: 'No, I'm not playing. No one plays a dead rubber. No one. I'm not risking myself getting injured on slippery glass just for a match no one cares about and it makes no difference whether I win or lose.' I got a text message from my brother at 4.30 in the morning after that. It said: 'You're a feakin' embarrassment to your country. I can't believe you won't just suck it up and play one dead rubber. You're a disgrace.'

So I said: 'OK, I'll play the match'. But I was in a bad mood on the court. I didn't want to be there. I could have said that it was the biggest joke ever that I was playing that match, I could have said it was ridiculous, but the crowd gave me really great support and I managed to win in straight sets against Roko Karanusic, a Croatian player ranked outside the Top 100 at the time. So much for me being on television. The crowd probably thought I was being as moody as my reputation, but at least I had a reason. I said to John Lloyd afterwards that if I'm going to continue with the Davis Cup: 'I am only playing if the other guys on the team are giving 100 per cent, practise hard and play hard. I've worked way, way too hard to get where I am in tennis to put up with other players not giving everything they have. It isn't fair on me. I have worked *so* hard to get where I am. I am not going to go and risk it by playing three matches in five days when you've got other people on the squad who aren't trying hard enough.'

I stand by that too. Instead of being about 'Andy', why wouldn't they step up and win a Davis Cup match themselves instead of having a go at me about it? If Britain is to have a bright future in the Davis Cup, I do believe it's time for some of the other guys to step up to the plate as well.

Jamie Baker did, actually. He beat Agustin Calleri in straight sets in Argentina, but it was the fifth match and a dead rubber by then. Argentina were already leading 4–0 after Jamie – Baker, not my brother – led off by losing 6–1 6–3 6–3 to world number nine David Nalbandian, followed by Bogdanovic losing easily to Calleri. My brother and Ross Hutchins held three set points in the second set of their match against Nalbandian and Acasuso in the doubles, but lost in straight sets. The final result was 4–1. It was a pretty sound beating they took, but everybody was expecting that. Maybe some good will come out of it. Some people will realise the depth of the team is not up to scratch. Without Tim and Greg, we don't have a team that merits being in the World Group.

Eventually the whole argument died down. My brother and I were fine afterwards. I called him on his birthday. We sent each other texts when we both won tournaments the following week, me in the singles at Marseilles, him in the doubles at San José. He obviously still believed in the things he said. He never did back down in the press. But it was fine. He was entitled to do that, not that I agreed with it. If he was looking at things from his point of view, he was disappointed. If he had put himself in my shoes, he wouldn't have reacted like that. I was hurt but it is something you move on from. All brothers fight about things. It is just a shame it was in public. The only explanation I've come up with is that he's never played three five-set matches in three days and he's never played a singles match for five sets on clay.

Some people said to me afterwards: 'You said you couldn't win a tournament after playing Davis Cup, but Jamie won a title the very next week.' I couldn't believe what I was hearing. Jamie was playing doubles. With the new scoring system – first point after deuce wins the game and the third set has been replaced with a 10-point tie-break – the average match lasts about an hour. Plus he wasn't playing a Davis Cup singles on the Friday or the Sunday, and he was playing the following week in an ATP event in America, in a similar time zone, not over in Europe. It was the most ridiculous argument ever. It was not even close to being accurate. I ought to be used to it by now, but sometimes I feel as though regardless of what I do, I'm going to get criticised. That's just the way it seems.

Not long after this I logged on to my website and there was a discussion about an article a journalist had written in the *Guardian*. Somebody wrote that it was 'the most scathing attack on Andy Murray I've ever read', so naturally I was curious to see it. I called it up on my phone and sat there reading it and laughing. Basically it said I'm an idiot. It began with the question: 'Can Andy Murray and Jamie Murray really be related?' comparing Jamie's smile with my scowl and Jamie's pleasing face with my 'Donald Duck features'. It also said my features were 'dolichocephalic', but I didn't know what that meant. (I found out later it's 'having a relatively long skull'.)

Kim was sitting next to me. 'What are you laughing about?' she said. 'I'm just reading this.' I showed her. 'Yeah, I read it earlier but I didn't say anything to you because it's not very nice.' No, but it was hilarious. By the end, he'd had a go at my personality ('terse, impatient, sour'), my looks ('bum-fluff tache') and not beating Roger Federer in Marseilles. To be fair, it would have been hard to beat Roger in Marseilles as he wasn't playing there, but maybe the guy thought better of me when I did beat Federer two weeks later in Dubai. Then again, he probably didn't.

I remembered that I'd met him before – Simon Hattenstone – when I was doing a sponsor day some time ago for David Lloyd Leisure. The first interview I did was with a couple of ladies from a woman's magazine, and one said: 'I can't believe how nice you are.' So I can't have been incredibly terse, impatient and sour that day. Then this guy comes and was swearing throughout the interview and was just generally weird, following me around with his recorder after we had finished talking. According to his article, I was the most charmless person he had ever met. I thought he was the strangest person *I* had ever met.

As it happens, I was more amused than upset about his story. None of it mattered. It just put into context some of the more violently critical pieces that were written after the Davis Cup. It just seemed to keep coming for a while, not least the sarcastic stories about my knee being strong enough to play a bit of football at the National Tennis Centre when apparently it wasn't good enough to go to Argentina.

As I seem to say very often, maybe I shouldn't have done it, but I wish people had understood that there is a huge difference between having a fun kickabout on a patch of grass for twenty minutes and playing a three-to-five-set match on clay. I know the limitations of my knee when it's inflamed and I know which movements could cause trouble. When I'm messing around or training I can avoid them, but when I'm in a match, that's not possible. I am sure when people are injured they don't sit around doing nothing. No one completely shuts down. When I hurt my wrist I didn't avoid a tennis court for two months. I went and hit balls over the net at 10 per cent speed instead. You still practice. You're still in the gym. Maybe I shouldn't have played football, but *only* because it resulted in some bad public relations, not because it was bad for my health.

If everything goes well, I will play Davis Cup against Austria in September, if I am asked. I really do enjoy playing it. I think most players agree it comes at a very difficult time and it isn't easy to fit into your schedule, but if people question my heart to play for my country, given the way I have played in the past, I think that is a little harsh.

I played against Serbia and Montenegro in Glasgow in April 2006 when really I should have been in bed. It was a pressure thing again. I was told: 'If you don't play, the team's going to lose.' The tie was in Scotland for, I think, only the second time in history and everybody was looking forward to it, especially me. Then I became ill with swollen glands and a fever and was advised by my doctor that I would be unlikely to recover in time for the tie. I was at home in Dunblane in bed for almost a week leading up to the match. I thought it would be better for someone else to play rather than me at less than 100 per cent. Well, I could have given a hundred per cent but only for about twenty minutes. The team came across to see me on the Tuesday before the Friday start, but it can't have been much of a sight. I was downstairs on the couch under my duvet, feeling horrible and taking antibiotics. It was so frustrating because I really wanted to play. It was a big match against a good team and everybody was really excited about it.

I did turn up for the pre-match press conference two days later. I wanted to be there to support the team. It took my mind off being ill, but when I arrived home again I was still feeling horrendous. The team doctor had said I was well enough to play singles on the first day, but luckily, there was another doctor there, one who my physio at the time knew pretty well, so we went to him for a second opinion. He checked my throat and temperature and his reaction was: 'No, you shouldn't be playing. You are not well.'

It wasn't the first time my body had disagreed with the official doctor. In a previous Davis Cup tie in Switzerland in

2005, when I played Federer for the first time, in the doubles, my back was feeling a little bit sore. The physio reckoned I would be fine with massage and manipulation, but the doctor came over and insisted I took anti-inflammatories. I said: 'No, I'm not keen on them to be honest.' He still insisted so I took one, held it in my hand and then threw it on the ground as I was walking to the court. Half-an-hour later the doc came back again. 'How's your back?' he asked. I told him fine. 'Good,' he said. 'That will be the anti-inflammatory kicking in now.' I've smiled about that a few times to myself.

I wish I could have felt better in Glasgow, but I knew the second doctor was right. So I approached the captain, Jeremy Bates, and said: 'Look, I really can't play on Friday.' He understood. Then he said: 'Can you play in the doubles on Saturday?' and my immediate reaction was: 'Yeah, I want to', even though I knew I wouldn't be best prepared for it because of the illness. That was my attitude towards the Davis Cup. I was proud to play for my country and I really wanted to. No one seemed to remember that when the Argentina affair happened, but that's another story.

So I played in the doubles with Greg Rusedski against Ilia Bozoljac and Nenad Zimonjic, who were not exactly high-profile players. Zimonjic reached a career high of 176 in the world in 1999, though he was a Top 100 doubles player, and Bozoljac never quite cracked the Top 100. Even so, Greg and I managed to lose 3–6 6–3 3–6 4–6, and, according to the press we were going to be fined £100,000 and thrown out of the competition for three years because of my bad language. I did swear when we were leaving the court and unfortunately there was a microphone under the umpire's chair and so my rant came across on everyone's TV. That was the occasion I called the umpire 'fucking useless'. I was disappointed that we'd lost. I was disappointed I played badly and I was disappointed with the umpire's performance. I really felt that a couple of wrong calls that he made against us in the third set had affected the outcome of the match.

In the end, we were hardly fined anything at all and we were nowhere near getting thrown out of the competition. It was ironic that this tie (which we lost) should be remembered for that, when in fact it went some way to proving how desperate I was to play for my country. I had lost a lot of energy through the illness and had had very little time to prepare for the match – all of about twenty minutes on the Friday evening after the first day's play. I didn't win, but I really tried to do my best. That was why hearing your brother say: 'If you really pushed yourself you could play,' over Argentina was so hurtful. I had pushed myself that time in Glasgow and I had done badly for the team. I had also set my recovery back another week. I'd remembered that. You would be stupid not to learn from that experience.

It was also ironic that around this time, the LTA were exploring the possibility of Novak Djokovic, the Serbian teenager, changing nationality and becoming eligible to play for Britain. That was the talk of the press conference at the time. My view, when they asked me, was: 'Imagine how good our Davis Cup team would be!' It would be great from that point of view, even if it all seemed a bit strange.

I don't really agree with people changing nationalities, unless they have a mother or father in that country or a long residence there, but I think the issue arose because my British teammate, Alex Bogdanovic, who moved here when he was about eight, was also Serbian. He didn't get a British passport till he was thirteen. Maybe they thought they could do something similar with Djokovic, but, for whatever reason, it didn't happen. Imagine if it did. Britain would have had its first male grand slam champion in seventy-two years when Djokovic won the Australian Open in 2008, even though he was born in Belgrade and lived in Monte Carlo.

Believe it or not, I have had some really happy times in the Davis Cup. My favourite was my debut when David Sherwood and I came together to play one of the best doubles teams in the world, Jonathan Erlich and Andy Ram, in front of a noisy partisan crowd in Israel. I was seventeen at the time, it was my first major exposure to tennis at senior level and we could hardly have been greater underdogs: two young Brits with no form on the tour and hardly any experience.

When I look back I realise it was the only Davis Cup match I've ever played when there has been very little pressure. I had been playing horrendously beforehand in Futures and Challengers, but I walked on the court and my tennis was literally awesome for the whole match.

It was the same for my partner, a tremendous athlete and the son of two Olympic medallists. Dave's dad, John Sherwood won the bronze medal behind David Hemery in the 400 metre hurdles in Mexico, and his mum, Sheila, won the silver medal in the long jump. That was some pedigree.

Neither of us had ever played Davis Cup before, we didn't even know each other at the start of the week and neither of us was expecting to play, but Bogdanovic had lost badly in the first singles and the team captain just said: 'Are you guys up for playing?' We said: 'Sure'. This was during the period that Tim Henman had decided to give the Davis Cup a break for a couple of years, and so the choices were more limited than usual.

The crowd were incredibly noisy. I had been used to playing tournaments where even if there were people watching, they weren't usually bothered who wins. This time there were 6,000 people all cheering against us, except my dad, my mum, and my mum's friend Laura who had come with her.

I remember this particularly because there had been a cocktail party for the British tennis team when we arrived. Laura was introduced to Greg Rusedski at some point during the evening and then she seemed to disappear. It was only later, when there was a lull in the conversation, that you could hear a woman's voice in the corridor outside the room, absolutely shouting down the phone to her husband: 'You'll never guess, I've just met Greg Rusedski!' I suppose all of us were pretty new to this world.

Dave and I didn't need five sets to win our match. Neither of us were intimidated. On the first point I hit a backhand return winner and pretty much everything I did after that just clicked. I was loving it. The home team were defeated 6–4 7–6 2–6 7–6 and when we finished I was so excited I threw my racket up in the air – but then I didn't know where to run or what to do. It is probably the most excited I have ever been in my life after a match. The video is hysterical. I just ran in a circle like a headless chicken. I hugged Jeremy. I hugged David. We celebrated as if we had won the whole tie instead of just the doubles. It was so, so special and that night Jeremy asked me if I would play the fifth and deciding rubber if Laura's friend Greg didn't win the fourth match. But he did and so I didn't have to play.

The night after the match I didn't really sleep, partly from adrenaline and mainly because Dave phoned me every half hour because he was watching Sky News repeat the highlights in their bulletins. He kept calling me from his room, shouting: 'Did you see that shot!' and I did because I was watching it too.

I look back on those days with great affection. That was the start, when everyone was so positive, so upbeat. They were also the days when you didn't know how to say no, when you agreed to everything because you were so naïve.

I wish I could say that I played brilliantly afterwards but it didn't happen. I went straight back to playing horrendously again. Something had changed though. After that match, I realised I could play at a high level after all. Even if it was just doubles it had given me an extra boost of confidence which may have made the difference when it came to my debut at Queen's and Wimbledon the same year. Maybe everything stemmed from that match.

I played with David again, at Wimbledon that year, but we lost in the first round. We kept in touch for a year or so afterwards and we still played some of the same tournaments. Then he stopped tennis altogether. I don't know what went wrong. He was probably one of the finest athletes British tennis has produced in the last twenty years. He won a round in the singles at that same Wimbledon, and then I think he went into coaching. Maybe he found the grind of the smaller tournaments a bit depressing after having a match like the one we had had together in Israel.

So my Davis Cup experiences are far from miserable. In many ways, that first one was inspiring. Even further back, when I was invited to join the squad for a tie in Luxembourg in April 2004 when I was sixteen and injured, it was pretty cool. I was suffering from my bad knee but they invited me along just to watch and learn. It was great to be helping on court with Tim and Greg, both of them were really nice, but the main reason I phoned my coach Leon was to gloat about the fact I was staying in a five-star hotel with a room to myself. Leon and I were used to junior competitions with five to a room or bunk beds. I kept telling him about the DVD player.

However, you get over those days of being amazed by the luxury. As my Davis Cup career went on, it wasn't so much the flat-screen TV in the hotel that excited me as the chance to play high-profile matches against decent teams in front of passionate crowds. Whatever happened with Argentina, that feeling hasn't changed. Tennis is about nothing if not playing, winning matches and making your name in some of the biggest arenas in the world. You get all that in Davis Cup.

I would never say I'm not going to play Davis Cup. I am not going to pass up the opportunity to play huge matches for my country. I'm not like that. I love it. I have only objected to the tough timing of the ties. I don't know whether that is the fault of the International Tennis Federation who oversee the Davis Cup or the ATP that represents the players, but they are obviously not working together as they could.

Not one of the players who skip Davis Cup regularly would ever say they don't like the competition. They do, but its place in the calendar makes it hard for the top players to make a commitment to compete. If a few things were tweaked it would be so much easier. I don't think giving ranking points for playing in the Cup would help. It is a great competition as it is – just change the dates.

Mark Petchey

It was a crazy time. Andy's life changed out of sight after Wimbledon 2005. For anybody aged eighteen to go through all that craziness in such a short space of time was amazing, and for ten months of that time I was riding shotgun as his coach. It was an unforgettable experience for both of us, and despite the fact that it came to an end (and I thumped him once in a car), I'm sure we'll be close friends for the rest of our lives.

I'd been involved with him at arm's length before that famous Wimbledon, while I was working for the Lawn Tennis Association. I was well aware of him and his talent but I didn't know him on any kind of intimate basis. I knew he'd split with his former coach, Pato Alvarez, before the French Open, and someone came up with the idea that I would hook up with him to help him through the grass-court season – Queen's and Wimbledon. I assumed that is where our association would begin and end. We had absolutely no way of knowing what would happen next. The wins at Queen's, the cramps, the fame, the five sets against a Wimbledon finalist – it was all completely unpredictable.

His rise was phenomenal. Nothing short of it. To go from being 350 in the world to 50 in ten months was almost unbelievable. It began with a bang at Queen's, where he won two matches and then at Wimbledon, where he was two sets up against David Nalbandian in the third round, the last Brit standing in the tournament. Within seconds of every match ending, my mobile phone went into meltdown. Probably the best thing that happened to us was being able to go away on the road for ten weeks, to get out of Britain and escape the publicity.

I never for one moment expected to be caught up in all this. I had a good job with Sky Sports TV commentating on tennis. I was just planning to leave the Federation, where I was manager of men's national training, because I wasn't seeing eye-to-eye with the performance director and Tim Henman's former coach, David Felgate. Sky gave me a lot of freedom and I had a good life with my wife and our two little girls after years of being on tour or holding down two jobs at once. There was no way I could say to my wife: 'Right, I'm volunteering to go away for ten weeks at a time again.'

Well, there was one way. After his amazing success at Wimbledon, Andy asked me if I would join him as his full-time coach. It was a massive decision, as I already had an idea of what it would involve. I'd spent two years coaching on the women's tour, with Sylvia Talaja of Croatia and the Slovenian Tina Pisnik, when Sylvia went from about 90 in the world to 17, and Tina rose from 150 to 55. So, when Andy asked if I would work with him as his coach, I knew — to a degree — what I was taking on. As much as it was a fantastic opportunity — which it was — it was also a huge commitment and meant walking away from a solid job at Sky.

My wife was obviously a huge part of the decision. She had our youngest girl when I was away for those two years with Sylvia and Tina. It was tough on her, very difficult. But I was an ex-player with a mediocre career having reached 80 in the world (although I beat the former Wimbledon Champion Michael Stich in the first round of the South African Open 1994) and I had to find something to do. If I was going to be away again, with Andy this time, my wife had to buy into it. She did. She was phenomenally supportive.

On the plane to the States, Andy and I must have been as surprised as each other – it was definitely a shock to my system. A week or so after Wimbledon, I found myself sharing a room with a teenager eighteen years my junior. It was a culture shock, I can tell you. There was a moment during that tournament week in Newport, Rhode Island, when I asked myself: 'What's happened to your life that you're suddenly back on the road with an 18-year-old instead of at home with your family and a fantastic job with loads of freedom at last?' But soon the answer became clear.

It may have been intense to share a room with this kid, but it was also fun. Put it this way: it was never boring. The grass courts at Newport were shocking and, Andy being Andy, he said so, which didn't endear him to the tournament director who had given him a wild card. But the amusements were great. We played basketball and video games. I realised immediately just how competitive Andy was – and always would be in everything he did.

It didn't matter what we played, he needed to win. There were no two ways about it. He needed to win. If he lost, he was 'fine' but you could see the disappointment. He tried to keep a lid on it, but I didn't mind – it is being so fiercely competitive that makes him such a great tennis player.

To quell my mounting sense of inadequacy, we started playing backgammon. He hadn't played an awful lot at that stage and I was winning a few games which he, in his inimitable way, put down to pure luck. As time went by, I felt I should teach him some of the tricks and patterns of the game, which I hadn't let him know at the start to preserve my dignity. That was an obvious mistake. As with everything, he started getting better and better, and then the matches were dangerously competitive.

I never *let* him win at anything – he won anyway. In fact, the only time I eased up on him and let him win deliberately was on one occasion in South Africa, when we played a set of tennis and I sensed he was struggling a little bit for various reasons. I had a feeling that if I won the tie-break, it wouldn't be conducive to his mood. But on the games front, I never let him win. As for video games, he was in a different league to me. He bought me a Tiger Woods golf game and remained forever frustrated by how useless I was.

On the road we did virtually everything together. We trained together, ate together, shared rooms together. He had that ankle injury which meant I had to make sure he used a wobble board every day to strengthen the joint. I spent a lot of time throwing a ball to him. I started picking up his likes and dislikes, including food. That was pretty straightforward. He had pasta arrabiata or fillet steak and a Sprite every night. America must have been struggling for cows by the end of our trip.

Our next stop after Newport was Aptos in California, a smaller Challenger event, where we stayed with a family. We stayed in one of their spare rooms with a dart board, and played horseshoes with our host in the back garden. I remember thinking how surreal this was, chucking horseshoes around in a Californian yard a million miles away from Wimbledon. It didn't seem like the same life. Once when we went to a Mexican restaurant with the family, we were asked: 'Do you know what Mexican food is?' Andy and I suppressed smiles and resisted the urge to ask: 'What's a nacho?' We always had a rapport in any funny situation.

That's how the bonding starts. I look back on that time and realise that Aptos was important in many ways and especially because Andy won the event. There was a lot of pressure on us both. Many people felt I wasn't the right person for the job. I understood that. You've got a kid clearly going places fast and he's decided to go with a former player who didn't make it beyond 80 in the world. 'What does he know?' and 'What the hell did he do?' were the questions being asked of me. There was pressure on Andy to prove I was the right choice for him at that stage of his career.

I also heard a lot of negative stuff about Andy and his attitude. People from clothing companies said they didn't want to sponsor him because he didn't hit the ball hard enough. Coaches said: 'He'll never do anything. He's too soft'. Very few people were positive about where he was going. I'd said to potential sponsors about eighteen months before all this: 'You sign him up, he's going to be something a bit special', but they just said: 'Nah, I don't see it.' There are a couple of people out there, I'm sure, regretting their decisions now.

That's why that Aptos week was very important. Even the resident racket stringer there said to me: 'Jeez, he's something else, isn't he?' I said: 'Yeah, there's a bit of genius there.' He agreed. 'I've been saying to everybody at the club: "Make sure you take a good look at him this week because he won't be back".'

Incidentally, no one – journalist or sponsor or coach – has ever come back and said to me: 'Sorry, we were wrong about Andy.' I was absolutely vilified for my comment at Wimbledon that he could be bigger than Wayne Rooney; I was crucified in the newspapers for that. Of course, I know that football's a bigger sport but in terms of individuals – if you look at the headlines Andy's generated in the last three years – I think to some degree I've been vindicated. All I did was go out there and try to emphasise how talented this kid could be. And boom! I was knocked back straight away. I wasn't upset. I thought: 'Ok, time will tell.' And it has.

The tournament after Aptos was a tour event in Indianapolis where Andy lost in three sets to the American, Mardy Fish. He'd been a break up in the final set but it was boiling hot and he was shattered. It wasn't all bad: we had a decent, comfortable hotel now we were on the main tour and, more important than that, we found a Starbucks. That was one of our things. We'd drive miles to find a Starbucks where Andy, without fail, would have a chocolate cream Frappucino without the chips. We always got a funny look. '*Without* the chocolate chips?' This genuinely baffled the Americans. But Andy is not someone you argue with. Sometimes we'd drive out of a town for miles to find the Frappucino. It became a sort of ritual.

From Indianapolis we went to Canada, where my family joined us for a holiday. I couldn't join them for an earlier trip to Disneyworld because I was away with Andy and this was my attempt to make it up to them. No Mickey Mouse but they had Andy to play with and, as they loved him to bits, that was fine. They'd mess around together and play card games and he was really good with them. We went on bike rides round the lake and he would always do just enough to beat me. It was never a leisurely cycle; it was always full-on or not at all.

By now, I was really getting to know Andy. As a person, he was one of the most sensitive kids I knew. There are some very precious moments we had together that will always remain private, but I can tell you that the person I know is far removed from what people see on the tennis court. The guy you see on court is a competitive animal, but that isn't him. That is just his rage to be the best he can be.

He gained a reputation later for shouting at his coach, but he never did that to me. Never ever. We had a chat about his behaviour once at Indian Wells the following year, but I don't have any complaint about the way he treated me. He vented his frustration, much of the time, because he is a perfectionist. I could handle that. In fact, you *want* to see that in someone you're coaching. It's better than being satisfied with being second best.

Vancouver was next and I had to fly back home for three days to be at my best friend's wedding. Andy stayed on and reached the quarter-finals and then we met up again in New York and took a hire car to Binghampton, somewhere upstate that I would respectfully describe as the back of beyond. This was a considerable change from the tour events. It was stinking hot, we were in a public park, the changing room was a caravan and there was nothing else but the tennis going on. Plus, in the second round, he was six match points down and out on his feet against a guy from India ranked 263. But that animal within him would not give up. I still, to this day, remember the backhand pass he hit to save one of those match points. I just sat there staring, thinking: 'My god, how did you hit that?' He came back and won the match and the tournament, earning himself a wild card to Cincinnati.

Off court, life had been equally eventful – this was the time I hit him. Luckily, we laugh about it now. The area around the tournament was a little rough. One day we were driving through a street of boarded up windows and came to a set of traffic lights. Andy leant over and honked the horn. He is always trying to wind you up, that is his modus operandi, but on this occasion I thought it was distinctly unwise.

I said: 'Don't do that', because we were behind a beaten-up old Cadillac at a set of traffic lights and it hadn't moved even though the lights had gone green. He honked the horn again.

Now, maybe I'm slightly paranoid because once when I was staying in Atlanta I'd been told about guys who travelled at night in their cars looking for people to shoot or whatever, and I had a whole fear of flashing lights and honking horns at unknown cars behaving strangely. I said to Andy: 'Look, you don't know who's in that car. They might jump out in a fit of road rage and smash our car up – or worse – us.' He took absolutely no notice and honked the horn again.

I warned him in my sternest tone: 'I'm telling you now, just don't do it.' He did it again and at that time, pushed beyond endurance, I prodded him hard with an elbow. It's funny now but at the time I was just desperate to protect British tennis's greatest asset from being beaten up by a 7'6" giant. Can you imagine the headlines? Sometimes he was just a kid having fun, and I had to find a balance between having fun and making sure I discharged my responsibilities to him, his family and world tennis. I may have been way too paranoid, but I was trying to guide him through some of the perils of being on a worldwide tour.

The episode did him no harm. The next thing you know, he's playing Marat Safin, the world number four, in Cincinnati – and taking him to three sets. He had moved up about two hundred places in the rankings already, an incredible jump. I was amazed. But to Andy, it wasn't a surprise at all. He always knew he was going to be good. He wasn't scared. Not at all. He loved playing in front of a big crowd. He was much more likely to struggle somewhere that had no audience and no atmosphere.

The other thing I had learned is just how tactically aware he was. He would watch an opponent play matches, apparently uninterested, but at the end he would say: 'Right, this is what he does and this is where I think I can hurt him.' He was very, very astute. That is why I felt quite encouraged going into the US Open that year. Here was a kid who just gets it. Tennis isn't just about playing well, it is about making your opponent play badly. Andy understands that in a big way.

When he played Andrei Pavel, a phenomenally experienced player, in the US Open first round, and beat him in five sets, it was something a bit special. After the summer he'd had, all that travel, a new coach and an exhausting set of matches fresh out of the juniors, it spoke volumes for him as a competitor that he could go out there and win. It was lovely to be part of it and Andy was so excited. He really couldn't have been any happier.

COMING OF AGE

We never did have any stand-up fights, Andy and I. After our road trip in America, he came home to stay with me and I think it must have been nice for him to be around normal family life. The stability was good for him when everything else was going a bit manic. It was just rather ironic that having rushed off to the States to escape the Wimbledon factor, we had an apartment (belonging to Pat Rafter's ex-girlfriend) in Wimbledon. There was no escaping the tennis connection.

There are certain moments that stand out vividly from our time together. I was with him when he cracked the World Top 100 in Bangkok. To remember his face after that match against Soderling still makes me well up with emotion. You can hardly understand how big that was to him. He was down and out when he called me after splitting up with Pato in the spring. He was low and really struggling. To go from there to being inside the Top 100 in the space of a few months was incredible. This was a kid who had only one thing on his mind: to be successful at tennis. His achievement made us both pretty emotional, but the really amazing thing was the way he continued to play that tournament when he had already achieved one of his major goals. He was thrilled to bits but he still had a job to do.

In the semi-final against Paradorn Srichaphan, the massively supported local favourite, he hit an unbelievable winner down the line on match point and I told him so afterwards. 'Nah,' he said. 'If I hadn't hit that, I don't think I'd have ever forgiven myself. I saw the size of the gap down the line and I didn't think I could miss.' I'd been looking at the same gap, and it looked less than a centimetre wide to me. I told him: 'I've seen some real genius in the way you played today.' His belief in his own talent is overwhelming.

But, inevitably, problems appeared. We made a difficult start to the following year. Part of that was due to the South African holiday I had booked before I signed the contract as Andy's coach. When I took the job, I told Andy and Judy that I had booked the family holiday and, after missing Disneyworld, I owed it to them to make sure this one happened. Andy and Judy both said it was absolutely fine and, when the time came, Andy wanted to come too.

On one level, it was the best time we had together because it was all about family and friends and we had a great time. However, there was no one there for Andy to practise with except me. We tried, though: I played with him every day; I sprinted with him; we even ran together on Christmas Day. Afterwards, a number of people criticised the way we'd worked. They said some horrible stuff. It was tough, but the kid was eighteen years old. Was it going to be a career-breaker? I didn't think so, but there is no doubt it caused the year to begin badly.

Then there was the business of the so-called sexist remark in Adelaide, when Andy said, as a joke, that he'd been serving like a woman. He meant that his serve had been broken too many times. The outcry was ridiculous and that's where people don't understand Andy. To some players, the reaction to that remark would have been like water off a duck's back, but it really affected him. That was a very hard trip for us on an emotional level and the match he played at the Australian Open against Juan Ignacio Chela, which he lost in straight sets, was the only bad match he played in our entire time together.

It was huge pressure. He was playing in a grand slam event against a well-established player in front of hordes of people and it was very difficult for him. For me, the defeat was no big deal. I just said: 'That was a learning experience. It wasn't great. Move on. Next tournament.'

Obviously, I was criticised for not being with him in San José the following month, when he won his first tournament on the tour. I was on half-term holiday with the girls, but I also thought, after our tough start to the year, it would do us the world of good to have a break.

I believed I was doing my job properly by not making him reliant on me. By the time he was winning match point against Lleyton Hewitt in the final, I was at Atlanta Airport ready to meet him again, trying to follow the match on the phone with Patricio.

Later Andy told me that once Lleyton had missed his first serve on match point, he knew he'd won the title. I told him that it was only when Michael Stich double-faulted on match point that I'd known I'd won that famous match of mine. That is the difference between us as tennis players.

It was difficult towards the end of our coaching relationship because he was obviously questioning whether I was the right man for the job. I think the world of him because he made the right decision, but it must have been very hard for him, given the closeness of our relationship. It was a courageous decision. For him to find somebody with Brad Gilbert's experience was good and I never resented that. Our time had run its course and it was right for him to move on.

We made the final split in Monte Carlo. We had a conversation about it in a little seaside café and then I met my wife and the girls who were over on holiday. I knew the news was going public at 4pm and was bracing myself for the response. Sure enough, my phone started ringing at one minute past four. My youngest daughter wanted to know what was going on. I told her: 'Andy and I aren't working together any more.'

'Who's calling you?' she asked.

'People want to know what I think about it.'

She screwed her face up. 'What, because you lost your job?' My wife and I were in tears of laughter and it was a fantastic reminder that life goes on.

I'm sure some people find it hard to believe that Andy and I could split so amicably and remain such close friends, but that is the reality.

When Andy and I speak now, we hardly mention tennis at all. We talk as friends and that is the way it will always be.

I wasn't on tour to see how his relationship with Brad worked out at close quarters, but I suppose I wasn't surprised when they decided to call it a day. When you know the two characters involved, it was obviously going to work for a while but eventually become too much for one or the other. Brad had a firm belief in what he brought to the relationship. And Andy has a firm belief and confidence common to all the top players that he is going to do it his way.

I've followed his career ever since we parted and I'm convinced he is going to make it to the top of the sport. But I did say to him once: 'I don't envy you as a person. You're going to go through so much in your life that will be difficult. You're going to be incredibly successful and yet often you're going to read stuff that makes you sound like a failure.' That will be difficult for someone as sensitive as he is. I don't think people know what they do to him when they say critical things. He has sometimes been very badly misjudged.

My description of Andy might surprise the people who judge him only by what they see on the court, but if someone asked me to sum up the young man I came to know intimately, I'd say this: He's sensitive, passionate, stubborn, competitive beyond ultra and, ultimately, a very genuine human being.

Chapter Ten:
One and One

You could say I have a pretty broad taste when it comes to coaches. There was the grand slam-winning American talka-holic, the Essex-born TV commentator whose career-high ranking was 80, the veteran clay-court guru who once coached Ilie Nastase, the young Glaswegian with an earring who now works for the LTA, and my mum. Currently, it is the former British Davis Cup player, Miles Maclagan, who was born in Zambia and raised in Zimbabwe, plus a bit of help from the former world number two and French Open runner-up, Alex Corretja from Spain.

Every change had its reasons. I like to think they were good reasons, but often I would look at the headlines and discover I was being called a 'Tennis Brat' for moving on to someone else. However, if there is one thing that makes me happy about my career so far, it is that I have remained friends, close friends, with most of the people who have coached me. That's good, especially when I'm related to one of them.

I started playing tennis with Mum as soon as I was old enough to walk around and swing a racket. She would tell you that I was much easier to coach than my brother. I always enjoyed it because it was never stressful. She was really positive and supportive. My games with her were much more relaxed than with other coaches. It was fun. Jamie and I both enjoyed making her run and she obviously enjoyed it as well, but when we reached a certain age it became a bit boring. We hit the balls too hard and she couldn't reach them any more.

Mum and Dad loved doing sports with us. That is how we spent our time as a family. We didn't read books or watch movies. We played golf, squash or five-a-side football with Dad. We played tennis with Mum. She coached Jamie and me until we were eleven and twelve years old and then, in my case, I started to work with Leon Smith, a very young Glaswegian guy who, up to that point, didn't have much experience, but my mum thought he would be fun for me to work with.

Leon was awesome. He was young, he wanted to travel and he wanted to learn. He had loads of energy and even though he was about ten years older than me, we played a lot of football, pool and snooker together. We enjoyed the same things. It was a bit like my time later with Tim Henman. We'd enjoy any game as long as it was competitive, even just throwing balls as hard as we could at each other. It was pretty immature stuff, but so much more fun than sitting around talking.

Leon could hit the ball reasonably well, so we'd practise together. He would come and pick me up from school when I was allowed time off subjects like Religious Education, PE and Art to go training at Stirling University. We got on really well because he was an unbelievably nice person and I guess he was someone I looked up to.

He was a bit of a poser back then: tall, good looking with bleached blond hair. On one of our trips he acquired an earring too. He went into Claire's Accessories for it, which was quite funny because it involved him standing in a queue with a huge crowd of little girls.

I would imagine he had quite an effect on me because I used to bleach my hair a little bit too, with a spray lightener. I'm sure it was horrendous for my hair: it made it go rock hard, and sometimes ginger if it went wrong. Fortunately, that wasn't Leon's only legacy. He gave me the enthusiasm to carry on with my tennis. Most kids stop playing before they're sixteen in the UK. The numbers are quite frightening. Maybe more than half give up the sport in their mid-teens.

I have always said the most important thing when you are young is not to have pressure on you to play from your parents or from your coach. I think it's important to be disciplined, but I also think it's very important for your coach to be positive and supportive, not critical and negative. That's the age when you start to get a bit self-conscious. If someone's getting down on you, you stop enjoying the sport. It hurts your feelings much more than when you're eight years old and criticism goes straight through your ears without stopping.

I enjoyed playing when Leon was around in my teens, and that is why we stayed together for such a long time. It was a new world for both of us. Obviously we didn't travel together all the time. Sometimes I'd be part of a GB team and then one of the LTA Age Group captains would travel with us, but when we were together we had a great time.

Our parting – my first as an employer – wasn't nice, but in sport you feel there comes a time when you need to move on. I'd been working with him for about six years, and it just seemed to get a little bit stale. It was tough to decide to make the break, but also I was training in Spain by then. I'd been working with different coaches in Barcelona, I'd go to tournaments all over Europe and Leon wouldn't be there. It wasn't his fault. We just didn't have the money to fund it.

It was a tough decision, but I think it was the right one. Some people might find it a little odd that someone sixteen years old would be prepared to make such a major decision but I thought it was a sign that I was growing up. I decided I needed a coach who was going to be there most of the time. It was just being practical.

You know how good the relationship was between you and your coach by what happens after you've parted. If you don't speak to them ever again, then obviously the relationship hadn't worked out. If you do stay close, then you can say the relationship was solid. Leon and I stayed in touch. We still get on and speak to each other. At my first Wimbledon in 2005 he was in my box for every match. He works much of the time in London and comes round for dinner at my new flat in Wandsworth. I'm sure we'll always be friends.

He reminds me of things like the time I played about thirty-six drop shots in one match. It's probably true. I enjoyed things like that. There were lots of times, especially playing domestically, when I'd be winning matches so easily I'd be trying to make the ball spin back from one side of the court to the other, and I'd keep trying until I did it. That might have been frustrating for my coach, but I don't think Leon minded too much.

After Leon, came the Colombian 'Pato' Alvarez. This was a case of moving to the other extreme. Where Leon had been young, inexperienced and was mainly used to the rain and indoor hard courts of Scotland, Pato was sixty-nine years old, had coached forty Top 50 players including Nastase, and in Spain they called him 'El Guru' of clay-court tennis. It is a bit of a cheat to say he was my coach really, because we only worked together for six months and it was always in the company of other players, but still, we did work together and at the beginning it seemed to go very well. When we travelled to Spain at the back end of 2004, I won two Futures tournaments.

Then I started to up my level of competition and I was struggling. We were travelling with the two other players from the Sanchez-Casal Academy and there was a bit of an age gap there too. I was seventeen, they were twenty-two and twenty-four. It wasn't much, but it was significant. I wanted to feel more independent. I wanted to have my own coach with me. At the start of 2005, we were playing Challenger events on clay in South America against difficult opposition in unfamiliar conditions, and I didn't want to be left alone, but Pato would get up and leave me mid-match to check on the progress of the others. There was no direction. You'd look up to find a friendly face and there'd be no one there.

I was a junior grand slam winner, but that didn't mean anything in this situation. I was playing qualifying Challengers in Chile and not getting anywhere. In one tournament I lost in the last round of qualifying, in the next I lost in the first round. We realised the arrangement wasn't working.

By now I knew I wanted to leave Barcelona. I had been there at the Academy for nearly three years and training was becoming very repetitive. It was great for a certain amount of time, but then I started to get a little bit bored with it. I wanted to spend time back home. Pato lived in Barcelona. I knew it wouldn't work if he continued to coach me because I couldn't ask him to leave his home and his family in Spain. Plus, his preference was obviously to work with a group of players. He used to coach Emilo and Javier Sanchez and Sergio Casal all at the same time and it worked for them, but I didn't want that. I wanted an individual coach.

I've heard it said that our parting was awkward and perhaps that is how it seemed, but that might have been because Pato didn't speak English that well. The press called him and he said a few things, but it might have come across as more aggressive than he intended. I wasn't hurt by what he said. I didn't believe he'd been deliberately nasty. He seemed to say that I wouldn't make it as a player if I continued with the same flat mentality, but the reason I was like that on and off the court was the fact I was unhappy with our arrangement. It is pretty tough to work and travel with someone aged seventy when you are only seventeen.

We also had a disagreement about my style of tennis. Every single tournament I played with him was on clay. I felt that if I wanted to be one of the best players in the world it was important to play on all surfaces from clay to hard to indoor to grass. I'd played on clay for six months in a row and it seemed to me I needed to have a more complete game.

His teaching style works best on a clay court and he believed there was very much a set way of playing. It worked for me when I was younger, then I started to develop more shots and understand how I could hurt the opposition more with a flexible approach. Pato believed there was a 'correct' way to play tennis. You should begin every rally by playing to a guy's backhand, for instance – but what if he had a weak forehand? I felt I needed to do things differently.

But we were both philosophical about it. Splitting up with coaches is one of those things in tennis. In fact, the following year, when I went to play the tournament in Barcelona, Pato came along to watch me and as I had no coach at that time, he stayed on to help me – he even took me to see a Barcelona football match. (He supports Real Madrid really, but has a couple of season tickets at the Nou Camp as well. I guess he goes along to watch them lose.)

I only made the second round at the tournament but we talked on the phone a couple of times and he was saying: 'These are the things you need to do better and I think you can be world number one.' I still get on absolutely fine with him. I'm sure that whatever was said at the time must have been his English letting him down. He's a great coach; I still speak to him and still have huge respect for him.

For a period I went without a coach. So does Roger Federer from time to time. It is something that happens. Mum filled the gap at Roland Garros, where her main responsibility was making sure my kit was clean and buying me those great French baguettes and smothering them with chocolate spread, but it was obvious I was going to need someone to help me through the grass-court season and, in particular, my first senior Wimbledon. Turning to Mark Petchey, then the head of men's tennis at the LTA and now a Sky Sports commentator, proved to be an inspired idea.

He had always been supportive of me in his LTA role, even though the first time he ever saw me play was the semi-finals of a Futures event in Edinburgh when I was absolutely hammered 6–2 6–1. He told me that I'd be a Top 10 player after that defeat, when anyone else might have thought I'd be lucky to get a job as a ball boy. He was always the person most supportive of me at the LTA and agreed to help me through the grass season as part of his LTA job. I didn't need to be told how to play tennis, but having someone with me all the time, to be positive and help with strategy would be very valuable.

I was enjoying playing. It was fun on the court again, after the last difficult days with Pato. Mark and I weren't getting deeply into technical things, it was just a relief to be out there playing with freedom. It was also a relief when he helped share the burden of press attention. British tennis was struggling quite badly that year – no change there, then – and everyone wanted to know if I was going to be any good. Mark decided to make a splash by saying I could be as big as Wayne Rooney, which seemed ridiculous to people at the time. But, a few years on, he still loyally stands by his prediction.

Wimbledon was little short of mad, with me reaching the third round against Nalbandian. Mark and I hardly had time to get to know one another properly, but what happened next threw us together virtually every minute of every day for ten weeks. I had asked Mark if he would consider being my individual coach. That would mean him leaving the LTA and many weeks on the road away from his young family. I knew it would be a tough decision for him and I was really happy when he agreed to do it. We headed off right after Wimbledon and hardly stopped. It was like a road movie. We went to America together and I played virtually every type of tournament you could think of – Challengers, tour events, a Masters Series, a grand slam – week after week for nearly three months, criss-crossing Canada and the States by plane and hire car until we almost forgot where we were.

We ate together, stayed together, practised together and he remains a very close friend. When we came home, he invited me to stay with his wife and two daughters in Wimbledon and it was the first time I'd been close to someone with young kids. I'm not too good with babies, I don't know what to do with them, but once they're four, five, six years old I can start to play with them, mess around, wind them up a little bit. That's what I used to do with Mark's two little girls, Nicole and Myah. I used to get them completely hyper then give them back to their parents and go to bed.

Sometimes we'd play outside on little scooters. They'd shout 'Let's race!' and I would gallantly say OK. All the time my head was saying: 'Make it close, make it close, make it close', but at the last minute I couldn't. I just couldn't let them win. I know it was terrible of me. Two little girls and I couldn't let them win.

Well, I say it's terrible but I don't believe in letting kids win. I think it's fine for them to lose as long as it's not by a massive distance. Mum and Dad used to say I'd go nuts if I lost when I was younger, but I still lost. You need to learn how to lose. If you win everything when you're a kid you get spoiled and when you're older you don't know how to deal with losing.

It was a measure of how happy I was with Mark that we were virtually living on the road and at home together all the time. In that winter of 2005 I even decided to go with him to South Africa to train because he had booked a family holiday there. It was my choice, because he had told us when he took the job as my coach that he couldn't break the commitment to his family holiday. However, it didn't quite work out as we planned.

We had thought a few of the Swedish players might come down and train in the same place, but they didn't show up that year and I was short of practice. Everything was good off the court. My Mum came over for Christmas, I was getting to know Kim Sears who became my girlfriend, the weather was great and the fitness work was fine – but there were no players there and I had a tournament in the first week of the year. To go from playing with Mark, who obviously hit the ball well but not to the same level as some of the guys I would be playing, was going to be difficult. I struggled in the first weeks of 2006 because I hadn't had enough tough match practice.

I think both of us knew it should have been better. It wasn't annoying me, but both of us knew that having no one to hit with wasn't the ideal preparation for my first full year on the tour.

I lost in the first round of the Australian Open and then Mark told me that he would not be able to come with me for the tournament in San José. It was half-term week and he was doing something with the kids. That was fine – so fine I won the tournament. Kim came with me and I spoke to Mark before all of my matches. He watched my progress online. It was all good. Everyone was happy.

I went to Memphis where I met up with him again and did OK (lost in the quarter-finals to Robin Soderling). Mark claims he beat me at pool nine times in a row in Memphis but I have no memory of that at all. Maybe that is what shifted my mood because when we went on to Las Vegas I suddenly felt really tired, as if I didn't want to be there. I played a bad match against the Spaniard, Tommy Robredo, and lost easily in straight sets. He was ranked higher than me, so the result was hardly surprising, but I knew I had made a really weak effort. I hate that more than anything. The following week at Indian Wells it was a little better. I beat a Greek player ranked nearly a hundred places below me and then lost in the second round to Nikolay Davydenko in three sets.

For both Mark and me things were getting a little stressful. There was a lot of tension building up about little things. They were probably petty, they shouldn't have mattered, but when you spend so much time together, on and off court, you begin to lose perspective. It is like the beginning of the break-up of any relationship, you can argue about minor things to disguise the major problem.

We'd been on the road across America, I'd lived with his family in Wimbledon, we'd been on holiday in South Africa, we'd gone down to the Australian Open and now we were back in America again. I wasn't ungrateful. I'd enjoyed being around him, his awesome kids, his lovely wife – I was lucky they had asked me to stay – but now I was just starting to feel tired. I didn't really know the reason for it. I was getting angry in my matches like I never had before in our time working together.

It stopped clicking and I decided I had to do something about it. For me, that was by far the hardest decision I've ever had to make in relation to a coach. Mark had been more than a coach to me. He had been a friend and a confidant and a companion. I had become close not just to him, but his whole family. With Leon, it was just the two of us. With Pato, I had never met his family. With Mark it was a personal relationship that took in everything.

It ended pretty quickly in Monte Carlo. He had sent me a text saying: 'Can you let me know. Do you need me at your practice on Thursday?' I sent one back saying: 'No, I don't. Let's speak when I get to Monte Carlo.' I think maybe he then had a word with Patricio, to clarify the situation, but no way would Patricio have told Mark the initial news on my behalf. When I'm close to someone, as I was to Mark, and to Leon, I wouldn't want them to hear something like that from anybody else. No way. I'm big enough to deal with it. If I've got a problem I'm not scared to open my mouth and tell them. When

I know it is the right decision for me I'm more than happy to say so.

Obviously people will think 'Davis Cup – Argentina' and, as I have admitted, in that case perhaps I should have called John Lloyd, the team captain first. If I'm honest it crossed my mind that he might say: 'You could play if you really wanted to. You could risk the next tournament . . .' And then I might have started to feel guilty. And yet I knew I'd made the right decision, and if I had said: 'OK, fine, I'll come to Argentina,' I might have been absolutely snapping and not wanting to play when I got there. Perhaps that was one of the reasons in the back of my mind that stopped me from speaking to John, but there was no reason not to face up to Mark when he arrived in Monte Carlo. I met him in a hotel just before the tournament. I spoke about the things I felt I wanted on the court and why I felt I needed a change. It was horrible. I was really, really upset and the break-up affected me for a long time. I didn't really enjoy playing for the next month-and-a-half during which I hardly won a game. I even spoke to Mum and Patricio about not wanting to play tennis any more. I was really down.

People tell me I'm the most sensitive person in my group of friends and family. I'm a pretty caring person and I don't like it when I have to do things that might upset someone else, even if it is for the best. Far from being the ruthless coach-sacker, as I am sometimes portrayed, I don't like hurting people close to me. I think it's a horrible thing to have to do – but, then again, sometimes in professional sport you do have to.

I was affected by not being around Mark any more, never seeing his family, travelling to tournaments on my own, not having a coach. I was feeling pretty sorry for myself. I played Barcelona, Rome, Hamburg, Roland Garros and I didn't start enjoying myself again until I came home for the grass-court season and could see my friends and family.

Mark's legacy to me is an enduring one. He was great. When we met I was ranked around 350 in the world and not enjoying my tennis. With him I jumped about 300 places in the rankings in the space of eighteen months. I was on the tour that I had always dreamed of. I was in big tournaments without having to worry about wild cards. I won a tour event and people were hailing me as a future grand slam champion. He gave me the belief that I could be a success. He helped me realise the dream of being ranked in the World Top 100. He still gets quite emotional when he remembers the day I beat Soderling to break that 100 barrier. It meant so much to both of us. He is a sensitive guy as well and one of the things I like so much about him is that he would defend me down to the ground if he had to. It is a trait he shares with quite a few football managers, who always defend the players in their team. Some people would disagree with it, but for the individual being defended that kind of loyalty is fantastic. I will always remember him going ballistic in America when he discovered that the US Open wanted to give me a wild card but Wimbledon wouldn't trade a wild card back to an American player because they said it was 'tacky'. Mark was going nuts. He was really devastated.

We were new boys on the tour together. He hadn't really been on the men's tour much during his playing career and I suppose we built up this bond from the experience. I owe so much of what I did to him. We spoke about loads of things, often way beyond tennis. He was and is a really, really close friend.

I suppose some people wondered why I didn't engage

another coach straight away. The thing is: it didn't feel right. The decision to find my next coach – the right person to take me from thirtieth in the world to the Top 10 – would be a very important one. I wanted a coach who had worked with the best in the world and/or a grand slam champion. That's what I was looking for. I wasn't going to be rushed. I'd be spending a lot of time with this person. I wanted to find someone I could get on with really well.

And so, enter Brad. I was really excited when I first started working with someone who had the credentials of Brad Gilbert. Everybody knows him on the tour: the Californian who reached a career-high number four in the world, wrote a book called *Winning Ugly: Mental Warfare in Tennis* and then coached Andre Agassi to six grand slam titles and an Olympic gold. It could hardly be a more impressive CV.

The circumstances were a little unusual when we got together. The LTA, bankrolled by the money they receive from Wimbledon every year, offered a contract to a number of high-profile coaches, Paul Annacone, Peter Lundgren and Brad among them, to work with British players. I was told that I would be travelling with Brad about twenty-five weeks of the year – I even went through the calendar to pick out the best weeks for us to be together – and the rest of the time he would be working with other British players. That was fine. As I say, I was excited. Within a year of working with Andre Agassi, Andre had gone from thirtieth to number one in the world. It was a phenomenal record. I was going to be working with one of the master strategists in the game.

We began the arrangement after Wimbledon 2006 and it soon became clear that I wasn't going to be sharing him much after all. We went to Washington together and I made the final.

We went to Toronto and I made the semis. We went to Cincinnati and only lost to a player Brad used to coach, Andy Roddick. I made the fourth round of the US Open. Still together, we went for a while to his house in California, and then I won both my matches in the Davis Cup tie against Ukraine. Then we went on to Asia for a couple of weeks. Just the two of us – no physios, no fitness trainers – and it was the start of an intense relationship.

He's not an intense character himself, he is very upbeat, but for some reason he is intense to be around. He is known for his ability to talk. At the beginning I was happy just to sit and listen. One of his favourite subjects was American sports. I enjoyed hearing about them, and tried to understand them better myself, to take more of an interest, so I could participate in the conversations. They were a bit one-sided because at the time I didn't know anything about sport in the USA.

People talk about our personalities grating, but off the court I would say we were getting on fine at first. Some days were better than others. He does talk a lot, but he is in a good mood all the time. He is always up for a chat about most things. Perhaps we made a mistake when I spent the off-season at his house. We even shared the same villa when I went to practise at the Nick Bollettieri Academy in Florida. Basically, we were seeing too much of each other and I felt I needed a bit of space.

I learned a lesson: you want to be close to your coach, but there also needs to be some distance so you don't get tired and fed up. I never really did find that distance with Brad. It is fair enough to spend part of the off-season with your coach so that you can work on things, but when you've just spent three months with someone and then go and spend another four weeks together when you need to be relaxing, it just isn't going to work.

We spent days together, evenings together, ate dinners together. Imagine sitting next to someone at work in an office for eight hours a day and then going home and having dinner with them every night. It's like groundhog day – the same over and over and over. I guess I just got tired of it.

It was probably my mistake for not changing the arrangement. It went on for too long. I should have known: after eighteen months with Mark Petchey, things had begun to go stale; after eighteen months with Brad, same thing. I suppose I could have told Brad I wanted to chill by myself sometimes, but I think it was very important to him that we had a close relationship. He wanted to generate the feeling that a coach is always there for you when you need them. However, it's about judging what's enough and what's too much in that sort of relationship.

Maybe I could just have said: 'Brad, please be quiet,' sometimes. It might have worked. But I liked listening to him a lot of the time. I had fun hearing about his experiences. He had loads of funny stories, but I was listening and listening, and after a while I didn't want to listen any more.

Patricio always says to me: 'You're way too nice,' but I am sensitive to the fact I don't want to upset or annoy someone by saying something like: 'I don't want to spend so much time with you.' Once the relationship started out like that, I found it difficult to pull back from the situation.

On the court, I cannot deny I was doing well. Brad is renowned as a great tactician and a thinker, and I don't think it was a coincidence that my ranking started to move upwards. He believes it is all about having no excuses, about finding ways to win even through the bad days when you are not playing well. Funnily enough, I didn't lose a three set-match for the first four months of 2007, even when it went to a tie-break as in the quarter-final against Tommy Haas (ranked 9 to my 14) in Indian Wells.

We didn't argue that much about tennis. I understood what he wanted me to do: mainly put on some muscle and speed up my serve. He employed an NBA trainer, Mark Grabow, to help with the physical improvement, and then we worked on some of the technical aspects of the serve. I understood what we were doing. I made sure I did. I was always asking him what the reason for any drill might be, maybe to the point of driving him slightly mad. I didn't just do anything because he told me to.

He wasn't too worried about rankings and targets. He thought they would take care of themselves if I played hard and well. He just wanted to keep it simple and drive home the idea that tennis is like boxing: you will be the winner if you pound the other guy harder than he is pounding you. Being a massive boxing fan, I understood that philosophy.

However, after twelve months, around Wimbledon time, I knew that things weren't right for me. I wanted to be more professional, to have a physio and fitness trainer on the road so that I could always be working on getting stronger and getting over any niggles more quickly. Maybe that wrist injury I picked up in Hamburg would still have happened even if I had gathered a team around me sooner. The risk is always there, but maybe it could have been reduced.

There were little rows behind the scenes. We didn't argue that much about tennis, it wasn't the on-court stuff that was a problem, it was just becoming obvious I wasn't enjoying myself on the tour as much as I should be. I'm lucky I spend my life touring the world, doing what I do purely because I'm good at sport. If I wasn't happy off the court, there must be something wrong.

Occasionally I shouted at Brad during matches. I had never done that to Mark. I don't think it's the right thing to do. It only happened a couple of times but, after that, even if I was shouting at myself, I think people imagined I was aiming the comment at him. I'd always shouted on court, often in the direction of friends, family and coaches in the players' box. I'd been doing that for years. I always find it easier to get my emotions out if I'm looking at someone I know. If you watch any of my old matches, you'll see that I'm shouting in the direction of my mum or Patricio or my brother or Kim. Even so, in connection with Brad, it wasn't the right thing to do. It was immature and silly.

It was heat-of-the-moment in a pressure situation, but that is no excuse. I wouldn't dream of doing something like that off the court. You let it all out and afterwards you think: 'I shouldn't have said that.' My habit attracted a bit of attention at the ATP Tour event in Doha at the start of 2007 but Brad just said when asked: 'I know he doesn't mean it.' I don't think he was too bothered about it, to be honest, and it certainly wasn't the cause of our split.

Maybe the bookies knew something was wrong before we did. After Doha they were offering odds of 2–1 that the partnership would break up by the end of 2007. And, as it happens, they were right. The relationship ended ten months later and it didn't end too well. My wrist injury had obviously been a frustrating time for us both and I think it's possible Brad misunderstood the best way to handle it with someone like me. When I went back on the tour after missing Wimbledon it still didn't feel quite right. I had two heavy defeats, one in Canada and a thumping one in Cincinnati by Baghdatis, and I was pretty downhearted at the whole situation.

Brad said he thought I was depressed. He thought I needed psychological help to get out of it. I did see a psychologist, a little later, and he confirmed I was not remotely depressed. Brad even wondered about the cause of my anger on court, whether it was related to something in my past rather than just my frustrated perfectionism as a tennis player. I know he meant all these things as a form of motivation and he had the best of intentions. They are just not the sort of things that work for me. I didn't really want to hear that I was 'one of the most negative people' he'd ever met. I didn't think I was. I didn't think I was angry either. I asked around all my friends: 'Do you think I'm an angry person off the court,' and not one of them said: 'Yes.' If anything, I'm completely chilled.

I suppose that's what people meant about our 'clash of personalities'. Brad believes in being upbeat all the time, which is a good thing, but I don't think he was really listening to me. There was always a lot of talking going on, but not much understanding. I think he thought I wasn't extrovert or carefree enough. He said that I didn't have any vices – I don't like drinking and I don't like going to clubs – so it would be good for me to go bungee jumping or skydiving or even – but I'm pretty sure he was joking – rip all my clothes off in public.

I flew back home after Cincinnati to see a sports psychologist that my Mum had found for me and it did help to clear my mind. In many ways, I had been thinking about the wrist too much and we just talked about other things. Maybe that is what Brad had meant, but there is no doubt we misunderstood each other.

I just thought I was being protective, having endured long-term injuries before. He may have believed I had issues with negative thinking that were holding up the healing process. I don't think he has much patience with injuries. He is more a believer in fighting through things. That's fine, but I'm a different type of person. Sometimes, if I'd just lost in a tournament, he'd just leave a note under my door at the hotel and fly off home. That's fine too, but it wouldn't be the way I'd handle someone like me.

It was one big mutual misunderstanding, not helped by the fact that he had clearly believed I could have played Wimbledon. I wasn't trying to duck the tournament. I was really desperate to play, but the advice from everyone except Brad was that to play would be to risk greater injury. It could have been a nightmare if I'd played and made things far worse.

People seem to think that I'm too stubborn or strong willed to listen to a coach, but I wasn't like that with Brad at all. I respected him. He said hire his fitness trainer. I did. He said see a psychologist. I did. He said come over and train in California during the off season. I did. It wasn't entirely easy staying at his house because we only had each other for company and at one point he went away and left me for a couple of days but I don't want to sound ungrateful. It was a generous offer and his wife was really lovely. She cooked for me and helped out and it can't be the easiest thing to have another person in your own home.

Brad also wanted me to stop working with Jean-Pierre, the physio I had trusted ever since my knee problems in 2005. They didn't get on. He didn't want to travel with him any more after Jean-Pierre had come over to Australia and then the States with us. Brad thought he was a bad influence. It was probably a huge coincidence that I injured my wrist after Jean-Pierre had gone, but you can never know these things with absolute certainty.

I probably should have spoken to Brad when we parted but by then there was a huge breakdown of communication. Brad wasn't speaking to my agent. Instead he was talking to the LTA, which is fair enough because they were paying him. But I think the one-on-one relationship between player and coach is really important and that had more or less collapsed.

I had to do something about it. I spoke to one of the guys at the LTA, Bruce Phillips, the head of communications. I said: 'Look, it's not working out any more. I don't want to work with Brad. Thanks for all your support but it's done.'

That might seem abrupt but it seemed reasonable to me to talk through the LTA because they were the ones employing him. Obviously I had taken quite a lot of flak about that earlier, people said I should be paying his wages myself, but at the time we started working together I could never have afforded to pay it. It's as simple as that. There is no chance I could pay his salary, plus bonuses, plus travel, plus expenses. Obviously tennis players do make good money, but I'd only been in that position for about eighteen months. You've only got about twelve years to make a good living from your career and if you're spending that much on a coach, there wouldn't be a lot left.

I don't know what else I should have done. All I thought at the time was: 'Brad Gilbert. God, what a great opportunity for me.' I was excited and respectful and sometimes you just learn the hard way that these things aren't enough on their own. Another lesson learned.

At the end of the year I decided to do things differently. I hired Miles Maclagan as my coach, a British Davis Cup player who had been in the Top 200 as a player and went on to coach Kevin Ullyett and Paul Hanley to a couple of grand slam titles. I thought we'd get on. He is closer to my age, plays well, keeps in good shape and although he was born in Zambia, he's Scottish. However, I decided not to work with him alone. I wanted a fitness trainer and physio to travel with me as well, and I wanted each of them to have a back-up. I also decided to bring in specialist coaches, like Louis Cayer to help improve my net game, and Alex Corretja, twice a French Open finalist, for the clay season.

It caused quite a fuss, people said the idea was radical, but I don't see what's radical about a team of people to support you. It was mistakenly reported that I'd have this massive entourage of people around me all the time, as though I'd need to hire a private 747 just to get them all to tournaments. Michael Stich, the former Wimbledon champion, was one of the guys who said it wouldn't work – but it is not like that at all. I am never going to have more than one coach, a fitness trainer and a physio with me. I don't want to have five coaches, six trainers and three physios. It is just that I know what it's like to be on the road all the time with one person, and it does get quite stressful. I wanted to be in a position where I had a couple of coaches, a couple of trainers and a couple of physios who all get on well with one another and are good at what they do. Then they can rotate. That way, if one gets tired or wants to go home or wants to see his family, I can just say 'fine' and ask the other one along.

When I announced what I was doing at Christmas in 2007, some people said: 'Look what happened when Rafa Benitez (now manager of Liverpool Football Club) tried rotation.' I said: 'Yeah, the Spanish League, the Champions' League, the UEFA Cup and the FA Cup.' That pretty much ended the argument.

After Brad, I needed someone I felt I could sit down with and have a discussion, not someone who would tell me what to do. I wanted to be able to put my opinion across, let them put theirs, and then we would come to a decision between us. I felt I was starting to understand this game of tennis and I didn't need to have everything spelled out for me any more. A few people might say I'm a difficult person to deal with, but I am open to ideas. I will listen. I am definitely not interested in yes-men. If people are thinking that I am, then they don't know me. I don't want to have coaches around me saying 'Yes, Andy, you're right.' I want to get better. I want to become one of the best players in the world and I'm not stupid enough to think I'm going to get there by listening to people telling me I'm wonderful.

I think this is the best way to improve. Get fitter, get stronger and find ways of doing even small things better. I'm a very good tennis player. I've been ranked in the Top 10, but there are lots of little things to improve that are going to make all the difference between being ranked 11th and being in the Top five – or third – or at number one in the world.

Judy Murray

I'm the pushy mother. I know that's what a few people think because I've had some horrible letters over the years, accusing me of all sorts of things including 'inciting violence' due to my 'aggressive' fist-pumping during matches and even humiliating my sons with my support. People like that just don't get it. I don't mind what they say for the same reason I tell Andy not to mind when they criticise him: these people don't know us.

Anyone who knows me can tell you that I'm not pushy at all. I am not a control freak. I'm not sacking Andy's coaches behind the scenes. I don't try and dominate the lives of my sons. I've always been a believer that if you make a decision yourself and it's a mistake, you're going to learn much more from it than if someone makes a decision for you.

I've always seen the difference between people who push their kids to do things and people who push to make things happen for their kids. I admit I've often had to push to create opportunities for my kids but if they didn't want to take them I would back off. When it came to tennis, they never wanted to back off.

It wasn't just tennis either. When they were little, it was anything that involved having fun: playing swingball in the garden, chasing the ducks round the pond in the park, flying down the chutes at the swimming pool in Dundee, riding their trikes like mini Valentino Rossis round the Dunblane Tennis club house. It would be pointless me saying I don't know where they get it from. I know very well. I used to take them to those indoor activity centres with ball pools, tunnels and slides. The other mothers sat and had coffee. I went on everything with them, ignoring the signs that said 'For Under-10s only'.

These days, my two little nieces just start screaming when they see me. I play hide and seek with them, I go on the trampoline, chase them round the garden. I get them completely hyper. My sister-in-law, when it gets close to bedtime, says: 'Can't you just read them a story?' I do, but it's nowhere near as much fun.

This may partly explain why Andy's first eighteen months were the hardest of my life. It was a little bit of a shock to discover I was pregnant again when Jamie was only five months old. I had found the whole birth thing such a horrific experience that if I hadn't done it again quickly I wouldn't have done it at all.

We had moved to Dunblane two weeks before Andy was born, back to my old home town and not far down the road from my parents. I'd had to give up my job in retail sales and my company car had gone back. I felt completely trapped. I was used to doing a job and loads of sport and suddenly there was no escape. I was stuck in the house with these two little tiddlers and it was an absolute nightmare.

It wasn't post-natal depression or anything like that, it was just the frustration of an active person suddenly surrounded by mashed vegetable. They were both good babies, although I wouldn't say they slept. I was up and down in the night with both of them. More with Andy, if I remember rightly. It just killed me the next day, and I still had a toddler running round to cope with.

I've been on the women's professional tennis tour, I've been through a divorce, I've watched both my sons win and lose major tennis matches and still I would say that Andy's first eighteen months were the toughest I've ever known.

Nothing has been that hard again, not even during the first couple of months of 2008 when Jamie was so furious with Andy for pulling out of the Davis Cup tie in Argentina. All brothers argue, but not many end up with newspaper headlines exposing the fact splashed all over the world.

I felt for both of them: for Andy as all he was trying to do was protect himself from unnecessary injury, and for Jamie because he was thrown in the deep end of a press conference without being properly informed. When he found out from the Davis Cup captain, John Lloyd, when the team were already over in Chile that Andy wouldn't be joining them he was visibly, audibly, livid. In the infamous press conference called shortly afterwards, Jamie had a rant against his brother to the press.

He obviously felt really strongly to have spoken out like that, but it had been caused by a horrible lack of communication. He was fielding all these questions about Andy's withdrawal and he barely knew anything about it. He was being asked as though he should know, since he was family, but he didn't. We had inadvertently put him in a very difficult and exposed position.

It all arose because Andy's knee had been bothering him on-and-off during December and January and it became clear that the worst thing he could do would be to play a succession of intense matches on clay where there is a lot of sliding and pressure on the knee from changes of direction. The result of a scan and the advice of his physios and trainers was that it would be taking an unnecessary risk to play in Argentina.

When Andy finally decided not to go, Patricio called John Lloyd, and we just forgot that Jamie didn't know. I understand from Jamie's point of view that he was put in a difficult position. I also think that Jamie felt very strongly they had a chance of winning the tie with Andy's contribution. Without it, they had no chance.

Perhaps people thought it was strange that the boys hadn't spoken to each other anyway, but, although they're brothers, they don't communicate on a daily basis, and especially not about tennis. They might send each other messages on MSN, but that's just banter. When they are together, they just have fun. They rarely talk about tennis at all.

I was relieved when they started speaking again. It didn't take long. They are brothers after all and blood is thicker than water. On the 13th of February the first thing that Andy said to me on the phone was: 'It's Jamie's birthday today, Mum,' so I knew he was thinking about his brother and that everything would be OK. They met for the first time afterwards at the tournament in Indian Wells and it was fine. I think Jamie now understands Andy's reasons for withdrawing from the team, but these should have been communicated to him personally before the announcement. It was obviously wrong that Jamie had to find out from John Lloyd.

You have to put everything in perspective. They've been competing – or wrestling or arguing – since Andy was old enough to walk. Most of the time they are polite young men (believe it or not) who enjoy each other's company. These things happen and, anyway, I understand the pressures of life on the tour.

I was on it myself once, not for long though. I had left school, just turned seventeen, and I really wanted to give it a try. It was completely different in those days. There was no one in Scotland to help. No coach, no training facility, no other full-time players. You had to do everything on your own. I had no money for flights and accommodation. I often had to take buses and stay overnight in a tent which, on one occasion in France beside the tennis club in Antibes, collapsed in the pouring rain.

The worst time, for sure, was at quite a big tournament in Barcelona when I was on my own as usual. I had just played Mariana Simionescu, who was Björn Borg's girlfriend at the time, and lost. In those days your opponent would always buy you a drink afterwards in the club-house bar. It's crazy to imagine that now. Justine Henin saying to Venus Williams: 'Would you like a beer?' after beating her in the Wimbledon quarter-finals is hilariously unimaginable. Anyway, we were on our way to the bar when Mariana said: 'We have to go to the locker room first.' I asked her why. 'Because Björn doesn't like to see me smoke,' she replied, lighting up a cigarette. 'I can't smoke in front of people or else he'll find out.'

So we stopped for her nicotine break, then had our drink together and it was a good job she was paying. I was so short of money I then had to go into Barcelona to a Spanish post office to collect extra funds that Mum and Dad had sent me. It was all I had in the world. Coming back from the city, the bus was mobbed. I had my handbag over my shoulder and, of course, when I got off the bus my bag was open and my wallet, including my passport and my ticket home, were gone.

I just stood there on the pavement in sheer horror and disbelief. I couldn't move from the spot for a while, but then I forced myself to go and find a policeman, who took me into a shop to find someone to speak English and eventually I found my way to the British Embassy who organised a little money and a passport home. When I arrived back in Dunblane, I was so distraught about the theft that my dad basically said: 'That's it. You can't do it on your own any more.'

It was hard because I loved tennis and, within Scotland, I had a successful career. I went on to represent Great Britain at the World Student Games in Bucharest in 1981. The reason I remember it so well is that I played mixed doubles with a guy named Bill Gowans against the Romanians who consisted of Virginia Ruzici (who was number ten in the world at the time but listed as a student by the home country) and Florin Segarceanu (who went on to become Romania's Davis Cup coach). We lost 6–4 6–3 in a great match with a big noisy crowd. Ruzici was a great athlete, a beautiful gipsy-like girl, with big gold hoop earrings. Bill kept drop-shotting her and she would invariably run up and smack the ball right at me. After she had done it about half-a-dozen times, I suggested to him it might not be the greatest tactic. He said: 'I know, but I just love to see her running towards me!'

All together I won sixty-four junior and senior titles in Scottish tennis, which is no big deal and I never talk about it to Andy or Jamie or anybody else. All Andy knows is that I was good enough to play with him until he was about twelve, and then he started beating me.

However, I am glad I tried for those few mad months on the tour. At least I have no regrets and it probably made me grow up fast. Doing things on my own made me stronger. When I see kids having so much provided for them these days, I think: You have no idea how lucky you are to have this chance. You learn so much more when you make your own mistakes. You try that bit harder if everything isn't given to you on a plate.

There was a gap between abandoning the tour and going to university, so I took a crash course in shorthand and typing, and then took a series of temp jobs like working as a secretary in a glass factory and later in a car insurance office where I maddened my boss by typing 'Ford gear' instead of 'Ford Ghia' from his dictaphone every time. How was I supposed to know? I had never owned a car in my life.

I studied French and German at Edinburgh University before switching to French and Business Studies, because, to be honest, the

German was so boring. For a while after that I was a trainee manager with Miss Selfridge and then I was employed as a sales woman for a confectionery firm with my own company car. It was that car – or one of its successors – I had to give back when I discovered I was pregnant with Andy.

Life changes with children in unimaginable ways, not just because you are looking after them but because pretty soon you discover the new characters that have arrived in your world. In many ways both boys were very similar, and yet they were very different too: both sensitive and fuming, but Andy with a stubborn streak so that it was always very difficult to tell him what to do. Whether he thought something was right or not, if you forced him to do it, he would dig his heels in and say 'No.' You have to find the right way to approach things with Andy. With Jamie you could always be a little bit more direct.

Jamie, now, is the extrovert. He loves going out in a crowd and being the life and soul of any social situation. That has only come in the last few years, boosted by his famous win at Wimbledon in 2007 with Jelena Jankovic and by the success he has enjoyed on the men's tour in the doubles. Andy isn't shy but he is more the introvert. He likes going out with a smaller group that he's very comfortable with. He is very happy with his inner circle, and has a really good relationship with his girlfriend, Kim and has a few very close friends from his junior tennis days. He is very level-headed and he's quite good at sussing people out.

I remember Paul Annacone, the LTA men's head coach, saying something to Andy like: 'When you're eighteen, you have to do xxx . . .' and Andy just said 'Well, why?' He will not follow instructions blindly. He won't just accept what somebody tells him. You have to prove it to him first.

Both boys are quite sensitive, but I would say Andy's the more sensitive of the two. He hates seeing people begging in the street, he hates cruelty to animals. He is more inquisitive than Jamie and he *can* be more argumentative – not in a bad way, but he likes to reason things out.

He has always been very sensible. When he went away to Spain I didn't have to give him a pep talk about potential vices. I trusted him. He never expressed any interest in drinking. He is so like me in many ways.

Apart from one time, I never, ever wanted to drink, even all the way through university. The only time I did was in a bar in Edinburgh the night before we were due to catch the London sleeper en route to a three-month stay in France as part of my degree. Someone encouraged me to try a Southern Comfort and lemonade. I agreed to try one, then two, three, maybe even four. When I tried to move away from the pillar I was leaning against, I couldn't walk. I then fell down a flight of stairs – it wasn't until the next morning I discovered I was covered in bruises – and I was violently sick on the train. The girl in the bunk below has never forgiven me!

I have never done it again. I never want to have that feeling again. I don't get it – how can people want to feel that terrible? I am pretty sure Andy is the same.

We're certainly similar on the tennis court – both seriously competitive. There was a family doubles event at our club in Dunblane which we would play in from time to time. I also remember us playing a fun summer tournament in North Berwick together. At that time I was a Scottish internationalist and I actually remember being quite nervous before our match because I didn't want to let Andy down. He was eight years old and he wanted to win. It was a handicap event and I knew he'd be thinking: 'My mum's one of the best in Scotland, so we should win.' In the end, we didn't and I felt thoroughly annoyed with myself. He tells me that I was swearing under my breath at the back of the court all through the match – and I probably was!

I know it was supposed to be a fun tournament, but I am not good at playing sports socially. I can't hit a bad shot and then laugh about it. I just can't do it. There is a myth that when I was a youngster I was such a bad loser that my mother once confiscated my rackets. That's not true, but she did leave me at a tournament once to find my own way home when I smacked my only racket on the ground during a match and broke the frame.

Maybe Andy gets some of his competitiveness from me, but when I watch him play I can see he has something that I never had as a player: an amazing self-belief. He plays to win, I played not to lose.

Going on to become the Scottish National Coach was not something I planned, it just happened. My dad always said he thought I would make a great coach, but I was too busy when the boys were small – setting up a lingerie and Italian jewellery business or helping Mum in her children's toy shop – to do anything about it. It came about as a happy accident.

There was a junior tournament at Stirling University and because I had been Scottish number one (and probably because I was local) they asked me if I would present the prizes at the end. I said OK, I would. In a rash moment, handing over the awards to the under-12s, I said that the winners – two boys and two girls – could come and have a hit with me for an hour in Dunblane as a bonus. They all took me up on it and afterwards the parents asked if I would do it on a regular basis. That's where my first four pupils came from.

Two of them were a brother and sister from Falkirk and part of the deal was that their mother would look after Andy and Jamie – take them over to the park in their buggies – while I coached her children for two hours. All four of those pupils went on to be Scottish Junior Champions and one of them reached the Top 500 in the world.

It turned out that coaching kids was something I loved to do. I have very happy memories of Jamie Baker, another British Davis Cup player, coming round to our house when he was really young and playing table tennis on our kitchen table, with the boys using a cornflake packet as the net. There was always something sporty going on in our house. Ornaments had a pretty poor survival rate.

Andy has talked about the sacrifice he made to leave home at fifteen and go to the Academy in Barcelona. He felt it was the right thing to do, and we supported him completely. It was an easy decision and, in some ways, a very hard decision too. Letting your children go away from home in their early teens is always difficult and we had already been warned that it could go horribly wrong.

I'm sure that Jamie's lack of confidence before his latter success as a doubles player stemmed from the miserable time he had at the LTA training school in Cambridge when he was only twelve. For a long time after that he didn't want to be away from home for any great length of time. Between the ages of about sixteen and twenty, when he was really struggling around the lower levels of the men's tour, it would have been very easy for him to have moved away from tennis and never blossomed into the outgoing character he is now.

I feel tremendous relief about that outcome because I definitely felt guilty about Cambridge. I look back and understand what happened, but at the time we just didn't know what to do for the best. He had been offered a live-in place at Bisham Abbey to train with Pat Cash's old coach, Ian Barclay, and he was desperate to go. He had pretty much had his bags packed for six months. Then, one month before he was due to start, the LTA announced that they were closing Bisham Abbey down and the Cambridge option came up instead. We had a look at it and he wanted to give it a try.

However, he was leaving his friends, his school, his home, his parents, his first coach and all that is secure about life. You have to feel absolutely certain that where your child is going is the right environment, not just on the courts but twenty-four hours a day – and it wasn't right for Jamie. He used to be in tears on the phone, but he wanted to tough it out. I didn't know whether to leave him there or bring him home, it was a terrible dilemma. That's why I am a great believer now in establishing much better regional set-ups. Many children won't thrive a long way from home at such a young age, and yet at that age you need high-quality sparring partners, not just a few local kids and your coach.

In the end, after a few months, we did go and fetch Jamie back and I could immediately see his game had deteriorated, or his interest had, and he seemed far less happy on the tennis court than he had ever been before. It was heart-breaking. That is why we had to be sure about Andy's decision to go to Spain and, when he loved it, why we worked so hard to afford it.

We got some funding from the LTA, sportscotland, and from Tennis Scotland in the first year, but were still left a lot to find ourselves as costs for training, lodging and competition were around £30,000 a year. We also had a little sponsorship from Robinsons, but it's difficult to encourage big firms to invest in potential. It is much easier when you have actually made it. It was sometimes pretty stressful trying to find the funding over the three years Andy was at Sanchez-Casal, and it was a massive relief when RBS came onboard to sponsor Andy during that time, but in many ways I am glad it was tough because it made it a real challenge and kept us all working hard.

We have proof that hard work pays off. I'll never forget the day he beat Soderling in Bangkok in 2005 to make it into the World Top 100. He sent me a text afterwards that just said: 'I did it Mum.' I remember crying as I read it. I was just as tearful when he beat Tim Henman for the first time, in Basle, at the end of the same year. I wasn't there, but I knew it would be a really big thing for Andy because Tim was so much a role model to him. I listened to him sounding so humble in radio and TV interviews afterwards and I thought: 'Andy, you have handled that so well.' I was really proud of him.

I think the most recent time I cried was when he won in St Petersburg at the end of 2007 after coming through that really difficult time with his wrist injury. He'd struggled physically and mentally, missed four full months of competition and he had had some horrible results in the run-up to the tournament. It had been a long, long haul, but he won and I remember thinking: 'He's back.'

I keep these moments to myself. I don't think Andy would ever have seen me cry at one of his tournaments. If he did, he would just give me a row. 'What are you crying for, you stupid woman?' I am pretty sure about this because at Christmas 2006 he gave me a card that said: 'I'd like to thank you Mum . . .' and he listed a whole pile of things like '. . . for always believing in me, always supporting me, always letting me make my own decisions . . . but I most want to thank you for being the best Mum in the world.'

Of course, as I am reading it, tears are running down my face. He took one look at me and said, genuinely mystified: 'What are you crying for? You are so stupid.' He is very affectionate, but he would never say nice things like those to my face. I don't think most teenagers would, but just the thought that he is appreciating what we do for him, meant a great deal to me.

The joys and perils of being on tour with Andy are pretty numerous. I don't go to many of his tournaments because I have a job and he has a coach, but when I do go there is always something to do. At the 2007 US Open he suddenly turned round and said: 'Mum, I haven't got any clean shirts for my match tomorrow,' despite the fact that there's a laundry service at the courts. So – not for the first time – I had to wash out his dirty shirt in the sink, hang it up and blow-dry it with a hotel hairdryer.

Then there is the story of the shoes. He wore through his tennis shoes at the Madrid Open while winning a three-set match against Ivan Ljubicic which finished at 6pm. The shops shut two hours later and although he tried everywhere, he couldn't find the same make in his size. He had to play the next day, an evening match, against Djokovic and so Brad called me and said: 'The kid's got no shoes. You're going to have to find some and bring them over here.' At that precise moment I had just checked my bags on to the Heathrow–Edinburgh flight after working in London for a few days. My battery was dying on my phone and I had no charger with me. First I had to try and locate new shoes. It was 7pm in the evening – no shops open – so I called Patricio who was on the way to a Chelsea match. He said there were shoes in his office in Fulham. I called Patricio's partner to ask if he would open the office at this time of night and get me the shoes. He did, and offered to bring them to Heathrow. Bonus.

While he was doing that, I caught the tube over to Terminal 4 to see if I could buy a battery charger. No luck, so I had to call Brad on a pay phone to say I had the shoes and would get a flight in the morning. I went to the BA desk to book a seat but there were only two left and they were business class. I'd never flown business class in my life, but I had no option. I had to stump up the £600. I then went to the hotel booking desk and found a room for the night. Another £140. I waited for the shoes to arrive, then had to hang around till about 10.30pm to get my bags off the Edinburgh flight, then jumped on the Hotel Hoppa Bus and got to bed just before midnight.

I was up again at 4.30am to catch the flight and made it to the tournament hotel in Madrid before he was due to set off for practice. I handed him the shoes and he said: 'I don't know why you bothered, there's nothing wrong with the ones I've got!'

Every cloud has a silver lining, though. David Beckham, then playing with Real Madrid, was at that tournament and I met him in the players' lounge after the match. Maybe it was divine justice for the journey I'd made to get there.

You might say life with Andy can be hectic. It can also be wonderfully funny. The Scottish boxer Alex Arthur came to Wimbledon 2006 to watch Andy in his match against Andy Roddick. He came up to the players' lounge with us afterwards with his wife and said: 'I'd rather go a full fifteen rounds than sit through that again. I've never been so nervous in my life.' He told us that he had been sitting behind this American guy who kept shouting: 'Way to go Roddick.' Every time he did, Alex shouted like an echo: 'Way to go Murray.' He said. 'I know it was really childish, but I couldn't help myself.'

Being Andy's mum is never boring, for reasons good and bad. My reaction when he is in trouble for swearing is the same as any other parent. 'Oh no!' It's embarrassing and you know it's going to lead to us having a 'conversation' about it, but I do understand why it happens because Andy is a fiery character. It means he is frustrated by something, like missing an easy shot or adopting the wrong tactic. He is only angry at himself and he has always worn his heart on his sleeve. He has always been like that. It is part of him. Unfortunately he gets wrongly portrayed as an angry young man when he is anything-but off the court.

I admit his language at the Davis Cup in Glasgow against Serbia in 2006 was embarrassing. He was perhaps a little bit unlucky that the microphone at the umpire's chair picked it up and broadcast his outburst to the nation on television. I'd rather that hadn't happened – but I think he really felt that a bad call had changed the outcome of the match and he was particularly fractious that day because he had been so ill with a bad throat (ironically!) that he shouldn't have been playing at all. However, he knows he made a mistake and he learned from it. He has never been in so much trouble since then.

People also noticed that Andy shouted at Brad Gilbert, when he was his coach, when things were annoying him on court. It caused quite a bit of comment, but Brad didn't mind. He said he preferred Andy to shout at him rather than shouting at himself: he thought it was a way of deflecting the blame for a bad shot on to somebody else and maybe that was a good way to handle it, that Andy didn't spend the rest of the match berating himself.

Andy has deserved some criticism for his behaviour, but I often think he is punished in the media more than he deserves. The accusation that he is anti-English is just nonsense. We both agree that there is nothing better than beating the English if you are Scottish, but my mum is English so I have absolutely no problems with anyone south of Hadrian's Wall. In sport, there is a wonderfully competitive element when Scotland plays England but, in the end, it is just a cultural joke. Andy was very unlucky that something he said as a joke – about supporting England's opponents at the 2006 World Cup – was taken seriously by a few people in the media.

The other criticism we have to contend with is that he's injury-prone. Sometimes perceived problems are just a combination of bad luck and sensational headlines. He has been a little bit unfortunate to turn the same ankle three times in his sporting career, but the first time he did it he wasn't playing tennis at all. He was a teenager playing football for a junior team, Auchterarder Primrose, and it wasn't repaired quite as well as it might have been because we weren't that savvy about injuries in those days.

Since then he's had the knee injury that kept him out for six months in 2004 but that was also unfortunate in that he was born with the bipartite patella and it was misdiagnosed as tendonitis for several months. For all I know I have one too, but I never did well enough as a sportswoman to have a single scan in my life.

I think people started to have a go about his fitness due to the cramping issues at Queen's and Wimbledon in 2005, and that was caused by a lack of understanding. Andy was perfectly fit for the rigours of junior tennis, best of three sets and pretty small venues, but the first time the cramping happened, he was playing a grand slam champion on the show court at Queen's in front of television cameras and a huge crowd, and he cramped up after waiting ages for treatment when he went over on his ankle again.

The second time it happened was in the fifth set against a Wimbledon finalist on the Centre Court at Wimbledon when he just ran out of energy after so much physical and mental exertion. That shouldn't have come as a surprise to anyone. It's normal It's happened to loads of other players when they step up from juniors to seniors. It happened to the Argentine junior, Juan Martin Del Potro, when he was playing Fernando Gonzalez in the Australian Open 2007. It happens. The only difference is that while the Argentines have a huge press corps following their matches, they have more than one player to write about.

I accept the fact that Andy will have to bear the burden of attention alone, as Tim did for so many years. I think he has handled it pretty well so far. I have just got to hope that some other British players will push through in the next few years, because he is pretty young to have to cope with all the attention by himself. I do wonder, though, where the next generation is coming from. British tennis has not always had the most healthy mentality. Sometimes it seems that success just means everyone gangs up against you.

I remember Andy playing in the final of a junior tournament. He was younger than the other players and I became very aware that most of the audience were supporting Andy's opponent – not because they wanted him to win, they just wanted Andy to lose. If Andy played a great shot there was no recognition of it. When he lost a point there was noisy applause. It was an unhealthy environment. That's when I started to think that the best place to survive would be out of it and Spain became the best option.

Being a tennis mum means more than just coaching. It is about looking at all the pitfalls and trying to avoid them if you can. Some people just don't seem to like visible tennis mothers. I remember the flak that Gloria Connors used to get, but what a great job she did with Jimmy. I admired her sense of determination and fighting spirit. I also remember the way the cameras used to focus on her when she was shouting: 'Go on, Jimbo,' in the crowd. I have learned over the years to keep my mouth firmly shut. Actually I react immediately when Andy hits a great shot, but by the time the cameras come to me I've switched back to sitting there as neatly and quietly as though I was related to the Henmans. It's a good trick and it works.

Naturally, not everything has gone quite so smoothly. We have had some rough times. Andy's injuries have been little short of 'hell' for the people around him, and one of those times was the wrist injury in 2007 when he was struggling so badly to get back to form that we arranged for him to see a sports psychologist.

Andy had started playing again in the August, having missed the French Open and Wimbledon, and it was obvious he wasn't hitting through the ball on his forehand side. He managed one win in Canada against Robby Ginepri and then lost easily 6–2 6–2 to an Italian qualifier that he would normally expect to beat. Watching him you could see, he was very, very tentative. He was quite down about that. The following week he went to Cincinnati and was absolutely hammered in the first round by Marcos Baghdatis. When we talked on the phone he said there was no point in playing any more matches leading up to the US Open. He said he didn't feel confident about hitting the ball. It wasn't a physical problem because the wrist wasn't giving him pain. It was mental. That is when we organised the psychologist, Roberto Forzoni who worked with West Ham United, and it really seemed to do Andy good. It helped that Roberto knew nothing about tennis so he talked about his feelings over many things not just the injury itself.

One of the problems was that Brad wasn't understanding how Andy felt about the injury. In Brad's mind it seemed to be a case of: 'The wrist's fine now so get out there and do it.' It was an unsympathetic response and Andy was really struggling with that. Most of the time when they travelled it was just the two of them and although the tennis expertise was great, there appeared to be little emotional support. 'The wrist's repaired now. What's wrong with you? Get going.'

I know that everything he did for Andy, Brad always believed was for the best. But it was a business to him. Whereas to us, this is our child, and good or bad, we will do whatever we can to help him get better. It's not just about results.

If someone said to me: What was the happiest day of your life? I think I'd have to pick three occasions when the boys have done so well. The most excited I've ever been was probably the first Davis Cup match Andy ever played, the doubles victory over Israel when he was seventeen years old and partnering David Sherwood. That was just unbelievable. Then there was the Davis Cup tie against Holland when both the boys were in the team at the same time. And, of course, Jamie winning the Wimbledon mixed doubles with Jelena – and Andy being so supportive of him – was incredible.

Now my ambition, apart from supporting Andy and Jamie in their careers whenever they need me, is to establish my own indoor/ outdoor training centre in Scotland for players and their coaches. I feel very passionately about tennis in Scotland. We've proved it doesn't really matter where players come from. If they've got the talent that is correctly developed, plus hunger and belief, coupled with the right direction and the right opportunities, then it is possible to produce world-class players.

It's a big challenge and it will need investment, but I'm hoping that between the LTA, sportscotland and corporate sponsors, enough funding will come forward to make it possible. Maybe a few years down the line it is something that Andy and Jamie might be keen to get involved with. Andy has enough on his plate right now but when his playing career is over, I can see him playing a part.

Both the boys love tennis and just want to go as far with it as they can. Jamie calls it 'living the dream', but I do worry about the weight of expectation. What they have done is already pretty special, but I think there is a general lack of understanding that there are a lot of good players out there. Every match is tough at the top level. Andy and Jamie are still very young, and they still have lots of improving to do.

Just because someone like Novak Djokovic, younger than Andy by a week, won the Australian Open in 2008 doesn't mean that Andy is failing by comparison. It just means he's not ready to win a grand slam yet. I can see so many areas of his game that Andy can still develop. He will improve, without doubt, because he's got a very exciting game and a great tactical brain.

To me, it doesn't even matter if he never wins a slam. We would love him to, but if it doesn't happen, he will still have been a Top 10 player at a very young age and he has emerged from a small country where tennis remains very much a minority sport. The future is bright for both the boys as long as we're not too impatient.

Chapter Eleven:
Team on Tour

It didn't seem too much to ask to have a relaxing holiday for a couple of weeks at the end of a stressful 2007. Kim and I went to Miami hoping to unwind and get some sun but it didn't quite turn out that way because I spent two days in a hospital bed hooked up to a drip. Some sort of food poisoning had seriously dehydrated me, and the doctors didn't want to take any chances. It was one way to relax, I suppose, but not quite what I'd had in mind.

I then embarked on the most hard-working off-season I'd ever known. So-called 'Team Murray' was being assembled – between track work and Bikram yoga with my new fitness trainer Jez Green, and on-court training with my new tennis coach Miles Maclagan, the winter in Miami went really fast. The yoga was incredible. It's the most difficult thing I've ever done because it's done at 42 degrees Celsius in a crowded studio, and just trying to stay balanced is really, really tough. Regular yoga looks just like stretching to me, whereas Bikram yoga tests you to hold your posture and concentrate all the time. A couple of times, Miles had to go out because he thought he was going to faint.

Having finished the 2007 season so strongly, I wanted to come back on even better form. There was no torture I wouldn't consider, including track work for the first time in my life. I'd done short, sharp sprints on a tennis court or running on a treadmill, but with Jez I started doing some work on the track at the University of Miami. He didn't really know what to expect of me. He'd say: 'Let's just see what you can do.' Then I'd do whatever it was and he'd say: 'Wow, I didn't think you'd be any good at that.'

I think people underestimate my athleticism, but to play tennis well, you have to be able to move well. We worked on that in Miami. I'd never done a 400-metre sprint in my life and so Jez set up my first session to run one 400 metres in under 80 seconds followed by an 80-second recovery – ten times in a row. Each session, we lowered the time by a second. My best was 75 seconds on, 75 seconds off.

That was tough, but the hardest session I've ever done was twenty 100-metre sprints, completed in 15 seconds each with a 45-second recovery. Now that is ugly. There's a video of it on my website and when it's over, I'm just lying down in a pool of sweat on the track with my arms out in crucifixion pose. When I stand up, you can see the imprint of my body on the ground.

I've never worked so hard in my life as I did during those weeks. We went to the gym, the track, the court, the yoga studio and, despite all that, I still put on weight because I started to eat much more than I've ever done. I was going out to dinner and eating forty-two pieces of sushi. I was eating massive amounts and snacking on balance bars (no bananas) to supplement the meals. I was 80 kg when we started work and by the end I was around 82 kg. Even now, I want to get heavier, I want to weigh 85 kg soon, so maybe sixty pieces of sushi is my target.

The one thing I won't do is bulk up on supplements. I've said elsewhere that I'm worried about taking things that could possibly make me fail a drugs test. These big pharmaceutical companies have so many products going through their laboratories and factories that there's always a slight chance there might be some contamination. That's one of my biggest fears. I'd hate to fail a drugs test. I don't really see how there's any way back from that in sport and I probably wouldn't want to play again.

I do take painkillers but I feel a bit uncomfortable about any other medicines, because you just never know. When Marion Jones was sent to jail for lying about taking drugs, I thought it was absolutely pathetic. If you were to win on drugs, I don't see how you could face your friends and family. OK, I'm sure you could put on a front, but when you got back and looked at yourself in a mirror, you must say to your reflection: 'What the hell was I doing?' It's just pathetic.

So, it was without any outside assistance – apart from my team – that I went to the Qatar Open in Doha for the start of the new tennis season. I sensed I was in the best shape of my life. I'd worked so unbelievably hard, the easy part was going to be playing the matches. I'd taken the pressure off myself and I felt ready to play good tennis.

My team that week – so much for my needing a minibus to get them around – consisted of Miles, my coach, and Matt Little, the fitness trainer I was leasing from the LTA. Kim was there (her studying for an English degree does not exactly qualify her as a tennis coach), also my brother, who was playing in the doubles at the time, and Ross Hutchins, who was playing in the doubles with me (not for long though, as we were outplayed by the top seeds Daniel Nestor and Nenad Zimonjic in the first round).

It was a good week. I played really well, winning one set 6–0 in each of the first three rounds. I knew I had to serve well, and sending down eleven aces against Olivier Rochus of Belgium in the first round told me I was on the right track. When I beat Davydenko in the semi-final in straight sets, things looked even better. I remember him saying I was difficult to play. He said I seemed to find some special shots when I needed them and that my slice to his backhand put pressure on him. That all sounded good to me.

I played my friend 'Stan' in the final. It was my third meeting with Stanislas Wawrinka, the Swiss Davis Cup player, and I had never won before. It wasn't easy this time either. I had to do a lot of running and it was a pretty tense match to begin with, but after going up 3–0 in the final set with two breaks of serve I won my fourth ATP title and collected the golden trophy.

I spoke on the court after the final about why my game takes a little longer to get together than most. I said that a lot of people on the tour have basic games and it takes them much less time to master their style of play. My game is quite complicated and I always knew it was going to take a bit longer to learn how to play the right way. It's taking me a bit of time, but it's exciting.

That was the gist of my speech. It turned out to be a premonition. I couldn't have guessed at the time that my results in the first part of 2008 would be so up and down. Great wins and tough losses kept alternating and I couldn't get a momentum going. But I knew I would; it was just taking time.

I was looking forward to the Australian Open. It comes so early in the year I'm surprised they don't give us Christmas presents, but that didn't stop me playing well the year before. I'd reached the fourth round and played probably the most thrilling match of my life against Rafa Nadal. But this time I was feeling good: I'd just won a tournament, I was ninth seed and my first-round opponent was the unseeded Jo-Wilfried Tsonga from Le Mans who everyone says looks like my hero, Muhammad Ali.

They'd changed the surface since the previous year from Rebound Ace to Plexicushion. I don't think it was the best of ideas because now it's very similar to the US Open, but it is still a surface that ought to suit me. I knew I had a good chance against Tsonga. As it happened, he had a good chance against me and emerged the winner 7–5 6–4 0–6 7–5.

Andy Roddick said after his match when he saw my result: 'I shudder to think what's going to be written about this tomorrow.' I knew what he meant: the British media were probably going to be hard on me after all the build-up. But I had only lost a match and not that badly either – I won more points than him (137 to 135), I won more games, and I had more breaks of serve. I just didn't quite win the match, but I ought to have done – Tsonga rushed the net over a hundred times, according to the stats; and by the end he could barely walk because of cramp, although it was hard to diagnose because he'd be hobbling one minute and then managing to chase down every ball I played.

There was, I think, one point that changed the match. After winning the third set 6–0, I had my momentum, and then I was 1–0 up in the fourth with a break point on his serve. I hit a passing shot which nearly beat him, but he returned a reflex volley that bounced off the net and fell on to my side of the court. He went on and managed to hold that game. If I'd won it, I think I'd have won the match.

I didn't play that badly. I didn't return the ball too well that day, even though the return is normally the best part of my game. Even so, it wasn't nearly as bad as in 2006, when I got absolutely smoked in the first round. I was disappointed but I wasn't panicking. I knew Tsonga had played really well and I still came close to having my chance against him. In a way, it gave me more confidence, not less.

I stayed for two or three more days in Australia. There was no sense in giving up the sunshine too early to come back to London in winter. For the last couple of years when I'd lost in Melbourne, I'd been go-karting, but this time I just went to the gym and practised. I had no urge to go and explore and I just didn't have time. I was due to go to Argentina to play in the Davis Cup and if I'd taken a week off to chill in Australia and then tried to get ready to play in 30-degree heat on a clay court in Buenos Aires, I couldn't have made the transition at all.

I suppose I should have taken even more heart from the fact that Tsonga went right through the tournament and ended up playing Novak Djokovic in the final. He didn't win that day but the way he beat Nadal in straight sets in the semi-final for the loss of only seven games made everyone think they'd found a new star of tennis. Apparently he even received a good-luck message from the new French president.

But it was Djokovic who emerged the new grand slam champion and because his birthday is a week after mine, a lot of people were saying that I had fallen behind. It's true he took big steps forward in 2008. He played really well last year too, reaching the semis of all the slams except Australia. He had separated himself from the pack chasing Federer and Nadal, the number one and two in the world. He was, for sure, the stand-out third-ranked player in the world.

We're called 'friends', Novak and I, because we've known each other since we were thirteen years old and we even played doubles in the Australian Open one year. But I don't spend that much time with him. He's obviously good for tennis and has a lot of personality. He's known as 'the Djoker' and does a good impression of Maria Sharapova, among others, at the player parties. I'm not really into the party scene so I don't always go. I missed the one in Monte Carlo because I was watching Barcelona v Manchester United, the first leg of the Champions' League semi-final, on the TV instead.

Meanwhile, it wasn't just me who was getting press attention for supposedly 'falling behind'; questions were being asked about the fitness of Roger Federer. I heard something about glandular fever, but I wasn't certain and it wasn't really my business. I did know that he had made it through to the semis in Australia without dropping a set – that didn't suggest a major loss of form. Djokovic obviously played well to beat him in the semis, but that's men's tennis. It certainly didn't look as though he would struggle for the rest of the year. If Federer is the most dominant player in tennis history, one defeat doesn't mean anything.

It was the same last year. He lost to the Argentinian Guillermo Canas in successive tournaments in the States, and everyone was saying: 'OK, that's it, Federer's struggling' and then he made the final of Monte Carlo, won Hamburg, reached the final of Roland Garros, won Wimbledon, the US Open, Basle and the Masters Cup. Some struggle. I wouldn't mind a year where I struggled like that!

It was around this time that I had a haircut. You may not be able to believe that I can't pinpoint when, because quite a fuss seems to be made about my hair, but I genuinely can't remember. I just went to the hairdressers in my apartment block in Wandsworth and asked for a trim. No big deal. It's just hair, isn't it?

More important was the row that had blown up over the Davis Cup and it's possible that I went off to the indoor tournament in Marseilles determined to play as well as I could and not be distracted by the fall-out from Argentina. Whatever the reason, it seemed to work. I won there, beating Mario Ancic, the 6'5" Croat (whose nickname is Baby Goran), in the final, and broke into the Top 10 again. I would have thought that was good news for British tennis but some people hadn't forgiven me for pulling out of the Davis Cup to protect my knee condition. One newspaper headline asked: 'So Andy, how is that knee doing?' The answer: OK, as long as I look after it.

After playing so well in France, I felt tired playing back-to-back tournaments in Rotterdam and lost to Robin Haase, a local hero, in the first round. Having inched up the ladder, I'd gone down the snake again and was back down to 11 in the rankings. There's no real excuse except the surface change didn't help me. The court in Rotterdam was probably the slowest I've played on since I joined the tour in 2005. I don't understand why all the indoor tournaments are not played on similar surfaces, but they're not. There's a lot of things i don't understand about the tour. Maybe I will one day.

Next, we packed our bags again and headed for Dubai, the tournament that all the top players make a point of playing because of the appearance money. Nine out of the top eleven players were there. I'm not against it. If a tournament really wants you, they should be free to do whatever they can to get you there. We were there in such numbers that – as an unseeded player – I ended up playing Federer in the first round.

I liked my chances in this match, I really did. I was asleep when the draw was done on Saturday. Someone sent the result in a text which woke me up, and I looked at it and went back to sleep. I wasn't worried.

There were, I admit, some differences between Federer and me: he was ranked 1, I was ranked 11. He was six years older, two inches shorter and had won over fifty tour titles to my five. He had earned $38 million in prize money; I'd earned $2 million. But then look at the stats that matter: he'd won our first match in straight sets in Bangkok 2005; I'd won the second in straight sets in Cincinnati 2006. We were matched one win each. As I said, I liked my chances.

I was right to like them. I played well and I was unlucky not to win the first set, which went to a tie-break. Before the match, Miles, Matt, my friend Carlos and I were playing football tennis on a court to help me warm up. Some warm-up. Miles and Matt ended up having an argument over a call and were effing and blinding at each other. Even as I was trying to get ready to play, they were still arguing. They didn't speak to each other for the first five games of the match. They just sat in the stands with their arms folded, not wanting to say anything. I'm joking when I said it distracted me. Actually, it was quite funny.

Federer hadn't lost a first-round match since a defeat to Dominik Hrbaty in August 2004, but I served so well he didn't have a break point on my serve the whole match. That probably hadn't happened to him for two or three years. Serving well was the key and I won 6–7 6–3 6–4. I must be one of the few players on earth to have held a winning record (2–1) against Federer in his prime.

Afterwards he had a few things to say about my style. He said I would have to 'grind very hard for the next few years' if I was going to keep playing that way. 'He tends to wait a lot for the mistakes of the opponent. He stands way far behind the baseline on the court and that means you've got to do a lot of running . . . I don't think he's changed his game a whole lot since I played him in the Bangkok final. Not that I'm disappointed but I really would have thought he would have changed it in some ways.'

I'll tell you what I thought about those comments: I wasn't that bothered, for the simple reason that I'd won the match. Also, I agreed with him. To play three or four metres behind the baseline every match is a tough thing to do and you get tired of running. But I don't do that every match, only in certain matches. I do different things against different players. If you go and watch my Australian Open match against Nadal, I was playing pretty close to the baseline and taking a lot of risks because I think that is the right way to play him. I'm not going to play that sort of game against Federer, who defends as well as he does. The result would suggest I was right.

I was feeling so confident after the win that I thought I might go all the way in the tournament. It wasn't to be, unfortunately. Davydenko beat me in the quarter-final, a reversal of our result in Doha. I wasn't too down. It had still been a good week for me, and just to prove that I wasn't the only one sometimes getting into trouble for firing coaches, Andy Roddick came out and told everyone that he and Jimmy Connors had parted company. It provided a little bit more

Wimbledon 2006 –
I played great to beat Roddick for
the second time that year...

... but it was horrible v Bhagdatis
in the fourth round

Backhand working well in my five setter v Rafa Nadal in the Oz Open, 2007

Launching the 2012
logo with Seb Coe

Hamburg 2007 –
wrist gone –
my worst nightmare!

Sept 2007 – Davis Cup team for World Group play off v Croatia at Wimbledon. Tim's final match

A spot of kick boxing at the Thailand Open in Bangkok

It's great to have your bro on tour – on and off court

Me and Rafa at the
end of court 0z Open
epic, Jan 2007

With our twin cousins Cora and Ailsa in fancy dress – them, not us

Wimbledon 2006 – chatting to boxing friend Alex Arthur in the player lounge after the Roddick match

(*Above right*) With Dani Valverdu, great friend and doubles partner in my junior days

(*Right*) Karting in Melbourne, 2007. Victorious, of course!

(*Above*) Debrief from Brad Gilbert after Davis Cup singles v Netherlands, 2007

(*Left*) Cricked neck at Davis Cup, Eastbourne, 2006. Had to sit out the final day v Israel. With my friend and physio Jean Pierre Bruyere

Qatar Open – my fourth title

(*Above*) My victory at Queen's was my 12th career title.
How big's the trophy?

(*Right*) Here's me and David Beckham teaming up for
the UK's Malaria No More campaign. We hit a few tennis
balls on the Wembley pitch. He was pretty good!

(*Above*) Warming up for Centre Court action at the Wimbledon practice courts.

(*Below*) 2009 US Open – having won Montreal I felt good going into
this tournament, but it just wasn't to be my year...

proof that player–coach relationships are tough to maintain even when one of them is a tennis icon.

I always look forward to going to America. This time I had even more reason. I'd played well in both US tournaments in 2007, I was going to go apartment-hunting in Miami, and I'd be seeing Gran, Grandpa, Uncle Keith and his wife at the Indian Wells tournament. Some people asked me if my family were there on a peace-keeping mission because it was the first time Jamie and I had met up since the Davis Cup row, but that wasn't remotely true. My uncle is a golf pro in Texas and my gran and grandpa, who hadn't seen him in two or three years, decided to fly over for a visit. It is always good to see the family. Gran bought me a tin of her customary shortbread and I ate the lot.

Jamie and I had said hi to each other already. I wasn't really bothered about the situation any more, and I didn't feel like we needed to say anything to each other about it. I just wasn't very happy about the way it had been reported. It went from being a disagreement between Jamie and me to reports of us hating each other and sparking a family feud. I can't believe he is such a fan of *Hollyoaks* on TV, but apart from that we don't disagree on too much.

It was a time for peace pacts all round. At the start of the tournament, Federer told the press that he hadn't meant to criticise me in Dubai. 'And if I was, it was at a very high level, so I'm sure he knows that. All I said was that I thought he was a more aggressive player and all he was doing was just keeping the ball in play. He can do both. I know it and he knows it, so I don't think we hate each other. We had a chat, so everything's OK.' We had, and it was.

On the tennis front, I played some good tennis at Indian

Wells, but not consistently enough. I was erratic against Karlovic in the second round when we split tie-break sets and I won the decider 6–3. It was the same against Tommy Haas in the third round. I played well but inconsistently and lost 3–6 in the third.

In Miami two weeks later, I had a couple of jobs to do as well as a tournament to play. I wanted to buy an ocean-front apartment, and I'd looked at about sixty places since the winter, but I had to put that on hold because of the mess in the American banking system, Also, I owed it to the ATP to make up with the Miami Dolphin cheerleaders. I'd missed an autograph-signing session with them the year before because it was raining and I'd gone back to my hotel instead and got a telling-off.

I realise that it may sound a little weird. Perhaps not many guys would miss a date with the Miami Dolphin cheerleaders because of rain, but it's not quite as miserable as it sounds. Practice courts are hard to come by in the rain, and I'd gone back to my hotel to use the courts there. It was a case of work before pleasure. That was my excuse, anyway.

So I kept my appointment this year and, to be honest, I don't know what's so special about cheerleaders. I signed stuff for kids, had some pictures taken and it was actually pretty awkward. I had to stand with a bunch of cheerleaders in front of a massive group of photographers telling me to strike a pose. That was not – for me – that much fun. I don't think Kim was that happy about it either.

But there was worse to follow. I had a really tough and ugly match against Ancic in the second round (the first round was a bye) and lost 2–6 6–2 6–7. I had two match points to win it and let them slip. That was the first time in my career that had ever happened to me, so I was pretty disappointed.

I was unbelievably flat, even in the first set I won. I tried to get myself going by losing my temper but it only worked to some extent. One of the papers said I was tearing at my shirt like the Incredible Hulk, which wasn't entirely the effect I was hoping for. I was trying to get pumped up. It's an old trick I learned from Tim Henman. Once in a Davis Cup tie against Jurgen Melzer of Austria, he lost the first set 0–6, and I saw him getting angry and pumped up. I thought: 'This is weird. What's Tim doing? It's not like him.' After the match I asked him what was going on out there. He said that sometimes you just have to get some emotion in a match by getting mad at yourself. He said you had to get really ticked off by something, either a line call or the umpire, and then it might fire up your game.

I thought I'd try it. I managed to turn the match around in my favour and I had those two match points, but I just didn't quite finish it off. I was criticised afterwards for playing too many drop shots but I thought that was blown out of proportion. It used to be something I did all the time – way too much, in fact – but I was barely hitting them now. Some people don't know what tactics are. I'd used them well in Marseilles against him; the strategy just didn't work so well this time.

I wanted to say to people: 'Look, I had two match points against the guy. If I was playing way too many drop shots, I wouldn't be having match points against someone of Ancic's calibre. The tactics were right, I just didn't play that well.' People that don't understand tennis are obviously going to think those drop shots cost me. They don't remember that at 6–4 in the tie-break Ancic used the drop shot successfully against me.

So, the drop shots were not the reason that I lost; I just served badly. I served like I had when I was eighteen years old: inconsistently and with insufficient power. It was only one match but just because my ranking drops, everyone says: 'Wow! Disaster.' But in the long run, it didn't make much difference. I went down to 20 in the rankings but I was coming into a period when I wasn't defending any ranking points because of my wrist injury the year before. I was looking to the future. If I don't improve on my ranking of 20 in the summer of 2008, that will be a terrible effort. If I'm in the Top 10 by the US Open in August, I'll be happy with that.

By now, I had an idea how 'Team Murray' was going and I was happy, but not everyone was convinced. A national newspaper ran a story that wildly exaggerated how many people were on my team. Fair enough, I had a coach (so do most top players), a fitness trainer (so do most top players) and a physio (so do most top players). But the paper was including Patricio, my former coach when I was eleven, and my brother, who last time I looked was a doubles player himself. It was ridiculous. I admit it may have been going over the top to take two fitness trainers to Australia. But at the big tournaments, I think it's nice to be surrounded by the people who have worked so hard with you. If I was to do well at grand slam, I thought it was the right thing to do.

After four months, I could tell that Miles and I were going to get along. He is a good person to practise with. We were similar off the court as well, pretty relaxed. I wasn't immediately as close to him as I had been to Mark Petchey, but it always takes a bit of time to get to know someone. The most important thing for me is to have someone who is similar in age and pumped to be playing in major tournaments. He is obviously excited to be on the tour but he doesn't have the sort of personality that makes him panic. He is pretty calm and relaxed and not so busy doing other things that he forgets the reason we're there. He is very different from Brad.

Miles has had his doubters. People said that because he had only reached the World Top 200 in his playing days, he didn't have the experience to guide me. That's how I know they don't understand tennis or sport. Jose Mourinho might be considered the best football manager in the world, but he was no Pele. In other words, just because you weren't a great player doesn't mean you can't be a great coach.

I think it's the players who had to work hard and weren't as talented as others who make the best coaches – they study tennis all the more because it doesn't come naturally. I think you should have played the game, but not necessarily to a Top 10 ranking. Brad Gilbert is a very good coach, but he hasn't worked with someone ranked 300 and brought them into the Top 40 in the space of eighteen months, whereas Mark Petchey has. But every coach has their own expertise, and some coaches suit certain players and not others. Think of Steve McClaren, the former England manager. Some people had a go at him when he managed England, but he did a great job with Middlesbrough.

I've worked with Mum, Leon, Pato, Mark, Brad and Miles and every one of them sees the game differently. The most important thing is that they understand the person they are coaching. If I'm going through a tough time, I'll phone my mum because she knows what I like to hear and what I don't like to hear. It is that kind of understanding that matters as much as forehands and backhands. Obviously I'm a very good player. I've been up there at number eight in the world, but there are still things I need to learn.

I tell Miles what I want to do and how long I want to practise, then he sets up the drills and we work on things. I study tennis: I watch a lot of matches and I know what I'm doing wrong. I don't just practise things I'm good at. For example, I want to play better on clay, so I brought in Alex Corretja to help me during the clay-court season. The Spanish former Davis Cup player has a great track record. He was twice runner-up at Roland Garros, as well as number two in the world and I just think it makes sense to call in the specialists to do a specific job.

This causes people to accuse me of being confused. I am not confused. I'm travelling with a fitness trainer to get me in better shape when I'm on the tour. What's wrong with that? I think it's a wise investment. I'm travelling with a physio because everyone's been complaining that I'm so injury-prone and this is a great way to iron out the niggles before they have a chance to develop into something more serious. What's wrong with that?

I was watching tennis on TV when the commentator mentioned that Djokovic was working with Mark Woodford, the prolific doubles champion, on his volleys. 'Great appointment,' said the TV analyst. 'It's something he really needs to improve.' If I employ someone to work on my volleys, or my clay-court game, then all of a sudden I'm described as confused. When we played in Monte Carlo, Djokovic had his family with him, his fitness trainer and his coach. Federer in Dubai had two coaches in his box, Jose Higueras, the Spaniard who used to coach Jim Courier, Michael Chang and Pete Sampras, among many others and the Swiss Davis Cup captain. So I'm not the only one; it is the way tennis is going. These people have the expertise. I don't know why you wouldn't want to work with them on a temporary basis.

My whole plan for the year is to work much harder on my fitness, get some input from some of the best players in the world and go through the season preventing injuries. I am also trying to gain those three kilos in weight which I think will make a big difference in years to come. I've been rather disappointed that the 'Team Murray' line has been blown out of all proportion. Am I supposed to tell my brother he's got to stop coming to tournaments because he's apparently part of my team?

So, there are all these professional questions to deal with and then you have to find the time to take a driving test. Kim can drive, even though she's six months younger than me, and although it's great to have a chauffeur, driving is something I really want to do. It's got to be soon because the theory test I did expires in November 2008. I don't think it will be too difficult. I've done a lot of go-karting. Basically, I've been behind the wheel quite a bit and I can drive fine. I've got good hand–eye coordination for a start.

It is funny trying to cram a little bit of normal life in to the hectic business of being on the tennis tour. This year will be busier than most, with (barring injuries) my first Wimbledon in two years, the Olympics in Beijing and the Davis Cup tie at home against Austria – which I am planning to play (I hope on a hard court).

I'd love to win Wimbledon, that's for sure. Everyone who watches the tournament would love someone British to win the singles there. I know I can play well on grass but a lot depends on the draw. Hopefully, I'll have my ranking up by then because Wimbledon does this weird seeding selection that doesn't work in my favour. Even if I'm in the Top 10 or

Top 15 by then, because I didn't play last year I'm going to get booted down the list to a lower seeding. But that's a minor technicality compared to the pleasure I get from playing there.

I do understand it's a special place. I've been going there since I was a kid to watch my hero Andre Agassi in my Lycra denim shorts just like his. I played the junior tournaments aged fifteen, sixteen and seventeen. I was in the seniors by the time I was eighteen. I reached the fourth round by nineteen. Every year, something happens, something changes.

And, of course, some things don't change that much at all. I remember hearing the story that a gateman once refused entry to Boris Becker, the three-time champion. That doesn't surprise me. At Wimbledon 2007, Kim and I went to the gate right next to the player's entrance with my entry badge. We were going to watch one of Jamie's matches in the mixed doubles and I needed to take her in so that she could collect her badge too.

'I'm just taking my girlfriend to get her badge,' I told the guy.

'No, sorry.'

'What do you mean?'

'No sorry, she can't come in.'

'Are you serious?' I asked in an unintentional echo of John McEnroe. He explained that Kim had to wait outside the gates, while I went in to get the badge. Then I had to come all the way out of the grounds with it, come back round to the entrance, and give the badge to her before we could go in. I understand the need for security, but this just seemed needless nit-picking. Yes, obviously Wimbledon is a beautiful place, but when you get rejected at the door it's not the nicest of feelings.

I don't think they do it any more, but in the past when you won at Wimbledon, you were given an honorary tie. I don't really know much about that kind of history – and I'm not a tie man. We have to wear them at Davis Cup dinners, which can be a nuisance because I can't tie the knot properly and I have to get someone else to do it for me. I can see why people enjoy Wimbledon's traditions – it's an amazing tournament – but I wish it could be just a bit more chilled and less expensive for the fans. I eat strawberries but not with cream, and preferably for less than a fiver!

The one thing I do love is the support of the crowd. I can play in some of the biggest stadiums in the world and get very good support but it is never quite the same passionate wanting-me-to-win that I find at Wimbledon. I know it's been for ever since a Brit won and I would love to change that. But, luckily, the last thing I'm thinking about on court at Wimbledon is the last time someone British won.

There's a chance I can win in 2008, but I'm not saying I'm going to. I'm definitely a better player than I was two years ago when I beat Andy Roddick, a Wimbledon finalist. It's possible, it's definitely possible, but there's a difference between having a slight chance of winning and actually doing it.

It won't be easy. Not with Roger Federer in the way, plus Nadal, Djokovic, Karlovic, Ancic, Roddick and all the guys who now play well on grass because it's not as fast as it used to be. I reckon there will be seven or eight guys going into Wimbledon this year who think they have a chance. The best thing I can say is that, all being well, I'll be one of them.

Chapter Twelve:
Me

I cannot give you the formula for success, but I can give you the formula for failure – which is: Try to please everybody.

Herbert Bayard Swope

I have never met Mr Swope. I don't know anything about him except I really like that quote. It sums up the way I feel. It also explains why I wanted to write this book when some people might think I am too young to have strong opinions. I don't think I am too young. In fact, I think I have pretty much mastered the art of having strong opinions.

Many things have been written and said about me that I wasn't happy with because they didn't reflect the person I am. Being able to tell my own story in this book has provided me with a very good opportunity to get my views across without any media distortion. Obviously, I have done some bad things in my time on the tennis tour, but at least now you know why I did them. It is not because I am naturally rude, or anti-English, or sexist; it is because I made mistakes as everyone does and then watched, amazed, as they were dramatised beyond all reality.

In no way am I saying that I'm perfect, but I would say that many things have happened to me that haven't been particularly fair. If I say to someone in the newspaper business: 'I'm really disappointed with what you wrote about me,' they are going to say: 'Really sorry,' and carry on acting like they're my best friend. Nothing happens about it. You don't have the luxury of saying 'That's absolute bollocks' in public after they get something wrong. Well, that's fine. But I wanted to get my side across too, and this book is the way I chose to do it.

It's not about making people like me. I know I'm not going to be everyone's favourite person – there are very few people in the world that absolutely everyone likes. It's not about being popular, it's about being me. When you are in the sporting spotlight, sometimes you deserve the chance to explain yourself. So this is it: I'm explaining myself. It is not to make you like me; it is hopefully to make you understand me a bit better.

One way of doing that, I thought, would be the sporting Q and A list. I often get asked to do these and it is a pretty good way of getting to know someone quickly. It might help to explain a few things about me and will probably convince you I've got an immature sense of humour, but it's still worth a try.

ANDY MURRAY'S QUESTIONNAIRE

Q: Favourite tournament?
A: US Open.

Q: Favourite tennis shot?
A: Drop shot.

Q: Greatest sporting moment?
A: Winning my first tournament in San José, 2006, beating Lleyton Hewitt in the final.

Q: Most difficult opponent?
A: Rafa Nadal.

Q: Best insult ever hurled at you?
A: 'Scottish wanker' was a good one.

Q: Favourite film?
A: *The Shawshank Redemption* and *Braveheart*, also comedies like *Wedding Crashers* and *Old School*.

Q: Favourite computer game?
A: Pro Evolution Soccer.

Q: Favourite music?
A: RnB.

Q: How many books have you read in your life?
A: I hate reading. Sometimes I scroll through books on the computer but only sports ones.

Q: If you weren't a tennis player, what would you be?
A: Footballer.

Q: What bores you?
A: Plane journeys.

Q: What's the worst thing about your job?

A: Not seeing family and friends that much.

Q: What's the best thing about your job?

A: Seeing new places all the time.

Q: What three things would you rescue if your apartment was on fire?

A: My sofa – so comfy – my wallet and PlayStation 3.

Q: What does life after tennis hold for you?

A: I'm interested in property and school sports.

Q: Which sport do you like least?

A: Bowling.

Q: What was your favourite subject at school?

A: Maths.

Q: What was the naughtiest thing you ever did at school?

A: Missing every homework I was ever given. I hated it.

Q: Have you ever seen a snake in your house?

A: Yes.

Q: Who is the sportsperson you most admire?

A: Muhammad Ali.

Q: Will you vote in the next election?

A: Probably not.

Q: Do you have any phobias?

A: Not really, but I don't like it when my limbs feel pinned down.

Q: Do you still get marriage proposals?

A: I haven't for a while. The last one was at Wimbledon 2006 – a girl came up with a banner that said 'Andy, will you Murray me!'

Q: Favourite holiday destination?

A: Miami.

Q: Favourite country?

A: I do like the States. Australia is very relaxed too.

Q: Favourite food?

A: Japanese.

Q: What's the best practical joke you've played on a mate?

A: Hiding his passport the day before he was leaving on a trip – his parents turned his room upside down.

Q: Do you think Scotland will ever make the football World Cup again?

A: Of course.

Q: Snow or sun?

A: Snow.

Q: Half full or half empty?
A: Half full.

Q: Sharapova or Ivanovic?
A: Sharapova.

Q: *Big Brother* or *Dancing on Ice*?
A: Both poor.

Q: Who is the most impressive person you have ever met?
A: David Beckham was awesome. Very nice, polite and normal as well.

Q: Have you ever considered a ponytail?
A: Never say never. I was close last year!

Q: What do you wear round your neck?
A: It changes. I had a cross, a foot and a little ball for a while. Right now just a ball because the strings broke on the other ones.

Q: If you were an animal, which one would you be?
A: I love dogs but maybe a snake. Something scary.

Q: What is your ambition in tennis?
A: To win a grand slam.

Q: What is your ambition in life more generally?
A: To have a happy family.

Q: What is the thing you most like about yourself?

A: My abs. Ha ha.

Q: What is the thing you most dislike about yourself?

A: My voice. Probably the most boring in Britain.

Q: What is your philosophy of life?

A: See Mr Swope's quote at the start of the chapter.

I was thinking the other day about throwing up. I don't mean throwing up then and there, I mean the time in Barcelona I got completely hammered on vodka, wine and champagne and threw up as an obvious consequence right outside a nightclub. I never drank again. It was, you might say, a formative experience.

It was during my Academy days in Barcelona when I was about sixteen. I was going out to dinner for my friend's birthday and just before I left the house, the son of the family I was staying with asked me if I'd like a drink. I said: 'Yeah, sure' and then, stupidly, left the room to go to the toilet. When I came back, there was this big glass with 'a little bit of vodka and Coke' in it. I drank it down in literally 20 seconds and went to catch the bus into town. I began to feel rather peculiar, which is not surprising considering I'd been given about half a pint of vodka with a few drops of Coke, or so I discovered later.

There were about fifteen or sixteen of us at the dinner, with wine and champagne flowing at the table, so I started drinking that too. It was fairly noticeable that I was not behaving normally by now so the others started feeding me crisps with chocolate cake on them. I didn't care. I knew what was going on and I knew it wasn't good, but I couldn't stop myself.

Then everyone announced they were going to a nightclub. Obviously I wasn't in the best shape to go with them and I had no expectations of getting in either. But I went along, shuffled to the front of the queue and just at that moment in front of the doors with loads of people around, I felt the urgent need to be sick. Instead of moving, I just tried to catch it in my hands. It went down my arms and legs and splashed on my shoes. Unbelievably, the nightclub let me in but I can only imagine that I wasn't a very popular clubber that night.

After that night, I decided it was possible to have fun without being drunk. You lose control and I hate that. I made an arse of myself in front of all my friends and, anyway, I don't like the taste of alcohol.

It is amazing how many things happen to you when you're young that have a knock-on effect when you're older. I always remember being petrified once that my temper had got me into real trouble. I was in the house on my own when I was about seven years old. My dad had gone to pick up Jamie from somewhere and I was on my bed playing a football game on my Nintendo and a PC game on Jamie's laptop at the same time. I'd been playing for a couple of hours and I wasn't winning. It was getting worse and worse and I was starting to get a little bit annoyed.

Then I went a goal down on the Nintendo and a split second later the same thing happened on the PC and that was it. In a fit of rage I whacked the screen of Jamie's laptop and broke it. The screen looked like a smashed windscreen. It was completely bust and I started panicking. I was crying as I phoned my dad and told an outright but necessary lie: 'I was playing on my bed and I just turned round and knocked it off by mistake.' We took it to the shop to try and get it mended, but it was completely dead. Dad probably had to buy Jamie a new one and, because I was so scared, I didn't tell Dad the truth until a couple of years ago – or Jamie, for that matter.

Dad tended to believe me when I was a boy and there was a good reason for that.

'Dad,' I called one day when we were in the house together. 'There's a snake in the house.'

'Be quiet, Andy,' he said crossly. He was on the phone, a business call, and he'd warned me sternly not to make any noise.

'But Dad, there's a snake,' I persisted, somewhat fascinated by the sight of a living, breathing snake slowly making its way along the floor.

He told me to shut up even more crossly than before. Then he came off the phone, looked down, went white and said: 'Oh my God.' He panicked and ran out of the room, and I think he took me with him even though I wanted to touch my new slithering friend by now. He phoned the RSPCA and the police, and it turned out that our neighbours in the adjoining house kept snakes and one of them had escaped, got under the floorboards and into our living room. It wasn't a dangerous one but I wasn't to know that, and anyway a snake's a snake. Since then, Dad has, pretty much, listened with respect to everything I say.

I would describe myself as mischievous rather than wicked growing up, and I always needed something to occupy me. Sitting around reading books wasn't an option. I am pretty much the same now. In Miami this year when we were bored, I started to do quizzes for everyone – not just about tennis, but a bit of everything. I refused to participate because I wanted to be quizmaster – in control – and I was impressed that they were all pretty good.

My favourite question was this one: Who's played more times: McEnroe v Connors or Sampras v Agassi? It's a trick question because they've played exactly the same number of times: thirty-four. Those pairings are probably the two best rivalries in tennis history and they have exactly the same win–loss record: Sampras won 20–14 and so did McEnroe. No one got the right answer.

I'm known as a bit of a statistician. I know pretty much what all the top players on the tour are doing, where they played, when they played, the scores. I couldn't tell you how many times they serve aces or hit forehand winners but I do know what the top players are up to.

If you ask me about Djokovic this season I'd be able to say off the top of my head that he played the Hopman Cup with Jelena Jankovic and lost in the final to the United States because Jankovic was injured. Then obviously fourth, played Gilles Simon, in Indian Wells, lost in the first round of Miami and went out in the semi-finals of Monte Carlo. He played Davis Cup in between against Russia and retired in the third set against Davydenko.

Knowing the players and their records helps me to prepare for matches, because I've always believed that winning the tactical battle is as important as hitting the ball hard. I think what's appealing about my tennis game is that it is not just about generating power off the racket. I like to defend – maybe too much sometimes. I try and use as many shots as I can. I hit flat, use high angles, slice, drop shot, and come to the net sometimes. I think that is the difference between me and lot of the other players right now.

I try and play a smoother game where you have to feel the ball rather than just muscle it. That's why people talk about me having 'good hands'. It's a timing thing. When I first started playing on the tour, it was a style I used all the time. Then I stopped doing it as much, but it's something I want to go back to because it's more fun to play. The alternative is just putting the ball back in court and hoping your opponent will make a mistake. But to me there is far more pleasure to be gained from putting up a high lob when you are pushed back on the defensive – the attacking defensive option is more fun.

I never saw him, but a lot of guys have told me I play like Miloslav Mecir, the Slovakian player they called the 'Big Cat' because of the beautiful way he moved around the court and the misleadingly gentle shots he used. I love watching players who you feel can produce a magical shot out of nowhere.

Obviously, you do need to play aggressively sometimes. For example, when I play someone like Nadal I am ultra-aggressive, coming forward all the time and trying to hit winners. It's about finding the right way to play against each opponent. You need to adapt. I love that about tennis. I love thinking my way to a win as well as just powering the ball over the net.

I think I'm quite bright when it comes to tennis but there is no argument that some people are much more intelligent than me. Kim Sears, my girlfriend, is one of them. I am always saying I don't know what she's doing with me. I met her for the first time at the US Open in 2005 when Mark Petchey intro-duced us. He knew Kim's father, Nigel, who coached Daniela Hantuchova for a few years on the women's tour and we've pretty much been together ever since. I'm lucky. I know she isn't with me because I'm in the spotlight. When we met, I was still playing qualifiers. She also understands the life of a tennis player because her dad is so closely involved with the sport.

I reckon it works as well as it does because we don't see each other all the time. She's away at university studying English and I'm away on tour, so when we get together we've always got stuff to talk about and the relationship always seems a bit fresher. She doesn't want to follow me around on the tour. She wants to have her own career, not just pose in *Hello!* magazine.

Obviously, I'm not much help with her English course – having read only a bit of The Rock's autobiography and a couple of Harry Potter books – but when she did drama I used to help her with her lines. I had to try and speak a bit of Shakespeare – *Measure for Measure*, she said it was – but I had no idea what I was talking about.

She is probably my first serious girlfriend and I know that many guys who play professional sport would prefer to go out with a thousand girls rather than just the one. But I think that's the easy option. And you end up having to go to clubs and bars to meet girls, and I'm really not interested in that whole scene.

Kim and I have been together a long time now, but we're still young. We've decided it's best to wait until she finishes her degree and then see what she wants to do. If she decides to go to Australia or somewhere, it's not going to work. But right now it's working really well and I hope it will do so for longer. I want the relationship to work. A happy family means a lot to me.

I accept that I see things differently from a lot of people my age. It isn't that I have anything against people who want to go drinking and find as many girls as they can – I know that's what most guys of my age do. I don't disagree with it, but it doesn't interest me that much. I don't know whether that's because I've got an older head on my shoulders or because I'm lucky enough to have Kim, but the last thing I'd want to do is go out looking for women.

I know a lot of people in their thirties who just can't get out of the habit. They say: 'I wanna settle down, I wanna settle down,' but they're still going to bars. It's tough to snap out of it. I'd hate to get to that age and think: 'Oh, I screwed up the only girl I ever really liked because I wanted to go and be with six or seven other girls.' I think you'd look back and regret it.

Maybe it is boring. This might be a boring way of looking at things. But, in the long run, I think I'm going to be much happier. And, anyway, the *last* thing I feel like doing when I come home from running ten 400-metre races is going out to a club, listening to unbelievably loud music, with a wall of smoke in my face on the way in and out, and people throwing up on me. That's not really my idea of relaxing.

I have quite a few pet irritations, but the worst by a long way is snoring. I absolutely hate it and I think it's totally unacceptable. I've never snored and I've always hated it when people around me do. In my life, I've had to share so many rooms and planes with other people, and if you are stuck there with someone who snores, it's a race to get to sleep before they do. Then you don't fall asleep because you're trying too hard and you end up being awake all night.

This is one of the things Matt Little and I argue about (one of many, many things). He says: 'I don't care if I snore.' And I say: 'Well, you should care because the people you're sleeping with can't sleep.' Then he says: 'How am I supposed to know when I'm snoring if I'm asleep?' And I say: 'You shouldn't lie on your back in bed. That's why people snore.'

We're always having arguments. We had an awful one the other day because he's a very average driver and we were driving into a tennis club with a narrow entrance road. He was looking way off to the right, while another car was coming head-on. 'Watch out,' I shouted. He just missed the car, we went off the road a little bit and he then said to me: 'Stop having a go at me when you haven't even got your licence.'

I said: 'Just because you haven't got your licence, doesn't mean you're a bad driver. I would rather be in a car with Lewis Hamilton before he passed his test than be in the car with you.'

'No way, they haven't got the experience.'

'Not the point. They know how to control a car.'

'No, no, no . . .' And so it goes on. Naturally, we then had to consult all the people around us for their opinion and then everyone was arguing. I think most of the time Matt does it just to wind everyone up. He takes what you say and then argues the exact opposite, whether he believes it or not. I accused him of that once and he denied it, but then I realised we were now having arguments about our arguments. It's funny. He does it most of the time to create a laugh, and he's loads of fun to have around. To have someone like that travelling with you is so good for morale.

But just to finish the argument, I have actually been in a car with an F1 driver and I can promise you that Nick Heidfeld, who drives for the BMW Sauber team, is a better driver than Matt Little. Driving with Nick was one of the scariest things I've ever done. We didn't have any helmets on and it was just a regular car he was driving round a track. But the speed was incredible. We were coming up to a corner, and I was thinking: 'Slow down . . . slow down', only there wasn't much slowing down going on – he decided to skid the car and it glided round the corner instead. It was not that comfortable.

I am not scared by much, as a rule. I'm not a huge fan of flying, but bugs, heights and, obviously, snakes don't bother me. I am not claustrophobic but I do hate not being able to move my arms and legs. I used to hate it when everyone jumped on top of me when I scored a goal in football.

I think it stems from the time I was swimming in a pool after some junior tennis tournament and a couple of older boys decided it would be really funny to dunk my head underwater. They did it for way too long and I couldn't move. I started to panic a little bit because I couldn't breathe. Normally kids do this kind of thing but it never lasts longer than 5 or 10 seconds. This felt like 30–40 seconds. Since then I've hated not being in control of my limbs. Control is one of my themes, I know. I like being in control of my life, that's for sure.

In some ways, I'm quite sensible by nature. I remember at the Sanchez-Casal Academy when the ice cream machine wasn't properly locked and loads of the guys nicked all the boxes of ice cream to hide in the fridges and freezers that some of them had in their rooms. But it was a totally stupid idea because there was no way they could fit them all in. Then they decided to hide all the extra cartons in their ceilings – they had those temporary slabs you could move – and they forgot about them so the ice cream melted and it was disgusting. As if the adults wouldn't realise that the twenty kids living five feet away from the broken machine were the ones responsible! But just before I sound too good to be true, I had better confess that the main reason I didn't steal the fruit pastille lollies I loved was nothing to do with morality: I didn't have a fridge.

Another thing I ought to do is apologise to Arantxa, the poor woman who was supposed to look after our corridor at the Academy. Carlos and I must have driven her mad playing Pro Evolution Soccer in his room on my PlayStation until two, three, four in the morning. Her room was at least 50 metres away, but we made so much noise when one of us scored a goal or missed an easy chance that we would disturb her sleep. As soon as we heard her footsteps down the wooden corridor, we'd switch off the screen, turn out the lights and I'd hide under Carlos's bed or in the wardrobe. She'd come in and find all mysteriously quiet and then go off again.

I'll never forget the night we heard those footsteps coming again. Usual ploy: screen off, lights outs, and me under the bed. She just opened the door, took the PlayStation, and left the room without a word. I had to admire her. She didn't give it back to us for quite a while either.

Contrary to my image, I do have a sense of humour. *The Office* is one of my favourite comedies and David Brent is simply the funniest character ever invented. It is so, so funny how much of an idiot that guy is. Sometimes I meet people who remind me a little bit of him and then I push them to try and say David Brent-ish things without them realising what I'm doing.

But I think the most amazing piece of television I've ever seen was the Christmas Special edition of *Extras* when Ricky Gervais has that famous rant about reality TV. His character is appearing on an episode of *Big Brother* and he suddenly bursts out with:

'And fuck you the makers of this show as well . . . No, the Victorian freak show never went away. Now it's called *Big Brother* or *American Idol* where in the preliminary rounds we wheel out the bewildered to be sniggered at . . . And fuck you for watching this at home. Shame on you. And shame on me . . .'

I watched it and I thought 'Wow.' That speech says everything I feel about the celebrity culture and why I never, ever want to be a celebrity. Maybe people think it's boring that I just want to be normal when I'm off the tennis court, but I don't think there's anything wrong with that.

Tennis is what I do for a few hours a day. The rest of the day, when I'm not playing tennis, I'm not in front of cameras and the only people around me are my friends and family. I'm pretty sure that if I changed and became this moody git that I'm supposed to be, the friends I've had since I was fifteen years old wouldn't be around any more.

It is true that I'm richer than I was at fifteen, but the last thing I've ever thought about on a tennis court is money. You get nervous about winning a tournament; you don't get nervous about winning the $100,000 prize. Money is not the most important thing to me, but I don't want to sound ungrateful. I do feel I am lucky to have done sufficiently well in my sport that I could buy my penthouse apartment with a roof garden in Wandsworth, and think about buying one in Miami too. One day I think I'd like a house in Surrey but I am not so sure about taking off to live in tax exile somewhere, because the money that you gain might be offset by the amount of time you miss with family and friends.

I've been asked in press conferences if I'm 'tight' because I'm Scottish. It makes me furious because it is obviously some sort of stereotyping. I answer back: 'I'm not going to say anything about the Scots being stereotypically mean. I'm surprised you're even allowed to ask that. If I said something negative about the English, I'd be absolutely slammed for it and you're sitting here in a press conference saying I am tight because I'm Scottish.' I'm never very happy about that.

And, no, I don't think I'm mean. I really enjoy buying presents, even makeup, but I draw the line at underwear. No chance. On myself, I haven't spent shocking sums of money but that's because I don't need anything. In America last December, I did buy a Mercedes sports car for Kim as a surprise Christmas present then promptly ruined the surprise.

You know how it is when you wake up after dreaming and your thoughts are still all jumbled up. I opened my eyes one morning while we were staying at Nick Bollettieri's academy in Florida and the first thing I said was:

'Do you like your Mercedes?'

She was saying: 'What?! What are you talking about?' To make it worse, I was still so dozy, I mentioned it again on the way to breakfast. I think maybe the complications of buying a car in a foreign country were preying on my mind and I just couldn't keep my mouth shut. Perhaps that, in some ways, is the story of my life.

Yes, I do get annoyed on court. Yes, I have done and said things I shouldn't – I am not disputing that at all, and I want to get rid of that behaviour. But many of the best players in the world in all the big sports have the same sort of hate-to-lose mentality as me and it does take them a while to get out of it. Federer is a perfect example. He was swearing and smashing rackets when he was a teenager. Even Tiger Woods is sometimes done a favour by the television companies when they turn their cameras away as he rants about a bad shot. Perhaps that is all it takes: just be as good as Tiger Woods and then everyone wants to keep you happy.

There are ways of getting around the problem of swearing out loud. After a long rally, you can use any word you like at the top of your voice when the crowd is applauding and cheering. I've just got to learn not to do it when I'm standing next to a microphone. Anyway, I don't think I've ever met anybody who doesn't swear about something, even if it's just dropping a glass. OK, maybe my gran doesn't – I'll have to ask my mum (who does).

When I first started on the tour, I had no idea about all the things that go with playing sport at the highest level. As you start to understand it a bit more, you try to protect yourself, and so your true personality doesn't come across any more. At that amazing first Wimbledon, I was described as 'a breath of fresh air' and they said how great it was to see such emotion on the court. That all changed pretty quickly and soon I was portrayed as a brat with appalling manners.

I'd like somehow to go back to the way it used to be with the press. I could be natural and they would be realistic in their portrayal of me. Tim managed all the attention in his own way and suppressed his personality completely. Few people saw his sense of humour and how nice he was. I don't really want to do that. I'd like to be me and trust the media to report me fairly – that's all.

There's a long way to go. I've still got another ten to fifteen years as a professional tennis player, all being well. Some people talk about me being a Pied Piper for British tennis, encouraging other young players, but I don't really think that will happen. I do believe it's important in sport to have some-one that kids can watch at the bigger tournaments, but I think the problems of British tennis go way deeper than that. It starts at clubs and schools and it is vital that kids are encouraged to play and continue to play just because they enjoy it.

I'm always being asked by parents of young tennis players what advice I would give to them. The only thing I can really say is that their children must get fun out of it. The more relentless drilling of young talent has worked in places like Russia but I don't agree with forcing kids to play tennis. When I was younger I played many different types of sport and that was really fun. The most important thing a kid should be thinking when they turn up for a lesson or at camp is: 'I'm going to love every second of this.' Often they don't. At thirteen or fourteen I would far rather have played football with my mates than have a one-on-one session with a coach.

I am not saying I don't want to be a role model – I am happy with that. When kids are already into tennis, it helps to have someone to look up to. But I am not going to make any difference to the six-, seven-, eight- and nine-year-olds in Britain. They just want to enjoy themselves and it doesn't bother them whether I've won a tournament in Marseilles or not.

I do think about this and one of the things I want to do in the future is to set up a foundation or a charity to fund a school, eventually more than one, that treats sport as seriously as the academic side. I'd have loved that when I was at school, because I adored playing sport and wasn't much interested in the classroom. I had to be allowed out of lessons to train. In countries like Australia and America they really value sport, and I would really like to do something to encourage a more positive view in the UK. We think sport is great in this country and yet we do so little to promote it to kids. I'd really like to help with something like that.

As for my immediate future, I think the most important thing I can say to people is just please give me some patience and time. I think I am still pretty young at twenty-one. There are players who have done great things at that age, no question

– Boris Becker was seventeen when he won his first Wimbledon, and Rafa Nadal has three French Open titles already. But I've always said I have a different game from most people's and it might take me a bit longer to get it together.

Matt Little had this sheet of statistics the other day – he is useful for something, after all. It showed every player in the Top 100 and their rankings since they were teenagers. The average age for peaking was twenty-three to twenty-five. That makes sense to me. That is when you are at your strongest physically, and more mature mentally.

So just try to be patient with me. If it wasn't for my wrist injury last year, I think I'd be ranked much higher already. But I'm still in the World Top 20 – not bad for someone my age. Obviously, I'd like to be better and I plan on winning a grand slam in my career. That's what I'm working towards. I'm not saying this year or next year, but it is what I'm aiming to do. And, believe me, I'll give it my best shot.

Chapter Thirteen:
The Next Step

A year has gone by. Fast. I come back to write this as someone who has done a lot of growing up. I think I'm a little wiser, more mature, more able to cope with all the things that life on the tennis tour throws at you. I no longer get riled by misunderstandings with the media. I just don't give them anything to misunderstand. You can make jokes about yourself but never about anything or anyone else. I've even put my spat with the BBC behind me and am definitely improving my time-keeping! That doesn't mean I'm not late sometimes. Just before Wimbledon I was due to appear live on Radio Five in front of an audience of about a hundred people and the only thing that held me up was the traffic at the Hammersmith roundabout. I had to jump out of the car and leg it to the studios but I made it in the end and actually enjoyed it. That is how much I've changed.

I have a lot of fun off the court these days. I play ridiculous practical jokes on the guys in my team like making them wear a skirt or a chest wig to dinner as a forfeit for losing at tennis football. Luckily I don't lose too often but I have been known to go out with my clothes on inside out! By Wimbledon 2009

I felt I'd learned to take a few more things in my stride. If I could scrub up well enough to stand on a catwalk to model my new outfit for Wimbledon, it proved to me that I'd come a long way in twelve months.

I've moved on and I think I can thank Maggie, my little border terrier, for that. Maggie came into my life – or, to be strictly accurate, into Kim's life – as a twenty-first birthday present, but I immediately claimed dual ownership. Getting Maggie – named after our favourite record, Rod Stewart's 'Maggie May' – was probably one of the happiest days of my life. I've always loved dogs. We play games. I hide under the duvet in the flat and she burrows underneath to find me. I chase her on Wimbledon Common and it's not entirely clear which one of us is having a better time; I've even taught her to jump up and lick my face. Sometimes Kim brings her to meet me at the airport when i come home from tournaments and Maggie gets so excited she usually pees all over my trainers. She's made a big difference to my general happiness. I'm a lot more relaxed these days!

The most obvious example of my maturity was Wimbledon 2008 which came after a run of absolutely average form on the European clay. We still had issues, the red clay and me. Despite those formative years in Spain, I was still slightly awkward in my movement on the stuff and impatient to finish points while the genuine clay-courters understood that you can spend hours out there just building a point.

I lost in the third round of Monte Carlo (badly, to Djokovic), the second round of Barcelona (Ancic), the second round of Rome (Wawrinka), the third round of Hamburg (a trouncing by Nadal) and then it was straight into the French Open. My first opponent was a French leftie, Jonathan Eysseric, ranked about

300, and it took me five sets to beat him. This was not exactly encouraging and I was right not to be encouraged. I lost in the third round to a tough Spanish clay-courter Nicolas Almagro.

The one good thing about that early loss was coming home to practise for Queen's Club. I thought my luck was changing when Sebastien Grosjean, twice Wimbledon semi-finalist, had to pull out of our match with an injury with me leading two games to love. Then the luck changed back again and I had to grant Andy Roddick a walk-over in the quarter-final when I injured my thumb after a fall in my match against Ernests Gulbis.

So now what would happen? Would it get better in time for Wimbledon? Had I gained enough match practice from my disappointing lead up to the summer? With no Tim Henman this year to deflect the patriotic attention away from me, how would I be received? I took Maggie for walks and wondered what it would be like.

I have a feeling that one day I'll look back and see that Wimbledon 2008 changed my life in some crucial way. It certainly changed my image. Before the Richard Gasquet match people tell me I was mostly seen as a bad-tempered Scottish brat who needed a hair cut. After the Gasquet match I became a much more acceptable British tennis player. But I still needed a haircut.

By mounting such a fight back against Gasquet, from two sets and a break down, something seemed to change in my relationship between me and the Wimbledon crowd. There was a huge momentum shift in the match when I could almost feel him wavering. He'd outplayed me for nearly three sets and then he double faulted trying to serve out for the match. It was his first hint of vulnerability. If you want to be a champion you have to be ruthless at times like that.

You have to take your chances. I won that third set with a backhand from so far out of the tramlines I basically finished up in the crowd. I wish I could remember more about it. Most matches I can tell you virtually every point of every set. But some – strangely – go missing. I can't remember things in detail about the Gasquet match at all. My memory must have been messed up by the massive adrenaline rush I felt as I stood there roaring at the crowd while the 15,000-crowd roared back at me. It was electric.

It was getting darker and darker as we went later into the evening, a likely three-setter now turning into five. The flash bulbs from hundreds of cameras were getting brighter in the gloom. Richard was complaining about the light. By the end of the match it almost seemed pitch black and the noise from the crowd was incredible.

I know the 'muscles' gesture was misread in some quarters but I don't apologise for it. I pulled up the sleeve of my tennis shirt and demonstrated, if I say so myself, a pretty decent bicep. I hadn't planned it. I wasn't showing off. It wasn't intended to strike fear into the tennis world. It was just a message to the guys in my corner to say: 'We've trained so hard, done so much work on speed and strength and this is my chance to show you that it has all paid off.' I suppose you might call it a 'thank you'.

When I went home that night to my flat in Wandsworth, I didn't feel physically tired, but I was so emotionally drained. One of the guys went out for sushi. I munched that and went to bed. No time for celebrations. Rafa Nadal, world number two, was up next. I'd made it to my first grand slam quarter-final, a little piece of history for me, soon to be trumped by Rafa's own epic progress to a second successive Wimbledon crown.

Good news, I'd reached the Wimbledon quarter-final, my first grand slam last eight, an achievement beyond my ranking at the time just outside the World Top 10. Bad news, Rafa was on fire and won in straight sets 6-3 6-2 6-4. A match that had been billed as the Battle of the Biceps (well, I asked for that) wasn't much of a battle at all.

I don't know why. It might have been a reaction to the marathon five-setter against Gasquet; it might have been the weight of shot from my opponent. It was disappointing but I wasn't dejected for long. Victories are what you play for but from defeats, you always learn.

I learned that against the top guys you have to be more aggressive from the very first ball. If you're a bit passive they'll make you do so much running, that you can't work yourself into a position to dictate the rallies.

But once the sting of the defeat subsided I realised that this was the most enjoyable Wimbledon I'd ever had. I had awesome support at my matches and I felt confident that next year I could do even better. More than that, I came away convinced I could string seven matches together and win Wimbledon one day.

I was even more convinced two months later when I defeated Nadal in the semi-final of the US Open, my most satisfying victory of 2008. For more reasons than one.

The Beijing Olympics in August had been a disaster. My fault totally. I screwed up. Annoyingly, the whole episode began a week earlier with one of the best results of my career, beating Djokovic (for the second time in successive tournaments) in the final of the Cincinnati Masters. He was an important scalp and that was a huge result for me. He led me 4–0 in head-to-head matches going into this American hard-court season. He'd beaten me easily three times in a row. That hurt because he was my exact contemporary. Our birthdays are only one week apart. If I'm honest, the manner of those defeats was the trigger for me to get fit. I knew I had to get stronger if I was going to compete at the highest level.

So those two victories over Djokovic were the demonstration of the growing strength that I needed. In Cincinnati the conditions were brutal – the court thermometer showed 104 degrees – but I hung in there and won in two long tie-break sets. That pleased me, but there followed a catalogue of self-inflicted errors that led to my miserable Olympic defeat.

Basically, I missed my plane. By the time I'd finished my media commitments after the final and arrived at the airport for my flight via Heathrow to Beijing, the plane was long gone. I had to wait for the next one and that one was delayed. As it happened, both delayed and bust. Six hours we had to wait while they were fixing the engine. We had to literally sit there and watch men in overalls trying to mend it. It was horrible.

We took off finally about 2.30am and I took a sleeping pill because I had so much travelling to do. I missed a couple of meals, didn't drink properly and became thoroughly dehydrated. Then I had another ten-hour flight, complete with an eight- or nine-hour time change.

When I arrived in Beijing obviously I wanted to be part of the Opening Ceremony. You cannot be at an Olympics and not want to be part of a gathering so vast and memorable. But it was stinking hot and so humid, and, having never done it before, I didn't realise it would take about five hours in total. After all that travelling and lack of proper food, I was now sweating loads and it was a late night. Three days after the Opening Ceremony I came out to play the first Olympic match of my life against Yen-Hsun Lu (ranked 77th) of Taipei and, basically, I was in terrible shape. I lost horribly in straight sets. Then I showered, crashed out to sleep for three hours and came back on court to lose the doubles with my brother, Jamie.

I was totally devastated. I was gone. One of the worst things about it was the perception from some people that I didn't care. I did. I cared passionately. Look at Federer. He was knocked out of the singles in Beijing by James Blake, a player he'd never lost to in his life. Sometimes it is possible to want something too much. But he was pumped up to win an Olympic gold medal, he ended up winning with doubles with Wawrinka. It may not be a grand slam event, but we understand that Olympic tennis can be just a once-in-a-lifetime experience. I may be lucky. I may have 2012. If I do you can be sure I won't walk on to the court a dehydrated wreck next time.

I may be an individual athlete, but I am used to operating in a team. Miles, my coach, was allowed to stay in the Olympic Village with me but it probably didn't help that neither Matt, one of my fitness trainers, nor, Andy, my physio, were able to join us. That might sound like an excuse and I make none. I was wrong. I have to take ultimate responsibility for looking after myself, and from now on, I make sure I do.

Next morning I went to weigh myself and I'd lost 4–5 kilos. I thought: 'What the hell am I doing. I've so screwed up here and it's all my own fault'. I was just really annoyed at myself and I make sure now I never fly without high protein drinks nor go through long periods of time without eating properly. The harder the experiences, the more you learn from them.

Maybe I'm a fast learner because I am convinced the Olympic experience stung me into form that took me all the way to my first major final at the US Open, still my favourite tournament. I had something to prove and I would rate my best performance of the year as the semi-final victory over Rafa Nadal. Four sets of outstanding tennis over two days in all weathers on two different courts. After the relatively easy victory he had over me at Wimbledon this was an awesome feeling. 'Revenge' might be too strong a word. 'Vindication' might be closer.

I just felt comfortable, fresh and mentally tough. I was more aggressive, took more chances. I always had the belief I could beat him but I went into the match with him leading our meetings 5–0. Sometimes when a player loses over and over again to the same guy, there comes a time when he almost expects to lose as he walks on court. I didn't feel like that. I wanted to introduce doubt into his mind. With this win, I accomplished that. It was very important for me.

That night I went out in Manhattan with the guys and Kim for dinner – shrimp starter, as usual, and a steak – and felt as satisfied as you could looking ahead to playing Federer, the four-times reigning US Open Champion, the next day for the title.

I make no apologies for the recurring shrimp–steak combo. You will find many tennis players find a routine and stick to it. I remember hearing that Pete Sampras could stand no noise at night, no glimpse of light and had to sleep in an air-conditioned room chilled to the point of refrigeration. I'm similar. I like a cool room to prevent dehydration and I like to get to bed reasonably early.

As it happens, I slept well the night before the final against Roger. My first grand slam final. I admit it felt a little strange in the locker room before the match. Not specifically because it was the biggest match of my career but because the atmosphere was so different. There was no one around. Everyone had left. The typical bustle and noise of Flushing Meadow had completely transformed into this slightly eerie silence.

For whatever reason, I didn't play my best tennis. Roger won in straight sets in less than two hours. I was disappointed but as I told the crowd afterwards, the tournament as a whole had been the best time of my life.

It wasn't a bad effort, reaching my first grand slam final at twenty-two. Then I nearly made tennis history for good measure. No one has ever won three Masters Series events in a row. Neither have I. But it was a close-run thing: victory in Madrid, same in St Petersburg, quarter-finalist in Paris. The run was halted by David Nalbandian, my old rival from Wimbledon 2005, still a very tough opponent ranked 8th in the world. After 14 consecutive victories I served badly, and probably deserved to lose. But you have to keep everything in perspective.

Going into 2009 ranked 4th in the world, relatively injury free, with a grand slam final experience, a great team around me and a loving and supportive girlfriend meant that things were looking pretty good.

On the whole, they got even better. I beat Nadal again in an exhibition in Abu Dhabi at New Year which maybe doesn't count in the scheme of things but was good for my confidence. I won Doha, beating Federer in the semi-finals. I won Rotterham in February, my third straight victory over Rafa, who was struggling with a knee injury, in the final.

But in the meantime I'd fallen short in the Australian Open, the first major of the year in January, an event for which some British bookmakers had me down as a favourite. I thought that was overstating my case. In my view Rafa Nadal and Roger

Federer are the two greatest tennis players of all time. (Apologies to John McEnroe, especially if I bump into him at Wimbledon). Perhaps I should be dismayed to be pitched into this era of Spanish/Swiss awesome domination, but I don't feel like that at all. It's a great and on-going challenge and I'd rather be here now than at any other point in tennis history. But it also means you have to be a little respectful and realistic when you bandy about words like favourite. Roger noticed: 'It surprises me that the bookies say he's favourite because he's never won a slam,' he said.

I couldn't argue and, unfortunately, I couldn't disprove it either when I lost to the Spanish leftie, Fernando Verdasco, who was on such a hot streak he almost upset Nadal in the semi-finals. It did not quite happen. The Federer v Nadal final was another see-saw classic which ended up with Rafa victorious, Roger in tears and my view of them both being the greatest players ever thoroughly vindicated.

If the general trend for me was upwards, I still had the odd swoop downwards. It felt as though an illness had been stalking me since Australia and, finally, during the tournament in Dubai I was so sick I had to pull out of my match against Gasquet. I flew home and was grounded by the LTA doctor for 7–10 days. The worst thing about it was the connotations for the Davis Cup tie against Ukraine. It was the second time the Cup had been played in Scotland. For the second time I was too ill to compete. Once is unfortunate, twice is a nightmare. But I accepted that certain people might construct a conspiracy theory round it.

After all the controversy of the Argentina tie the year before, this was another let down. I phoned the team captain, John Lloyd, and explained. He understood but the team went on to lose 1–4. I couldn't have played. I lost about 5 kilos and by the last day of the tie I was still stumbling about at home eating nothing but soup. I have to live with the suggestions that I don't care about the Davis Cup. I do. I care very much about playing for my country and one day I hope that will become more apparent.

I can't explain what it is about me and the United States but as soon as I arrived at Indian Wells in March I felt energised. I've always loved the bold, brash atmosphere of New York. Now it turned out California in the spring time was pretty good for me too. I reached the final and, although I lost comfortably to a rejuvenated Nadal, I compensated a couple of weeks later by defeating Djokovic (again in straight sets) in the final of Miami. With that victory I equalled the number of tournaments (11) won by Tim Henman which may have been something I mentioned in a text to him later.

Miami was also memorable because the organisers set up for me to have a knockabout game of street tennis with Venus Williams out on Ocean Drive to pre-promote the tournament. By the time Venus and I arrived there was a big crowd including a large group of TV crews and reporters and it was scorching hot. We jumped up onto the roof of a couple of cars and started to play. It was great fun, though not necessarily something I'd recommend to anyone who is looking to seriously improve their tennis technique! The publicity shots from this were published around the world, which was great as it showed that anyone can play tennis on a street just as easy as they can kick a football around. You don't have to join a club, or to be wealthy; all you need is a racket and a couple of tennis balls.

I was entering the clay-court season with my confidence as

high as it had ever been despite having very little time to prepare on the dirt and the results were genuinely encouraging. Alex Corretja joined the team again in Monte Carlo and persuaded me to stop treating the surface so gingerly. I tried to move and slide better and hit more patiently. Reaching the second week of the French Open was a real breakthrough.

I lost in the quarter-finals to an extremely useful clay-courter, the Chilean, Fernando Gonzalez, who was a set away from reaching the final. There was no shame in that. To my mind, it was a good effort but I have to accept the fact that the expectations on me can still be unrealistic. I'd barely won a match on clay in my life and yet here were people mildly annoyed I hadn't walked into Roland Garros and won.

In fact, I came away upbeat. It was a decent result and we had taught Alex Corretja, one of the all-time great clay-court competitors, to play a decent game of tennis football on the Roland Garros courts. He might have thought it was sacrilege at first, but he seemed to get over that.

An event that amazed the tennis world then happened: Rafa Nadal did not win the French Open. He had not lost a match there in five years, he was four-times champion, but this time he crashed into Robin Soderling who was on ridiculous form. What struck me was Nadal's attitude after his fourth round defeat. 'You need a defeat to give the value to your victories,' he said.

It was a great line, a consolation to himself and a reminder to me that what I most wanted was a grand slam victory to give value to my defeats. I was getting closer and closer. My goal in tennis was now utterly focused on winning a major. Becoming a grand slam champion was the only goal I had left for myself going into 2009. OK, that and passing my driving test.

It's a funny thing about tennis players. We often have cars before we can drive. I think I heard that Jennifer Capriati had a huge car at thirteen. I wasn't that bad. I bought my Range Rover Sport in 2008 but I never seemed to find the time to take lessons. It was a little annoying but I reckoned I would get around to it sometime. I suppose I could have a limo and driver everywhere, but no part of me wants that kind of celebrity lifestyle.

That was the first thing I told Simon Fuller, head of the management company, 19, that looks after David Beckham. He came round to my flat on his own and we just talked. I said: 'For me it's not about being a celebrity, it's about becoming the best tennis player I can be.' I told him that I don't want people to think I'm a fake person. I want people to appreciate what I do on the tennis court. To enjoy the way I play. I work hard and I'm dedicated. That is the person I would like people to see, not someone who goes to movie premieres and famous restaurants. That just isn't me. If there was a red carpet in someone's house I'd probably go round it.

Simon took all that on board and the change of management companies has worked very well for me. There is no criticism of Patricio Apey and ACE Group, but I think maybe like coaching, there comes a time for a change. I'm really happy with the way things are going. I've learned so much from them about the importance of image and planning for the long term. 19 have great people covering every aspect of the business and it's good to know my off-court stuff is in such good hands.

I don't want to make it sound like I'm some kind of hermit, nor a hypocrite either. Meeting great people is no bad thing. At the US Open semi-final I suddenly noticed on the giant screen that my favourite comedy actor, Will Ferrell, was in the crowd watching me. He even rolled up his sleeve and kissed his bicep, so I knew he was on my side! That was a weird moment. My brain took time out of the game just to register: 'Wow!' I met him afterwards and even though it was all a blur, I came away with the thought that he was a very good guy.

Then I joined up with David Beckham for the Malaria No More charity as a UK ambassador, something I was pleased to do because nearly one million people die of malaria every year. The charity tries to tackle the disease head-on, and by treating the disease and providing bed nets they say it's possible to reduce the death toll to zero by 2015.

They invited me to launch the campaign at Wembley Stadium with David where the world's largest mosquito net was hung across the pitch. I met David for the first time in one of the Wembley dressing rooms. It was the day after the FA Cup Final when Manchester United had beaten Everton and there were huge posters of Sir Alex Ferguson and David Moyes everywhere. David was completely at home and gave me a short guided tour before leading me out to the pitch.

We had time for a quick tennis knockabout and he was pretty good at getting the ball back. The day was completed by a visit to 10 Downing Street to meet the Prime Minister, Gordon Brown. A protest demonstration outside Parliament had closed one of the roads, so we were ferried in the back way. Mr Brown was there to meet us and he showed us around the Cabinet Room before taking us upstairs for the meeting with the charity.

This was all slightly surreal to me but I came away with the feeling that Mr Brown was a very nice person trying to do his best. I didn't feel sorry for him exactly but he has such a tough job. I couldn't believe he knew so much about what I'd been doing when there was swine flu and the recession to deal with. It makes me continually aware that you can't always believe what you read in the papers. Maybe I'm a little bit more sympathetic on his behalf because I discovered the hard way what it's like to be misinterpreted.

As for David, he's a really decent guy. He gave me a pair of his football boots which I immediately tried on and took some extremely average free kicks.

I'm glad Matt Little wasn't there, he'd have given me serious grief. I know a lot of people thought I was employing 'yes men' when I stopped working with Brad Gilbert and put together a team to travel round the world with me. I would say my decision has been proved right.

I never wanted or had 'yes men' or a bunch of friends to agree with every word I said and fall in with everything I wanted. I would hope if I was acting up they'd tell me. When I started pushing myself with Jez Green, I said: 'Look I've spent the last two years not pushing myself as hard as I should. If I don't do a session properly I want you to tell me straight out. Tell me: "Your attitude's wrong." Don't let me get away with anything.'

It's only happened once so far. There was one occasion when, trying to do ten 200-metre sprints, I wasn't able to complete the session. I ground to a complete halt after seven. I don't know what was wrong but I just couldn't do it. I was too tired. We sat down for ten minutes, had a chat, and then I somehow staggered through the rest of it. At least I finished.

Actually, it happened one other time as well, just before Wimbledon 2008. It was one of Jez's little tortures, attempting five 400 metres under 70 seconds each with just 140 seconds rest in between. It's pretty brutal but I enjoy the challenge. I did the first one in 63 seconds which was way too fast. The second in 67 seconds, the third in 69. Then I lay on the ground, just staring at the sky, completely gone. I wasn't getting enough oxygen. I didn't know where I was or what was going on. This was five days before Wimbledon. It wasn't good.

I decided to cut down on near-death experiences. Before Wimbledon 2009 . . .

By the beginning of May I had achieved another small milestone. I was now ranked number three in the world. It was nice but not any major cause for celebration. For a start, I was sitting at home watching TV when it happened. Novak Djokovic lost in the final of the Rome Masters against Rafa Nadal and, because he had won the event the year before, he dropped the few points that allowed me to leapfrog him in the rankings. Can't say I got too excited – reaching the World's Top 100 had meant more to me if I'm honest. If I ever get to number one in the world, I'll celebrate for sure.

History was not exactly on my side walking into Queen's Club for my first (of two) grass court championships of the year. It turned out that no Briton had won the tournament for 71 years, since Bunny Austin in 1938. That made me a bit nervous. I wish no one had told me.

Fortunately, one of the things I have learned to do with age is manage the nerves a whole lot better. Experience teaches you that being nervous is to be expected – if you're not nervous, you're not ready – but it shouldn't affect your game. I had a dream week at Queen's. No injuries, no worries, no dropped sets, and only two breaks of serve the whole week.

I felt good. I was walking on court for every match feeling confident. I beat the Italian Andreas Seppi, Spaniard Guillermo Garcia-Lopez, America's Mardy Fish and Juan Carlos Ferrero of Spain on the way to the final where I came up against the very likeable American James Blake. Except the press had uncovered the fact that his mother's father had once been the village policeman in Banbury, Oxford and were doing their best to turn him into a fellow Brit.

He was a tough opponent with a big serve and huge forehand, but my game on grass had come together so well that I managed to win in straight sets, 7–5 6–4. It was my first grass court victory and twelfth career title. Now I had one more than Tim Henman, which he was nice enough to acknowledge in a text.

But, as for the huge gold trophy, it didn't get anywhere near my mantelpiece, in fact I didn't even get to carry it off court! It was enormous. A bit like a giant FA Cup: unbelievably heavy and not exactly easy to lift. In the end they gave me a plaque to take home which is now on display in my games room alongside the table football, the pool table and my arcade games machine.

That's the other thing I'd done just before Wimbledon – move house. I'm told moving house is one of the most stressful things a human can do, but actually I didn't do a whole lot for it so it was fine. I left my flat in Wandsworth on the Tuesday morning to go training. My mum picked me up from the tennis centre around 6pm and drove me back to the new house. I just didn't get involved! Kim, Maggie and I were moving to a nice, quiet area of Surrey, which is something I've always wanted. I liked the feeling of being out of the way, having somewhere I could relax that was about half an hour by road from Wimbledon.

People wondered why I made the move at a time of maximum pressure, but if they had seen me the year before they would have understood. Wimbledon 2008: I'd get to bed about 1.30am after matches and be woken by the sun flooding in the window of the master bedroom of my penthouse flat in Wandsworth at 6.30am. OK, so then I'd sleep in the bedroom on the other side of the apartment and be woken by the noise of the skips down at the dump next door. Not the best preparation! All things considered, the pressure of the move (none) was a great deal better than that. Most of the rooms were totally bare: we only moved with two beds, a sofa and a coffee table (plus three cuddly toys that the press spotted) but I absolutely loved it straight away.

I realised how lucky I was to be able to do such a thing at twenty-two. Some might say it's extravagant but it's not like I'm into cars or clothes or jewellery or watches. Those things aren't that important to me. But I live in hotels most of the year and I've always wanted to have a nice house where I can have people to stay. I don't really like spending time on my own. I'm told there are quite a few Chelsea players around the same area, but I haven't bumped into them yet.

So the week before Wimbledon was pretty hectic to begin with. My short-lived career as a catwalk model began and ended with me walking on stage in my Fred Perry outfit for the Championships. I wasn't too bad. Maybe I was a little bit awkward but at least I didn't feel like a total prat. It was a coincidence that Fred Perry was the last British man to win Wimbledon way back, in 1936, so, of course, the comparisons were made, but I didn't let the pressure get to me.

I tried to keep the days leading up to Wimbledon very familiar and low-key. I'm pretty good at that, surrounded by my team, family and friends. I didn't even react when the news came through that world number one Rafa Nadal pulled out because of his continuing knee problems. Some people might have thought I'd be celebrating, but no part of me dared think that the task was now easier. It would have been disrespectful to the other guys in the draw. The strength in depth in the men's game is massive now and anything can happen in tennis on any given day, as I was to significantly prove.

I wasn't happy that Rafa was missing. I'm good friends with him. We've known each other a long time and my competitive streak is such that if I win a tournament I want to beat the best players in the world. I really hoped Rafa would be in good shape to come back soon after Wimbledon. One of the best ever, he's a player who gives everything every time he performs. It's such a physical game and he's been on tour for six years already. If he plays four more years that would be a ten-year career, and I reckon he'd be pretty happy with that.

But this was no time to be worrying about Rafa. The newspapers were full of guesswork about whether or not I was ready to win Wimbledon, but I decided to steer clear of reading them throughout the tournament. The hype was everywhere. But hype is just someone else's opinion multiplied by sensation-seeking.

So my fourth Wimbledon campaign began with me no longer a teen outsider with a reputation for being a temperamental Scot. Now I'm the British favourite. Now I'm seeded to reach the final. Now it's serious.

I walked in through the gates early (for me) at 11am, determined not to change my attitude or routine. I'd long since decided to treat Wimbledon as just another tennis tournament, if I could, even though the rest of the country sees it rather differently. So I warmed up with the guys on the indoor courts, playing our usual game of tennis football. Matt lost, which resulted in him walking around with a bin on his head for a minute. This was one of the punishments in our inter-team forfeit system. For a while it became the talk of the media. I was really hoping I wouldn't have to wear anything pink in public while the cameras were pointed at me.

So far, so normal. I practised with Miles for an hour on the Aorangi Courts in the grounds of Wimbledon and could hear the Chilean Fernando Gonzalez being his usual noisy self on a court nearby. Then I went into the gym for a stretch and was delayed a minute or two because I wanted to watch the end of Laura Robson's first senior match at Wimbledon. She lost to Daniela Hantuchova but considering Laura had only just finished her GCSEs, winning a set was a pretty decent effort. I had a feeling I was going to be asked about British tennis in my press conference the following day because, as is all too depressingly common, not many survived day two.

I remember lunch on that first day not because the chicken and pasta were remarkable, but because Matt Little was succumbing to doughnuts so early in the tournament. The banter was flying. My body felt good. I was ready for my first round match against Robert Kendrick, an American, ranked 76th in the world, the next day.

Robbie is a beach boy, appropriately for a Californian. He loves surfing in his spare time, but as a tennis player he's a potentially dangerous opponent who serve-volleys and really gives the ball a smack. This was the sort of match where I would have to concentrate hard. A certain match stood out on his CV when he took Rafa Nadal to five sets in the second round at Wimbledon 2006, hitting thirty-two aces. I'd played him on grass three years ago and won 6–0 6–0, but that kind of history was ancient. People can raise their games anytime at Wimbledon, especially when they have nothing to lose. The place can have that effect, as I can remember from my first visit in 2005. I was wary about this match, and I was right to be.

The rules at Wimbledon mean that only one coach is allowed in the locker room before a match, so we hung out in the nearby gym and just outside it. I prefer having my team around me. It relaxes me. But when the clock struck a minute to five I was walking on to Centre Court alone for my first match of the 2009 Wimbledon campaign. I'd be lying if I said I didn't feel butterflies.

It was warm. The famous new roof had been slightly shut to give the Royal Box a sunshade. I tried not to keep them out there too long but after I won the first set, Robert came back and won the second on a tie-break. That frustrated me. I'd had my chances but while this was not shaping up to be an easy match, I was staying calm. That was the key. In previous years I might have let my nerves overwhelm my game. By now, I knew better. I'd had plenty of experience of tight moments. It was annoying dropping that second set but not disastrous. I won long before the sun went down, 7–5 6–7 6–3 6–4.

As predicted, there were questions about the state of British tennis afterwards because, of all the Brit entries, only Elena Baltacha was still in the singles. I answered honestly. 'It's not great,' I said. 'The depth needs to get way better. It's not acceptable.' I didn't blame any one player. I watched some of them play and they played well. But they just aren't at the same level as many of their opponents.

Someone asked if it put extra pressure on me. I said no and I meant it. Whether there were ten Brits or just one in the tournament, I was going to take care of my own business. I went home pretty satisfied, but it was only the beginning.

Next day, we played tennis football on the indoor courts in

the morning. This time Jez Green had to walk around with a bin on his head. I noticed a girl on the adjacent court looking at us completely bewildered. The joke became even more interesting when Jez earned another forfeit and this time had to dress up like a cricketer at the Aorangi Practice Courts (packed with onlookers). I don't know why he had a cricket helmet with him (unless 6'10" Ivo Karlovic was going to be serving at him later), but he did. We made him walk all the way back to the players' lounge in that gear. The media were fascinated. I just told them he likes cricket.

After lunch I met some kids from the Make-A-Wish charity. I did this last year too and it made a big impression on me. It's obviously so sad to see children with terminal illnesses, but if you can make one day better for them by giving them a chance to see Wimbledon and meet a tennis player, then it's an absolute pleasure to help. I met a boy from Holland and a girl from the States, and we chatted for about fifteen minutes and watched some tennis on the TV in the RBS suite. We took some photos and gave them some of my T-shirts and caps, and I came away – as I did last year – pretty thoughtful. I understand how lucky I am. I am so grateful that I am fit and healthy and able to enjoy so much the profession I'm in.

I had an hour's treatment in the altitude chamber at the National Tennis Centre to round off the day. The final event was a dip in the ice bath. One of the guys had to go under for five seconds, which is seriously ugly. I was only glad it wasn't me.

I must admit, Jez seemed to suffer the worst kinds of punishment as the week went on. On the day of my second round match against Ernests Gulbis, the right-hander from Latvia ranked 73rd in the world, Jez and Miles had to kiss my feet having lost our warm-up game of tennis football. The snappers – as we call the photographers – knew to expect some kind of forfeit. There were back page pictures in the evening papers which made it far, far worse for Jez and therefore far, far funnier for us.

To pass the time before my match – third on Centre Court again (they must know I hate early starts) – I watched some of the Lleyton Hewitt v Juan Martin del Potro match. This really started something. My team and I competed with one another to find tennis player names that sounded like snacks. Things like Juan Martin del Pot Noodle and Mardy Fishcakes. I won't embarrass myself by discussing this further but somehow or other the media found out about it and everyone was offering suggestions on the radio. At Crisp Evert I tuned out.

The match against Gulbis was solid. I served really well, so did he in patches, but I won in straight sets 6–2 7–5 6–3 and someone in the crowd asked me to marry them. It's happened to me a couple of times at Wimbledon but I haven't accepted any offers yet. Not sure how Kim would take it.

In the press conference after the match I talked about the letter I had received from the Queen. She had written to me to say well done for winning Queen's and good luck at Wimbledon. That was the gist of it. I said I kept it separate from my pile of bills at home. The letter had arrived by hand when I was on a practice court. It said: 'To Andy Murray Esquire' on the front and had some sort of seal on the back. It was nice. Not everyone has their monarch writing to them just before they go to work.

Clearly I'm popular with formidable ladies. I got a big hug from my gran when I caught up with her and my grandpa later. They had been watching Jamie win in the mixed doubles. They have never missed a year when Jamie and I have played

Wimbledon. Now people were saying that if I make the final, the Queen might come along too. As far as I was concerned, it was way too early to think about that.

By now I felt I was in my Wimbledon stride. The routine of practice courts in the morning followed by late matches or massage in the afternoon really seemed to suit me. That was until Friday when I lost my first forfeit and had to tidy all the trays at lunchtime, including those on some adjoining tables at the players' restaurant in Aorangi Park. I got a few strange looks from staff, players and guests – must have seemed a bit odd to everyone, or maybe it was because I was a pretty rubbish waiter.

I was keeping life simple; in my own little familiar bubble. Nothing was different on the middle Saturday. More warm-ups, more forfeits, more food, followed by my third round match against Viktor Troicki of Serbia, ranked 31, who broke into the Top 100 last year. I'd never seen him play on grass before so I didn't quite know what to expect.

Anyway, it was decent. I won 6–2 6–3 6–4 in front of an array of Olympians in the Royal Box. To have the chance to play in front of them was nice, and afterwards I met fellow Scot Sir Chris Hoy, who won three gold medals in Beijing. I didn't really know whether to call him Sir and stuff. I think I called him Chris. He must have been fine with that cos he wished me luck for the rest of the tournament.

I had a long conversation with the press after the match. Inevitably they asked me about expectation. All I could say was that they couldn't expect more of me than I did. I had come to win the tournament. I was given a toy border terrier (wearing a pair of trousers and carrying a handbag) afterwards. I wasn't sure what Maggie would make of it. I was pretty sure I would never dress her in trousers.

On the Sunday – an off day at Wimbledon – I had a phone call from Sean Connery just to say 'well done' for the day before. Ever since he watched me from the Royal Box at my first Wimbledon in 2005 he has kept in touch and I really appreciated that.

I hit for an hour at Aorangi Park with Miles and Ross Hutchins, with Stan Wawrinka, my next opponent, on an adjacent court hitting with Andy Roddick. Little did I know then that Andy was preparing hard to go all the way to the semi-finals after an epic quarter-final with Lleyton Hewitt.

But I wasn't thinking about the future. One match at a time. As soon as you start to think about matches beyond the next one, you're in trouble. I wanted to distract myself. So the guys and I headed to Wimbledon village for a chicken baguette lunch at our favourite restaurant. The first people we saw were my mum, gran and grandpa. They left, luckily for Miles, before they could witness him trying to pay for everyone's lunch with his driver's license.

After the weekend, my Wimbledon warmed up in every way you could imagine. The weather was boiling, not so much that it made ice baths a pleasure but enough that spectators were being warned to wear hats. The humidity reminded me of those Bikram yoga sessions I used to do in Miami. I'd never experienced a Wimbledon so consistently hot, and it was just my luck that moments before I was due to go on court to play my friend and fellow go-kart fanatic Stan Wawrinka, the Swiss number two, a few spots of rain had convinced the officials to close the famous Centre Court roof for the first time in the tournament's history.

Our match was going to become a matter of historical record: the first to be played from start to finish under a thousand tonnes of steel and translucent fabric that shut out the night sky. The weather outside was lovely by night-time, but there had been a few rain drops fall on a women's match on the court earlier. They decided to shut the roof. Maybe they just couldn't resist the urge to press the button at last, whether it was raining or not.

People talked about it afterwards as looking like a spaceship. The pictures in the papers the next day were amazing. I admit it looked great.

It did change the conditions of the match, however. Despite the air conditioning, I thought it made the air very humid. I was sweating so much I could hardly hold my racket to serve and the balls seemed heavier. When I came off the court it was as though I'd been in a bath. It took me a while to get going in the first set but I didn't quite manage it. I lost the first set 2–6 and realised I was in for a fight.

Stan and I had played seven times before – I led the series 4–3 – but we had never played a match like this one. We were slugging it out for nearly four hours under the novelty of Centre Court floodlights in a transformed arena that echoed with noise. It was the latest finish in Wimbledon history. The crowd sounded like 150,000 sometimes instead of 15,000. It was a draining, intense experience but one that left me satisfied when I walked off having won 2–6 6–3 6–3 5–7 6–3.

I appreciate it was fraught for the crowd. Mum said the experience of watching it was like 'a cross between sea-sickness and a heart attack'. In my talk to the press after the match I made comments about the different on-court conditions and they made it sound like a complaint or, worse, an excuse. I didn't want that, so I called Ian Ritchie, the Wimbledon chief executive, the next day to smooth things over.

The only point I seriously wanted to make was that there ought to be more warning whether the roof will be on or off. The first word I had was that it *might* be closed. If it was opened there would be a thirty minute delay, if not we'd be straight on. How do you warm up for that? That was my point but I meant it as constructive criticism.

When I came off court I went straight to Andy Ireland for some physio on my legs and Jez went to try and find some food. Not an easy task – because of the late finish, the players' restaurant was closed. I went to meet the press. They asked me if the match had given me more confidence. 'No,' I said. 'I believe I can win Wimbledon. That's not changed since the first match. But I'm going to have to play great tennis to do it.'

The next day it was reported that, desperate for food, we went home via Pizza Express, which had actually closed for the night, but they fired up the ovens again just for me. Whilst this is a good story, the truth was subtly different. In fact, it was Mum and her friend Laura who walked up to Pizza Express, found it closing and then walked on to look for somewhere else. But a manager had recognised Mum and came running out to say they'd been watching my match on television and they would put the ovens on again for her. I'd eaten already, but OK I did share some of theirs. Margherita, nothing fancy.

I know they say you shouldn't eat cheese late at night but I went to sleep at 1.15am and slept like a dream until 10am the next day. I had a chat with Sue Barker on BBC television, having dumped my rackets outside the studio. No sign of Tim Henman, now a BBC pundit, but I did see him a couple of times in the locker room and he sent me a few texts of encouragement.

Obviously, the days of my BBC boycott are over. I'm much more composed now about media responsibilities. It's all part of the job. However, I'm not a completely softened character. If I feel people are rude to me, I won't talk to them, but in the day-to-day operation of player-media relations, I'm willing to play my part. But I'm careful, like Tim, so don't expect me to be controversial.

Next up for me was my Wimbledon quarter-final. It was a significant milestone. This was as far as I reached in the tournament last year when Nadal was just too strong for me. I felt ready to do better this time, but I would have to play well against the former world number one and French Open champion Juan Carlos Ferrero, who had entered the tournament as a wildcard.

His ranking had dropped to seventy after a few years when injury and chicken pox conspired to hamper his game, but I didn't want to take anything for granted. He was nicknamed 'Mosquito' for being so fast around the court, and I had a lot of respect for him as a former world number one and the last Spaniard to reach this stage of the competition.

I arrived at Wimbledon about midday and met up with the guys over at Aorangi. For a while I sat and chatted with my old coach, Leon Smith. He's heavily involved with coaching British juniors and he wanted to pick my brains. Before a forty-five-minute hit I had a massage with Andy Ireland and a laughing fit when Matt Little coughed in the shower and put his back out. Then I had lunch on my own in the locker room. I was keen to avoid the distractions you might find if you sit in the players' main dining room. Funnily enough, the person I was chatting with was my opponent. It won't surprise you to know it was about go-karts. He has a couple of his own that he races and so we were talking about them. It might seem odd, but there's no hatred or jealousy in men's tennis.

Federer had been playing on Centre Court before me, up against the huge-serving, 6'10" giant from Croatia, Ivo Karlovic. But Federer won in straight sets, taking him to his twenty-first consecutive Grand Slam semi-final. In every respect, he was going to be a big act to follow.

The crowd, though, were pretty welcoming when I got out there. I was told later that two Miss Scotlands were watching me. One of them, Katharine Brown, went to school with me in Dunblane and my mum coached her at tennis. I knew the press would go for the angle that a beauty queen was supporting me, but I was just happy that one of my school friends came to watch. I'd seen her at Queen's too and we'd already chatted together.

Among other members of the crowd was the golfer Sergio Garcia, rooting for his good friend Ferrero. I played well, if a little tentatively at the start. My serve was working strongly, I hit eighteen aces and, apart from one spell at the start of the second set, I was really feeling quite comfortable.

I won quickly – 7–5. 6–3 6–2 – and then had the luxury of watching my next opponent, Andy Roddick, get tied up in a long, hard five-setter with Lleyton Hewitt. The longer the better, I thought, while I was getting a massage next to my brother who had just won through to the semi-finals in the mixed doubles with Liezel Huber, his South African-born partner. I was so pleased for him.

The important thing about my Wimbledon semi-final debut was not to think about it. Obviously I could think about tactics and fitness and any other physical detail, but definitely not the occasion. I did a pretty good job of that. Andy Roddick is a nice guy and we managed to distract each other before we went on court by playing a game of computer putting on one of the games consoles in the men's locker room, whilst simultaneously keeping an eye on Roger Federer, who was winning through to the final against Tommy Haas.

I like Andy and I thought I knew what to expect from his tennis: power serving and endless aggression. But I didn't know his serving would be almost perfect on the day. In only the third game he hit a serve at 143mph, the fastest of the tournament. I thought I did well to get it back.

It was a close four-set match. Andy won the first set with a break when I played three bad points to lose my service game at 4–5. I was annoyed with myself and took a toilet break, which in fact gave me time to collect my thoughts. I came back with a clear plan of what I had to do and was ready to go. I won eight of the next nine points and it really was that close right through the match. Andy won a crucial point in the third set tie-break with a forehand volley that flew off the throat of his racket. But that is tennis life. I am not complaining. At one point the umpire mistook what I was saying to myself – 'Come on, pass!' – as an audible obscenity, which in retrospect is funny but wasn't at the time.

After just over three hours, Andy had two match points. I wasn't done. I hadn't given up. I saved the first with a cross-court backhand that made him dive in the old Boris Becker style, but he pulled me well out of position on the next one and my dream of reaching my first Wimbledon final had to retire for another year. I would have loved to have made it, but this wasn't the most disappointed I've ever been. I lost 6–4 4–6 7–6 7–6 but I felt I played a pretty good match. Seven out of ten, I'd say.

After the match, people came up to me and said consolingly: 'Tough luck' or 'You did so well', but I didn't feel up to responding. I think they were right though. I did do pretty well.

I hit more winners than Andy, made less unforced errors and the only difference was a few points here and there. But it was still a defeat. However, competitive people don't like to dwell on defeats so I turned it round. It became the foundation of my motivation. I'd just work harder from now on.

We had a family party at my house on the Sunday after the last match and my two little six-year-old cousins put it all in perspective when they asked: 'Why did you lose, Andy?' I told them that Roddick played better than I did and that was the end of the story. They didn't say anything, they just ran off, jumped in the swimming pool and didn't care.

I felt better by now. It wasn't as though I had let my family and friends down. I hadn't embarrassed myself. I hadn't demonstrated a bad attitude and Maggie still loved me. She was still bringing me her lead and endless smelly socks and dribbling whenever I came through the front door. It was around this time that she swallowed four pebbles – she'll eat anything, including plastic! – and had to have an operation to retrieve two of them from her intestines. (She sicked the other two up.) It was a pretty big operation and came close to maxing out my credit card.

A few days later, everyone was gone. I was by myself, training hard on the exercise bike overlooking the pool. My fitness trainers were both away on holiday and I was feeling really tired. 'It would be much easier to get off and just chill,' my mind tried to tell my body. Then I looked at the scene around me – the new house, the grounds, the view beyond – and I thought: 'OK, hard work has got you this far, don't stop now.' I kept going.

Now I faced a challenge that was going to change my life. Alright, it was only my driving test but it was still going to change my life. Never again would I have to ask for a lift to the shops, the airport or to training, or the running track, or anywhere else further than a five-minute walk. I wouldn't be a nuisance or dependent on anybody else sitting behind a wheel. I could do it myself. All I had to do was pass the test.

There was just one problem. I only had a week. Between the end of Wimbledon and going to America for seven weeks, there was barely time to pack my bags let alone learn to drive. But I took an intensive course where the instructor was with me all day for six days and I could drive to wherever I needed to go for training but then I could practise whenever I had free time. It worked really well and I have to say that I was pretty confident going into the test. Put it this way. I would have been seriously annoyed with myself if I failed.

What happened next was so embarrassing. The first thing you have to do in your driving test is open the bonnet and point out to the examiner simple things like where you would find the oil and the brake fluid. I'd done that a few times with my instructor. I knew what to expect. What I hadn't done was ever actually open the bonnet.

'OK,' said the examiner, 'would you open the bonnet for me please?'

I floundered around with the catch.

'It won't open!' I said in rising panic, painfully aware I hadn't even sat in the driver's seat yet.

'Pull the catch towards you,' advised the examiner in a low voice. I did. It opened. But it was clearly going to be one of those days. Going round a roundabout I was chased by an ambulance, lights flashing, alarm sounding, on call. Then I had cars coming at me from both directions when I was trying to reverse round a corner. Finally, the instructor asked me to 'turn the car round' and I didn't know what he was talking about.

'What's that?' I asked, worried that here was something to be performed I hadn't learned.

'A three-point turn, Andy,' explained my instructor wearily.

'Oh.' OK, I could do that.

It was a wonderful feeling – perhaps an unlikely feeling given the way the whole thing started – when the guy told me I'd passed my test. It definitely wasn't my name or fame that clinched it. He had no clue who I was. 'What do you do?' he said in casual conversation afterwards. I said I played professional sports. He asked which one. It was only when I said 'tennis' that something seemed to register.

So, at last, I was on wheels. My first outing was to drive in my little Volkswagon Polo to the running track where I train. I was so pumped. It was such a relief to be in a car by myself for the first time without the pressure of having to do everything perfectly. I had to make the most of it. The very next day I was going to the States.

Something of that celebratory feeling carried on once I was back on my favourite surface on my favourite circuit in North America. Ever since I was a junior I've loved the atmosphere over there. The first tournament was the Masters event in Montreal, Canada, where I went through to the final (in straight sets every match) to play the giant and improving, twenty-year-old Argentine Juan Martin Del Potro, little knowing that in a month's time he would be crowned the new US Open champion.

It was steaming hot on the day of the final and I was thoroughly glad I had spent the previous two weeks training with Jez Green in the sub-tropical temperatures of Miami. I don't think a cold August in London would have done me much good at the time.

We fought out the first set for over an hour which was eventually won in the tie-break by my younger opponent. But as the heat took its toll, my improved fitness levels began to make a difference. I served three aces in the second set tie-break and levelled the score. He was out of gas by set three. I won that one 6–1. I was pretty satisfied. I'd served sixteen aces overall in the match and this was my fifth title of the year. My form was looking good going into Cincinnati and on to the US Open.

The locals – who fly everywhere – thought we were crazy but Jez and I decided to make the trip to Cincinnati by car, but not just any car. We travelled the 1,120 miles in a Cadillac Escalade SUV and I was so comfortable, sprawled out across three seats, that I couldn't resist tweeting about how much sleep I was getting.

I arrived in Ohio well-rested and also ranked number two in the world. By beating Jo-Wilfred Tsonga in the semi-finals in Montreal, I had finally separated the incredible duo of Federer and Nadal. Obviously Rafa had taken a great deal of time off to rest the injury to his knees, and now he dropped to number three while Roger remained at number one. I was, statistically, the second-best tennis player in the world. It was a good feeling. I acknowledged that, especially as I was the first man to break up the Roger/Rafa domination in four years. But it wasn't my particular goal. That remained to win a Grand Slam title. That is what I was here to do.

Cincinnati went well. I reached the semi-finals before confronting Federer in aggressive form. I didn't help myself much by leaving the ball too short too often and the double fault on match point wasn't great either, but I was still confident heading into New York.

We did the usual touristy things for a couple of days: the

baseball batting cage, the tenpin bowling, the shopping and Times Square, but all too soon I was back to the same routine of tournament tennis. The omens were good. In the third round against Taylor Dent, the 195th ranked player in the world who had suffered a serious back injury and lay off, I only lost seven games.

Then I came up against Marin Cilic, the 6'6" Croatian I'd previously beaten in the fourth round of Roland Garros in the summer, and he produced stunning tennis to defeat me in straight sets 5–7 2–6 2–6. It was obviously disappointing. I said at the time it was the most disappointed I have ever been on the tennis court. But you have to learn from these things.

I learned that day you have to be in the best possible physical condition you can be going into a Grand Slam contest. I was a touch unlucky. I had a slight wrist injury. I didn't harp on about it. I didn't want to make excuses. But I had hurt my wrist during Cincinnati. It was diagnosed at the time as tendonitis and the only cure for that is rest. I wasn't about to relax and take time out of the sport with my favourite Grand Slam tournament looming. It was my decision. I wanted to play. Even now I'd do the same again.

John McEnroe, whose opinion you would have to respect, said I looked tired going into the match. He had also said going into the tournament that I was one of the favourites, so I'm hardly likely to discount his opinion. I agree with him. I was a little bit flat. That could have been due to a number of things, but I believe it's possible to over-analyse these occasions when something doesn't go very well.

There was criticism. There always is when a contender loses. People asked if I had 'the bottle' to win a major. But the critics and the pundits, who haven't played professional sports, are not always the right people to judge. Just because a twenty-year-old – Del Potro, a player I had beaten in Montreal – went on to beat Federer for the title in a huge five-set battle doesn't mean that my chance is lost for ever.

By the time I retire, if I haven't won a major I will have given it my best shot. That is all I can say. That is all I have ever said.

There is no such thing as a straight route to the top. There certainly hasn't been for me. I don't expect the passage to be easy. I continue to work, train and make sacrifices for my own remaining professional ambition. I want to win a major. The scale of the sacrifice I'm prepared to make can be judged by the fact I even ate bananas for energy at Wimbledon – and you know how much I hate bananas. They would be the last thing I'd eat if it was up to me, but that is what The Championships supply, so it is banana or bust.

I came home from the States, still disappointed, but realistic. It was hardly surprising I felt a little tired. Thanks to a relatively injury-free year, I had played twenty more matches than at this stage the year before. It does take its toll. Rafa had come out and admitted he was tired at the 2008 US Open when I beat him in the semi-final. We're not machines. Mentally, physically, emotionally we put in so much work, there are times that we just don't play so well. There seems to be a clamour that I should play more aggressively, that I should develop a 'B' game when the 'A' game fails.

All I can say to that is that, although there are more important things in life than tennis, when I am on the court, I give it one hundred per cent. That is all I ask of myself.

I picked myself up pretty soon. My first job on arrival home was to drive (on a motorway for the first time) down to Sussex to pick up Maggie who was staying at Kim's house. She'd been given a close-cropped haircut so she didn't look great but I knew she was pleased to see me because she dribbled all over the floor.

We also brought back a large painting that Kim has done herself for our house. It's like a flower, but don't ask me what flower. At least it looks like something. I've never been into modern art which to me just resembles some kind of paint spillage on canvas. She asked me what I thought of it and I said: 'It's fine.'

If I was to look back just five years, I might be astonished that I'd achieved so much in such a short time. From gawky junior to number two in the world, finalist at the US Open, semi-finalist at Wimbledon, with a fabulous house in the countryside, and, the most important thing of all, my great friends and family around me still.

But I don't look back. That is for the retirement years. I look forward. To more work, more training, more sprints, more games of tennis football, more forfeits, more weights . . . but it will all be worth it one day if I can say I'm a Grand Slam champion.